Benjamin Myers

Milton's Theology of Freedom

Arbeiten zur Kirchengeschichte

Begründet von

Karl Holl† und Hans Lietzmann†

herausgegeben von

Christian Albrecht und Christoph Markschies

Band 98

Walter de Gruyter · Berlin · New York

Benjamin Myers

Milton's Theology of Freedom

Walter de Gruyter · Berlin · New York

∞ Gedruckt auf säurefreiem Papier,
das die US-ANSI-Norm über Haltbarkeit erfüllt.

ISSN 1861-5996
ISBN-13: 978-3-11-018938-4
ISBN-10: 3-11-018938-0

Library of Congress — Cataloging-in-Publication Data

A CIP catalogue record for this book is available from the Library of Congress.

Bibliografische Information Der Deutschen Bibliothek

Die Deutsche Bibliothek verzeichnet diese Publikation in der Deutschen Nationalbibliografie;
detaillierte bibliografische Daten sind im Internet über http://dnb.ddb.de abrufbar.

For Elise

Contents

Preface

This book offers a new reading of Milton's poetic thought in the light of a detailed examination of post-Reformation theology. It aims to clarify and enrich our understanding of Milton's epic, *Paradise Lost*, and to open new perspectives on to the fascinating complexities of Protestant theology in the seventeenth century. I hope the result will, therefore, be of interest both to Milton scholars and to students of post-Reformation theology.

What Albert Schweitzer once said of the Enlightenment writer Reimarus may with equal truth be said of John Milton: "He had no predecessors; neither had he any disciples." Milton's poetry and thought tower above their time and context, consistently inviting historical explication, yet refusing to be explained away by any historical determinant. His poetry continues to resist interpretive determinisms, while his thought continues to challenge theological and philosophical determinism. Milton's work is thus a monument to the freedom of the individual and to the irreducible singularity of the creative impulse. Acknowledging this creativity and individuality is not, however, to argue that Milton's thought existed in a vacuum. On the contrary, Milton absorbed entire traditions of linguistic, literary and theological discourse; and having absorbed them, he transmuted them and freely pressed them into the service of his own creative vision. Paradoxically then, the historical and contextual positioning of Milton is essential if we are fully to appreciate his uniqueness and individuality.

It is, for instance, only by recognising Milton's appropriation of the epic tradition that we can appreciate the achievement of *Paradise Lost*, a work that transforms and transcends this tradition. Similarly, we can understand Milton's theological achievement only when we situate his thought within the context of the theological traditions to which he was indebted, especially the traditions of post-Reformation Protestantism. In exploring Milton's relationship to his theological context, I therefore endeavour to highlight the creative freedom of his own theological thought. In two respects, then, this book is a study of freedom: it is a study of Milton's theological vision of freedom in *Paradise Lost*; and it is also a study of the freedom of Milton's own theological creativity as embodied in the poem.

I should indicate at the outset that my own theological horizons are shaped principally by the traditions of Nicene trinitarianism and Reformed Protestantism—traditions of which Milton himself was by no means uncritical. As a result, I have often found myself disagreeing with Milton's theological formulations. Such disagreement has, however, remained silent throughout this study, since my purpose is not to contest, but to listen to Milton himself as openly and as sympathetically as possible. In any case, regardless of the criticisms I might make of Milton's theology, I feel only profound admiration for the work of this poet and thinker. If it is true that Milton had neither predecessors nor disciples, it is also true that he had few peers. His profound intuition, penetrating insight and uncompromising individualism set him apart from other writers and thinkers of his time. For this reason, I have found my engagement with Milton to be a unique challenge and a unique joy.

This book is a revised version of my doctoral dissertation, completed for James Cook University, Australia, in 2004. I am grateful to the staff and faculty of James Cook University's School of Humanities for providing so supportive an environment in which to work, and my gratitude is due especially to the Head of School, Greg Manning, for generously providing research and travel funds that enabled me to present some of this material at conferences in Sydney, Auckland and Grenoble. A postdoctoral research fellowship at the University of Queensland's Centre for the History of European Discourses has enabled me to complete work on the manuscript in an amiable and stimulating research environment.

Without the generous advice and encouragement of Anthony Hassall, I would have neither begun nor completed this book. He first encouraged me to attempt a study of Milton's theology, and as my doctoral supervisor he guided me through the entire process of research, writing and editing with enthusiasm and scholarly rigour. I am grateful also to Dennis Danielson, Beverley Sherry, Michael Bauman and Rosemary Dunn, who carefully read the entire manuscript and offered many valuable criticisms and suggestions. In addition, parts of the work were read and critiqued by Jason Rosenblatt and Edward Jones, and many discussions with John Hale have helped both to sharpen my arguments and to deepen my understanding of Milton's theology. In the final stages of preparing the work for publication, I received invaluable guidance from Michael Lattke, and also from Albrecht Döhnert of Walter de Gruyter. If this book has any merits, they are due in large part to the encouragement and advice of so many friends and colleagues; any remaining errors of fact or interpretation are my own.

Some material from Chapters 3 and 6 has appeared previously, as "Milton's *Paradise Lost*, Book 11," *The Explicator* 64:1 (2005), 14–17; "Prevenient Grace and Conversion in *Paradise Lost*," *Milton Quarterly* 40:1 (2006), 20–36; and "Predestination and Freedom in Milton's *Paradise Lost*," *Scottish Journal of Theology* 59:1 (2006), 64–80. I am grateful to the publishers, Heldref, Blackwell and Cambridge University Press, for permission to reproduce this material here.

Finally, my greatest debt is to my wife, Elise. Her wedding date was the anniversary of Milton's birth, and she has lived with Milton ever since.

Brisbane, March 2006

Abbreviations

ANF   *The Ante-Nicene Fathers*. 10 vols. Grand Rapids: Eerdmans, 1956–62.

Bentley   *Milton's Paradise Lost: A New Edition*, ed. Richard Bentley. London, 1732.

Bush   *The Complete Poetical Works of John Milton*, ed. Douglas
Bush. Boston: Houghton Mifflin, 1965.

CM   *The Works of John Milton*, ed. Frank A. Patterson et al. 18
vols. in 21. New York: Columbia University Press,
1931–38.

CPW   *Complete Prose Works of John Milton*, ed. Don M. Wolfe et
al. 8 vols. New Haven: Yale University Press, 1953–82.

Flannagan *The Riverside Milton*, ed. Roy Flannagan. Boston:
Houghton Mifflin, 1998.

Fowler   *John Milton: Paradise Lost*, ed. Alastair Fowler. London:
Longman, 1968.

Heppe   Heinrich Heppe, *Reformed Dogmatics Set Out and Illustrated from the Sources*. Ed. and rev. Ernst Bizer. Trans.
G. T. Thomson. London: Allen & Unwin, 1950.

Hughes   *John Milton: Complete Poems and Major Prose*, ed. Merritt
Y. Hughes. New York: Odyssey, 1957.

Muller, *PRRD* Richard A. Muller, *Post-Reformation Reformed Dogmatics:
The Rise and Development of Reformed Orthodoxy, ca. 1520
to ca. 1725*. 4 vols. Grand Rapids: Baker, 2003.

Newton   *Paradise Lost: A Poem, in Twelve Books*, ed. Thomas
                Newton. 2 vols. London, 1749.

NPNF   *A Select Library of the Nicene and Post-Nicene Fathers of
                the Christian Church*, ed. Philip Schaff. First Series. 14
                vols. Grand Rapids: Eerdmans, 1979.

OED   *Oxford English Dictionary*

PL   *Patrologia Latina Cursus Completus*, ed. J. P. Migne. 221
                vols. Paris, 1844–55.

Schaff   *The Creeds of Christendom: With a History and Critical
                Notes*, ed. Philip Schaff. 3 vols. New York, 1919.

Tanner   *Decrees of the Ecumenical Councils*, ed. Norman P. Tan-
                ner. 2 vols. London: Sheed & Ward, 1990.

Todd   *The Poetical Works of John Milton: With Notes by Various
                Authors*, ed. Henry J. Todd. 4 vols. London, 1809.

TRE   *Theologische Realenzyklopädie*, ed. Gerhard Krause and
                Gerhard Müller. 36 vols. Berlin: Walter de Gruyter,
                1977–2004.

Verity   *Milton: Paradise Lost*, ed. A. W. Verity. Cambridge, 1910.

A Note on the Texts

Where Latin theological texts exist in modern English translations, I
have generally cited these editions, but have often modified my citations against the original Latin. References to Milton's *De Doctrina
Christiana* refer both to the Latin text in the Columbia edition (*CM*) and
the English translation in the Yale edition (*CPW*). All citations of Milton's poetry are from Helen Darbishire's edition, *The Poetical Works of
John Milton*, 2 vols. (Oxford: Clarendon, 1952–55). Italics in citations are
from the original texts unless otherwise indicated.

Introduction

"No man who knows ought, can be so stupid to deny that all men naturally were borne free." This was Milton's characteristically uncompromising judgment in *The Tenure of Kings and Magistrates*.[1] Milton's lifelong dedication to the cause of human freedom is well documented. According to the early biographer John Toland, Milton "look'd upon true and absolute Freedom to be the greatest Happiness of this Life, whether to Societies or single Persons," and for that reason he "thought Constraint of any sort to be the utmost Misery." Toland relates that Milton himself would tell his friends "that he had constantly imploy'd his Strength and Faculties in the defence of Liberty, and in a direct opposition to Slavery."[2] If one were to seek for any intellectual conviction or principle that underlies the whole diverse scope of Milton's works, both poetry and prose, then Toland's "true and absolute Freedom" would surely be the most likely candidate. As G. A. Wood has said, regardless of the important ways in which Milton's thought changed and developed over time, "[i]t is the love of Liberty that gives consistency and unity to his life and to his teaching."[3] And according to Sir Herbert Grierson, Milton's entire corpus "begins and ends in the idea of liberty and its correlative duty"—that is, in freedom and responsibility.[4] As Susanne Woods has observed, "Milton's own lifelong interest in liberty" remains a point of agreement among Milton scholars, with disagreements arising only over the precise nature of his understanding of liberty.[5] In particular, Milton scholars remain divided over the question of whether Milton's theology of freedom was orthodox or heterodox.

---

1   *CPW* 3:198.

2   John Toland, *The life of John Milton* (London, 1699), 150–151.

3   G. A. Wood, "The Miltonic Ideal," in *Historical Essays by Members of the Owens College, Manchester*, ed. T. F. Tout and James Tait (London, 1902), 361.

4   Herbert J. C. Grierson, "Milton," in *Encyclopaedia of Religion and Ethics*, ed. James Hastings, 13 vols. (Edinburgh: T&T Clark, 1908–26), 8:647.

5   Susanne Woods, "Choice and Election in *Samson Agonistes*," in *Milton and the Grounds of Contention*, ed. Mark R. Kelley, Michael Lieb and John T. Shawcross (Pittsburgh: Duquesne University Press, 2003), 178.

Heresy and Orthodoxy

Over half a century ago, A. S. P. Woodhouse remarked:

> Nothing is more obvious in modern Milton studies than the emergence of
> two schools, one of which is so impressed by Milton's heresies as to lose
> sight of his fundamental Christianity, while the other ... insists on the tra-
> ditional character of the poet's religion and, where it cannot deny the here-
> sies, brushes them aside as peripheral.[6]

In spite of the ways in which the discussion of Milton's theology has
developed since the 1940s, Woodhouse's description of a radical–conservative divide in Milton studies remains broadly accurate.[7] Thus Stephen Fallon has recently highlighted the interpretive conflict between
those readers who emphasise Milton's "intellectual unconventionality
and even heterodoxy," and those who portray the poet as a "spokes-
person for orthodox Christianity."[8]

This conflict between radical and conservative readings of Milton is
exhibited in a striking way in the continuing debate over Milton's Arianism,[9] with some scholars arguing that Milton's view of the Trinity "is

---

6   A. S. P. Woodhouse, "Notes on Milton's Views on the Creation: The Initial Phases,"
     Philological Quarterly 28 (1949), 211. Similarly, see R. J. Zwi Werblowsky, *Lucifer and
     Prometheus: A Study of Milton's Satan* (London: Routledge & Kegan Paul, 1952), 1–2,
     who humorously contrasts radical portrayals of Milton as a "dashing Satanist" with
     conservative portrayals of "the conventional poet who would not say anything un-
     less seventeen people had said it before."

7   For concise summaries of Milton's theology, see Richard Luckett, "Milton," *TRE*,
     22:753–59; Flannagan, 306–9; and John P. Rumrich, "Milton, John," in *Encyclopedia of
     Protestantism*, ed. Hans J. Hillerbrand, 4 vols. (New York: Routledge, 2004), 3:1244–
     47.

8   Stephen M. Fallon, "*Paradise Lost* in Intellectual History," in *A Companion to Milton*,
     ed. Thomas N. Corns (Oxford: Blackwell, 2001), 329.

9   The Arianism of *Paradise Lost* has been contested in various ways by William B.
     Hunter, C. A. Patrides and J. H. Adamson, *Bright Essence: Studies in Milton's Theology*
     (Salt Lake City: University of Utah Press, 1971); James H. Sims, "*Paradise Lost*: 'Arian
     Document' or Christian Poem?" *Études Anglaises* 20 (1967), 337–47; Stella P. Revard,
     "The Dramatic Function of the Son in *Paradise Lost*: A Commentary on Milton's 'Tri-
     nitarianism,'" *Journal of English and Germanic Philology* 66 (1967), 45–58; and, most re-
     cently, Michael Lieb, *Theological Milton: Deity, Discourse and Heresy in the Miltonic Ca-
     non* (Pittsburgh: Duquesne University Press, 2006), ch. 8. The poem's Arianism has
     been affirmed and defended by Maurice Kelley, *This Great Argument: A Study of Mil-
     ton's De Doctrina Christiana as a Gloss Upon Paradise Lost* (Princeton: Princeton Uni-
     versity Press, 1941); Michael Bauman, *Milton's Arianism* (Frankfurt am Main: Peter
     Lang, 1987); John P. Rumrich, "Milton's Arianism: Why It Matters," in *Milton and
     Heresy*, ed. Stephen B. Dobranski and John P. Rumrich (Cambridge: Cambridge Uni-
     versity Press, 1998), 75–92; and, most recently, Larry R. Isitt, *All the Names in Heaven:
     A Reference Guide to Milton's Supernatural Names and Epic Similes* (Lanham: Scarecrow
     Press, 2002).

in agreement with the creedal statement of ... Nicene orthodoxy,"[10] and others arguing that the heretical Milton "rejected the orthodox dogma of the Trinity."[11] The same radical–conservative conflict is responsible for the fervour with which Milton's authorship of the *De Doctrina Christiana* has recently been contested on the one hand and defended on the other.[12] In contesting Milton's authorship of the treatise, William Hunter's underlying conservative intention is expressed in his description of a theologically innocuous "Anglican communicant" Milton, whose radicalism extended "only to church governance, not doctrine,"[13] and who should therefore be associated with what Hunter calls "the great traditions of Christianity."[14] Advocates of Milton's authorship, on the other hand, speak of his "heretical" and "idiosyncratic" beliefs, and complain of "the persistent desire to present Milton as an orthodox Christian."[15]

This continuing conflict between orthodox and heretical readings of Milton's theology forms the background to the present study. I was prompted to undertake this study when I became fascinated by the way in which the thought-world of *Paradise Lost* seemed to accommodate both theologically orthodox elements on the one hand, and idiosyncratic, heterodox elements on the other. I wondered then whether the sharp division between radical and conservative interpretations of

---

10 William B. Hunter, "Further Definitions: Milton's Theological Vocabulary," in *Bright Essence*, 25.

11 Maurice Kelley, "Milton and the Trinity," *Huntington Library Quarterly* 33 (1970), 316.

12 Studies contesting the treatise's Miltonic authorship include William B. Hunter, *Visitation Unimplor'd: Milton and the Authorship of De Doctrina Christiana* (Pittsburgh: Duquesne University Press, 1998); Paul R. Sellin, "John Milton's *Paradise Lost* and *De Doctrina Christiana* on Predestination," *Milton Studies* 34 (1996), 45–60; and Michael Lieb, "*De Doctrina Christiana* and the Question of Authorship," *Milton Studies* 41 (2002), 171–230. Defences of the work's Miltonic authorship include Christopher Hill, "Professor William B. Hunter, Bishop Burgess, and John Milton," *Studies in English Literature, 1500–1900* 34 (1994), 165–88; Barbara K. Lewalski, "Milton and *De Doctrina Christiana*: Evidences of Authorship," *Milton Studies* 36 (1998), 203–28; and Stephen M. Fallon, "Milton's Arminianism and the Authorship of *De Doctrina Christiana*," *Texas Studies in Literature and Language* 41:2 (1999), 103–27. There have been some attempts to mediate the controversy, especially the extensive report by the international research group: Gordon Campbell, Thomas N. Corns, John K. Hale, David I. Holmes and Fiona J. Tweedie, "The Provenance of *De Doctrina Christiana*," *Milton Quarterly* 31:3 (1997), 67–117. But such mediating attempts have drawn criticism from defenders of Miltonic authorship: see especially John P. Rumrich, "Stylometry and the Provenance of *De Doctrina Christiana*," in *Milton and the Terms of Liberty*, ed. Graham Parry and Joad Raymond (Cambridge: D. S. Brewer, 2002), 125–36.

13 Hunter, *Visitation Unimplor'd*, 16.

14 Hunter, *Visitation Unimplor'd*, 8.

15 Stephen B. Dobranski and John P. Rumrich, "Introduction: Heretical Milton," in *Milton and Heresy*, 1, 12.

Paradise Lost had in fact been fostered by the nature of the poem's theology itself. I wondered, in other words, whether this theology was altogether more complex, more variegated and more elusive than either straightforwardly orthodox or straightforwardly heretical readings have tended to suggest.

This study is therefore especially interested in identifying points of both continuity and discontinuity between *Paradise Lost*'s theology and its post-Reformation theological milieu. My aim is not simply to highlight the most daring and heretical aspects of the poem's theology, nor to play down these aspects in order to emphasise the more orthodox features.[16] Both these approaches suffer from the shared assumption that the essential character of *Paradise Lost*'s theology can be decided in advance, whether from a reading of the *De Doctrina Christiana* or from some other construction of Miltonic thought. Having thus already decided that *Paradise Lost* is essentially orthodox or heterodox, one need only highlight those features of the poem that most clearly illustrate this basic theological character.[17] In contrast, the assumption underlying the present study is that the theology of *Paradise Lost* should be encountered on its own terms, using both the seventeenth-century context and the context of Milton's other works (including the *De Doctrina*) as interpretive aids, but disallowing any commitment to a preconceived construction of either a radical or a conservative "Milton." Further, this study assumes that the theology of *Paradise Lost* is interesting for its own sake: it is intrinsically interesting, regardless of how conservative or how radical it might be. This does not of course mean that it is unimportant whether or to what extent the poem's theology is in fact orthodox or heterodox. On the contrary, it is precisely the points of continuity and discontinuity with the major traditions of the seventeenth century that reveal most about the character of *Paradise Lost*'s theology. Both the continuities and the discontinuities are intrinsically

---

16 For a notable example of a radical approach, see Denis Saurat, *Milton, Man and Thinker* (London: J. M. Dent, 1944), 91: Saurat seeks "to study what there is of lasting originality in Milton's thought, and ... to disentangle from theological rubbish the permanent and human interest of that thought." And for an example of the conservative approach, see C. S. Lewis, *A Preface to Paradise Lost* (London: Oxford University Press, 1942), 82: "*Paradise Lost* is ... Catholic in the sense of basing its poetry on conceptions that have been held 'always and everywhere and by all.' This Catholic quality is so predominant that it is the first impression any unbiased reader would receive."

17 Thus Stanley E. Fish, *How Milton Works* (Cambridge, Mass.: Harvard University Press, 2001), 18, rightly notes that some arguments for or against the authorship of the *De Doctrina Christiana* have tended to rest "on a conclusion already reached about the kind of person and thinker Milton is."

interesting; and both are equally important for a full appreciation of the poem.

In this study I am not therefore offering a kind of interpretive *via media* that seeks—by conceding too much to both sides and thereby satisfying neither—to reconcile conservative and radical approaches to Milton's theology. Instead, I wish to uncover the richness and complexity of *Paradise Lost*'s theology by investigating the ways in which the poem draws on and appropriates orthodox and heterodox traditions alike. As I will try to demonstrate, the poem's theology as a whole resists simple categorisation as either basically orthodox or basically heretical. Indeed, the important interpretive question is not that of orthodoxy or heresy, but rather that of continuity and discontinuity: to what extent do the various aspects of the poem's theology exhibit continuity and discontinuity with post-Reformation theological discourses?

Continuities and Discontinuities

The emphasis in this study on identifying continuities and discontinuities is indebted to broader developments within recent post-Reformation theological scholarship, especially to the very extensive revisionist studies of the American scholar Richard A. Muller, which have focused consistently on the question of theological continuity and discontinuity in medieval, Reformation and post-Reformation thought.[18] Muller's work, which to date has been curiously neglected in studies of Milton's theology,[19] has amply demonstrated how illumi-

---

18 See especially Richard A. Muller, *Christ and the Decree: Christology and Predestination in Reformed Theology from Calvin to Perkins* (Grand Rapids: Baker, 1986); idem, *God, Creation and Providence in the Thought of Jacob Arminius: Sources and Directions of Scholastic Protestantism in the Era of Early Orthodoxy* (Grand Rapids: Baker, 1991); idem, *The Unaccommodated Calvin: Studies in the Foundation of a Theological Tradition* (Oxford: Oxford University Press, 2000); idem, *After Calvin: Studies in the Development of a Theological Tradition* (Oxford: Oxford University Press, 2003); and idem, *PRRD*. For an early but still useful summary of Muller's revisionist approach, see Martin I. Klauber, "Continuity and Discontinuity in Post-Reformation Reformed Theology: An Evaluation of the Muller Thesis," *Journal of the Evangelical Theological Society* 33:4 (1990), 467–75.

19 As far as I can tell, the only exception to this puzzling neglect is Victoria Silver, *Imperfect Sense: The Predicament of Milton's Irony* (Princeton: Princeton University Press, 2001), who recognises Muller's scholarship but does not engage with it in any detail. For his part, on the other hand, Muller has not been inattentive to Milton studies: see for example his interaction with Milton scholarship and with the *De Doctrina*, in *PRRD*, 4:24–25, 97–99, 210–11.

nating the continuity–discontinuity question is, and has established that this question is crucial for an understanding of the character of a theological thinker or movement. The approach of Muller and his school, and the large body of their recent scholarship on post-Reformation thought,[20] offer fresh and exciting opportunities to engage with Milton's theological context in a more nuanced and more sophisticated way than was possible in the past.

The present study, then, with its grounding in the post-Reformation theological context and its attention to continuities and discontinuities, seeks to allow *Paradise Lost*'s theology to emerge on its own terms, so that its own distinctive contours, emphases and tensions are brought clearly into view. By highlighting the poem's continuities with its theological context, I seek to offer fresh insights into the theological traditions with which Milton has engaged, and into the distinctive ways in which he has appropriated these traditions. It is only against the backdrop of such theological continuities that the genuinely innovative features of *Paradise Lost*'s theology can be identified and appreciated.[21] And such original aspects of the poem offer revealing glimpses of some of the poet's most profound theological concerns and commitments.

Because this approach demands a close and detailed reading of *Paradise Lost*, an interaction with the large body of Milton scholarship and post-Reformation scholarship, and an extensive engagement with primary theological sources, the scope of this study is necessarily restricted to one central aspect of the poem's theology: its theology of freedom. In the judgment of most Milton scholars, the concept of freedom stands at the very heart of *Paradise Lost*'s thought-world. And although much has been said about the importance of free will in *Paradise Lost*, there remains a need for a new, specifically theological and contextual study of this dimension of the poem and of Milton's thought.

---

20 Muller's approach has been taken up and developed in different directions by scholars such as Eef Dekker, Willem van Asselt, Lyle Bierma, Antonie Vos, Carl Trueman and Martin Klauber.

21 On this methodological point, see Carl R. Trueman, "Puritan Theology as Historical Event: A Linguistic Approach to the Ecumenical Context," in *Reformation and Scholasticism: An Ecumenical Enterprise*, ed. Willem J. van Asselt and Eef Dekker (Grand Rapids: Baker, 2001), 256, who notes that only a deep awareness of "the continuities between Puritanism and the wider intellectual context" can enable us "to see where, if at all, Puritan theology makes a distinctive contribution." In the same way, a lack of attention to the continuities between *Paradise Lost*'s theology and its intellectual milieu has often led readers to misconstrue the poem's points of theological originality.

Contexts of Milton's Theology

Earlier studies of Milton's theology have engaged with a diverse range of theological contexts. Some scholars have attempted to ground Milton's theology in a more or less homogeneous "Christian" or "Catholic" tradition. Douglas Bush, for instance, has described *Paradise Lost* as "simply a poem of traditional Christianity, Catholic as well as Protestant."[22] Similarly, Miriam Joseph has argued that *Paradise Lost* embodies "theological doctrines in conformity with the Catholic Church," while C. S. Lewis has claimed that this "Catholic" poem presents "the great central tradition" of Christianity.[23] Most notably, C. A. Patrides has ambitiously attempted to position Milton's theology within a synthesis of the entire history of Christian thought.[24]

In more focused studies, writers like Golda Werman, Jason Rosenblatt and Jeffrey Shoulson have explored Milton's thought against the background of Jewish theology.[25] Others have concentrated on the patristic backgrounds to Milton's thought. Notably, Peter Fiore has discussed parallels between Miltonic and Augustinian thought, while Harry Robins has employed the thought of Origen as a "gloss" on Milton's theology.[26] According to Robins, Milton's thought "looked backward" to antiquity, and his theological views "were those of the Christian writers before the Council of Nicea."[27] William Hunter, J. H. Adamson and Patrides have also attempted to link Milton's theology to pre-Nicene thought, and, while contesting their conclusions, Michael Bauman has demonstrated the close parallels between Milton's thought and the Arianism of the Nicene period.[28]

Comparatively few studies have explored the medieval background to Milton's thought, although notable exceptions include Peter Gregory Angelo's Thomist reading of *Paradise Lost*, and J. Martin

---

22 Douglas Bush, *English Literature in the Earlier Seventeenth Century, 1600–1660* (Oxford: Clarendon, 1962), 401–2.

23 Miriam Joseph, "Orthodoxy in *Paradise Lost*," *Laval théologique et philosophique* 8 (1952), 249; Lewis, *Preface to Paradise Lost*, 82, 92.

24 C. A. Patrides, *Milton and the Christian Tradition* (Oxford: Clarendon, 1966).

25 See Golda Werman, *Milton and Midrash* (Washington: Catholic University Press of America, 1995); Jason P. Rosenblatt, *Torah and Law in Paradise Lost* (Princeton: Princeton University Press, 1994); and Jeffrey S. Shoulson, *Milton and the Rabbis: Hebraism, Hellenism, and Christianity* (New York: Columbia University Press, 2001).

26 See Peter A. Fiore, *Milton and Augustine: Patterns of Augustinian Thought in Paradise Lost* (University Park: Pennsylvania State University Press, 1981); and Harry F. Robins, *If This Be Heresy: A Study of Milton and Origen* (Illinois: University of Illinois Press, 1963).

27 Robins, *If This Be Heresy*, 176–77.

28 See Hunter, Patrides and Adamson, *Bright Essence*; and Bauman, *Milton's Arianism*.

Evans's analysis of the medieval interpretation of the fall-story.[29] On the other hand, Reformation theology has been related to Milton's thought in numerous studies, particularly by scholars by such as A. G. George, William Halewood, Timothy O'Keeffe and George Musacchio,[30] and most importantly in the theologically sophisticated work of Georgia Christopher and Victoria Silver.[31]

Studies of Milton's theology have also focused on a range of post-Reformation theological traditions. Paul Sellin has drawn parallels between Amyraldian theology and the *De Doctrina Christiana*,[32] while George Conklin, Nathaniel Henry and Michael Lieb have explored the heterodox Socinian tradition as a background to Milton's thought.[33] The Reformed orthodox context has received considerably less attention; but Maurice Kelley's extensive annotations to the Yale edition of the *De Doctrina* still offer a remarkably detailed and precise engagement with Reformed orthodoxy, and these annotations demonstrate the extent to which the *De Doctrina*, for all its heterodoxies, remains an artefact of Reformed theological discourse. As Hunter has also noted, "there can be no question" that Milton was "intimately familiar" with the Reformed orthodox tradition;[34] and Roland Frye has suggested that the

---

29 See Peter Gregory Angelo, *Fall to Glory: Theological Reflections on Milton's Epics* (New York: Peter Lang, 1987); and J. Martin Evans, *Paradise Lost and the Genesis Tradition* (Oxford: Clarendon, 1968): 168–91.

30 See A. G. George, *Milton and the Nature of Man: A Descriptive Study of Paradise Lost in Terms of the Concept of Man as the Image of God* (London: Asia Publishing House, 1974), 42–53; William H. Halewood, *The Poetry of Grace: Reformation Themes and Structures in English Seventeenth-Century Poetry* (New Haven: Yale University Press, 1970), 140–75; Timothy J. O'Keeffe, *Milton and the Pauline Tradition: A Study of Theme and Symbolism* (Washington: University Press of America, 1982); and George Musacchio, *Milton's Adam and Eve: Fallible Perfection* (New York: Peter Lang, 1991).

31 See Georgia Christopher, *Milton and the Science of the Saints* (Princeton: Princeton University Press, 1982); and Silver, *Imperfect Sense*.

32 Paul R. Sellin, "If Not Milton, Who Did Write the *De Doctrina Christiana*? The Amyraldian Connection," in *Living Texts: Interpreting Milton*, ed. Kristen A. Pruitt and Charles W. Durham (Selinsgrove: Susquehanna University Press, 2000), 237–63.

33 See George Newton Conklin, *Biblical Criticism and Heresy in Milton* (New York: King's Crown Press, 1949); Nathaniel H. Henry, *The True Wayfaring Christian: Studies in Milton's Puritanism* (New York: Peter Lang, 1987), 67–92; and Lieb, *Theological Milton*, ch. 7.

34 William B. Hunter, "The Theological Context of Milton's *Christian Doctrine*," in *Achievements of the Left Hand: Essays on the Prose of John Milton*, ed. Michael Lieb and John T. Shawcross (Amherst: University of Massachusetts Press, 1974), 272. Some early studies argued even that Milton's mature theology was essentially Calvinistic. See especially A. D. Barber, "The Religious Life and Opinions of John Milton: Part I," *Bibliotheca Sacra* 63 (1859), 557–603; idem, "The Religious Life and Opinions of John Milton: Part II," *Bibliotheca Sacra* 64 (1860), 1–42; and Joseph Moody McDill, "Milton and the Pattern of Calvinism" (Ph.D. diss., Vanerbilt University, 1938). Arthur Se-

theology of Reformed orthodoxy "forms the general background for Milton's work."[35] Kelley has engaged closely with the theology of the Reformed writer Johannes Wollebius,[36] who, along with William Ames, was regarded by Milton as one of the "ablest of Divines."[37] Following Kelley, both Hunter and John Steadman have continued to investigate Wollebius's relation to Milton's thought.[38] The Puritan theological context has been explored in studies by A. S. P. Woodhouse, Arthur Barker, Boyd Berry, Christopher Kendrick and, most notably, in the brilliant and idiosyncratic work of Christopher Hill, which sought to position Milton's thought within the theologies of the radical Puritan sects.[39]

While some studies have misunderstood or caricatured post-Reformation theology,[40] engagements with the post-Reformation context in Milton scholarship have become increasingly sophisticated since the publication of Dennis Danielson's pioneering study, *Milton's Good God* (1982), a work that engaged extensively with seventeenth-century sources, and brought to light the complexity both of the post-Reformation context and of Milton's own theology of freedom.[41] Following and building on Danielson's close attention to the Arminian context, many recent studies have continued to explore the relationship

well, *A Study in Milton's Christian Doctrine* (London: Oxford University Press, 1939), also argued that Milton's theology remained deeply influenced by Calvinism.

35 Roland M. Frye, *God, Man, and Satan: Patterns of Christian Thought and Life in Paradise Lost, Pilgrim's Progress, and the Great Theologians* (Princeton: Princeton University Press, 1960), 39.

36 Maurice Kelley, "Milton's Debt to Wolleb's *Compendium Theologiæ Christianæ*," *PMLA* 50 (1935), 156–65.

37 Edward Phillips, "The Life of Mr. John Milton," in *Letters of state, written by Mr. John Milton: ... to which is added, an account of his life* (London, 1694), xix.

38 See Hunter, *Visitation Unimplor'd*, 24–30; and John M. Steadman, "Milton and Wolleb Again," *Harvard Theological Review* 53 (1960), 155–56.

39 See A. S. P. Woodhouse, "Milton, Puritanism, and Liberty," *University of Toronto Quarterly* 4 (1935), 483–513; Arthur E. Barker, *Milton and the Puritan Dilemma* (Toronto: University of Toronto Press, 1942); Boyd M. Berry, *Process of Speech: Puritan Religious Writing and Paradise Lost* (Baltimore: Johns Hopkins University Press, 1976); Christopher Kendrick, *Milton: A Study in Ideology and Form* (New York: Methuen, 1986); and Christopher Hill, *Milton and the English Revolution* (London: Faber, 1977).

40 Reformed orthodoxy has especially been subjected to caricature. For example, Saurat, *Milton, Man and Thinker*, 103, blithely asserts that "free will has no place in Calvinism"; Andrew Milner, *John Milton and the English Revolution: A Study in the Sociology of Literature* (London: Macmillan, 1981), 99, contrasts "Calvinistic determinism" with the idea of "man as rational agent"; and Werman, *Milton and Midrash*, 133, suggests that the Protestant view of grace requires "that God be everything, and that man be nothing."

41 Dennis R. Danielson, *Milton's Good God: A Study in Literary Theodicy* (Cambridge: Cambridge University Press, 1982).

between Milton and Arminianism. A highly nuanced understanding of Arminian theology characterises the recent scholarship of Barbara Lewalski, Thomas Corns and John Shawcross,[42] and is especially characteristic of the theologically sophisticated work of Stephen Fallon.[43]

Furthermore, several studies have drawn Milton's theology into dialogue with modern theological contexts. Michael Lieb, for instance, has employed the theology of Rudolf Otto as an interpretive aid to *Paradise Lost*, while John Tanner and Catherine Bates have related *Paradise Lost* to the thought of the Danish philosopher-theologian Søren Kierkegaard.[44] In other studies, Anthony Yu and Roland Frye have noted parallels between Milton's theology and that of twentieth-century Protestants like Karl Barth, Dietrich Bonhoeffer and Paul Tillich, while, most recently, Joan Bennett has brought Milton into dialogue with Catholic liberation theology.[45]

The present study of freedom in *Paradise Lost* will engage in some way with most of the theological contexts mentioned here. I will seek mainly to locate the poem's theology within its post-Reformation context, with particular attention to prominent traditions such as Reformed orthodoxy and Arminianism. But post-Reformation theology is itself located against the complex background of patristic, medieval and Reformation thought; and, for a twenty-first century interpreter, it is also inevitably viewed from within the horizons of modern theological discourses. For this reason, throughout the present study I will interact with these diverse patristic, medieval, Reformation and modern con-

---

42   See Lewalski, "Milton and *De Doctrina Christiana*," 216–21; idem, *The Life of John Milton: A Critical Biography* (Oxford: Blackwell, 2001), 420–25, 432–33, 474–75; Thomas N. Corns, *Regaining Paradise Lost* (London: Longman, 1994), 78–86; John T. Shawcross, *John Milton: The Self and the World* (Lexington: University Press of Kentucky, 1993), 128–41; and idem, *The Arms of The Family: The Significance of John Milton's Relatives and Associates* (Lexington: University Press of Kentucky, 2004), 170–74.

43   See Stephen M. Fallon, "Milton's Arminianism and the Authorship of *De Doctrina Christiana*," *Texas Studies in Literature and Language* 41:2 (1999), 103–27; and idem, "'Elect above the Rest': Theology as Self-Representation in Milton," in *Milton and Heresy*, ed. Stephen B. Dobranski and John P. Rumrich (Cambridge: Cambridge University Press, 1998), 93–116.

44   See Michael Lieb, *Poetics of the Holy: A Reading of Paradise Lost* (Chapel Hill: University of North Carolina Press, 1981); John S. Tanner, *Anxiety in Eden: A Kierkegaardian Reading of Paradise Lost* (New York: Oxford University Press, 1992); and Catherine Bates, "No Sin But Irony: Kierkegaard and Milton's Satan," *Literature and Theology* 11:1 (1997), 1–26.

45   See Anthony C. Yu, "Life in the Garden: Freedom and the Image of God in *Paradise Lost*," *Journal of Religion* 60 (1980), 247–71; Frye, *God, Man, and Satan*; and Joan S. Bennett, "Asserting Eternal Providence: John Milton through the Window of Liberation Theology," in *Milton and Heresy*, 219–43.

texts, while maintaining a sharp focus on the post-Reformation context as the crucial backdrop to Milton's theological thought.

Dead Ideas

When in 1900 Sir Walter Raleigh famously described *Paradise Lost* as "a monument to dead ideas,"[46] he was right at least to see the great gulf that exists between Milton's intellectual environment and that of more recent times. Some critics have tried to overcome this gulf by playing down or ignoring the "dead ideas" of *Paradise Lost*, and by focusing instead on those aspects of the poem that seem closest to modern intellectual interests. Thus Denis Saurat, for instance, has attempted to find in Milton's poetry "a permanent [philosophical] interest, outside the religious and political squabbles of his time";[47] and, in response to Raleigh, Michael Wilding protests that "Milton the radical, Milton the pacifist—*that* Milton would have something to say to us today."[48] Saurat and Wilding may well be right, of course, to think that such elements of Milton's thought are of contemporary interest. But the question remains whether such a philosophically or politically interesting Milton can be fully appreciated if the "dead ideas" that inspired his thought are simply set aside.

Even if for no other reason, the fact that *Paradise Lost* can be described as "a monument to dead ideas" makes a theological study of the poem necessary. The description of Milton's ideas as "dead" need not be taken as a prejudgment of those ideas, but only as an indication of the historical distance that separates Milton's intellectual milieu from the present. The present study of freedom in *Paradise Lost* aims not to revive these "dead ideas" —not, that is, in Wilding's words, to prove that they still "have something to say to us today" —but only to make the thought-world of *Paradise Lost*, and especially the poem's view of freedom, more intelligible, and thereby to enable a better appreciation of the poem on its own terms. As William Riley Parker has said:

> there is one vast gap between Milton's basic ideas and those predominant in our own world; we shall never understand [Milton] by ignoring the gap and focusing our attention upon his "modern" views of censorship or di-

---

46 Walter Raleigh, *Milton* (London, 1900), 88.
47 Saurat, *Milton, Man and Thinker*, xi.
48 Michael Wilding, *Dragons Teeth: Literature in the English Revolution* (Oxford: Clarendon, 1987), 249.

vorce or education or politics. Milton's conception of human freedom was bound up inextricably with religion.[49]

Parker is not here suggesting that Milton's religious ideas are more interesting than his "modern" social and political views. Rather, his point is that an understanding of the former is a prerequisite to a full appreciation of the latter.

Similarly, the present study, with its closely focused theological reading of *Paradise Lost*, seeks only to complement, not to challenge, the range of contemporary political, historical, philosophical and ideological approaches to Milton's thought, all of which have deepened our ability to read and to understand his poetry. While adopting a theological approach to *Paradise Lost*, I recognise that it is often "impossible to say decisively" that Milton's poetic language "says only this or that."[50] It is neither necessary nor advisable to attempt systematically to pin the language of *Paradise Lost* down to a single determinant meaning. On the contrary, as perceptive critics like John Rumrich and Victoria Silver have recently argued, *Paradise Lost* embodies poetic indeterminacy to such an extent that the text itself will always resist the imposition of static, determinant interpretive grids.[51] In the words of Diane Kelsey McColley, Milton's poetry "is too open and subtle to become trapped in an ideology," so that it "springs away from categorical cages."[52] The present study, then, has no intention of constructing another such "cage," but only of offering a contextual, theological interpretation of *Paradise Lost* that can complement, and perhaps also enrich, other readings. Indeed, although the present study assumes that Milton's theology is interesting for its own sake, I hope nevertheless that it will invite further reflection on the social, political and ideological implications of Milton's theology of freedom.

---

49   William Riley Parker, *Milton: A Biography*, 2 vols. (Oxford: Clarendon, 1968), 1:vi.

50   J. Hillis Miller, "How Deconstruction Works," *The New York Times Magazine* 9 (February 1986), 25.

51   See John P. Rumrich, *Milton Unbound: Controversy and Reinterpretation* (Cambridge: Cambridge University Press, 1996); and Victoria Silver, *Imperfect Sense*.

52   Diane Kelsey McColley, "'All in All': The Individuality of Creatures in *Paradise Lost*," in *"All in All": Unity, Diversity, and the Miltonic Perspective*, ed. Charles W. Durham and Kristin A. Pruitt (Selinsgrove: Susquehanna University Press, 1999), 34. McColley is referring here to poststructuralist readings of *Paradise Lost*, but her caution applies equally to any interpretive approach to the poem.

Poetic Theology

In interpreting *Paradise Lost* within the context of post-Reformation theology, and in offering a specifically theological reading of this work, I am of course aware that *Paradise Lost* is a poem and must be read as such. As the Protestant theologian Augustus H. Strong has said, Milton is "a didactic poet" with a definite theological aim.[53] Such a statement is no longer controversial; few critics today would agree with Edwin Greenlaw's argument of early last century that *Paradise Lost* is concerned only with "moral allegory" rather than "poetical theology."[54] Indeed, it is now widely recognised not only that *Paradise Lost* is a distinctly theological poem, but also that "Milton wrote his ... theology most forcefully in his poetry."[55] This does not mean, however, that Milton's poetry can be read like "a doctrinal treatise," using the interpretive categories of theological prose[56] — a mistake into which even the most learned and judicious theological readings of Milton have sometimes fallen.

In my analysis of *Paradise Lost*'s theology, I therefore seek as far as possible to avoid not only the Scylla of insufficient attention to theological context, but also the Charybdis of insufficient sensitivity to the work as poetry. In keeping with this aim, my usual method throughout this study is to perform close readings of specific sections or passages of *Paradise Lost* in order to elucidate the poem's theological content, and to indicate the ways in which the poetic language itself expresses theological themes. Further, the basic structure of this study is shaped not by the theological concept of freedom systematically considered, but by the narrative structure of *Paradise Lost* itself. Thus I attempt not to impose a set of preconceived theological questions on to the epic, but instead to extract from the whole epic narrative the basic shape and structure of its theological portrayal of freedom.

This study begins, then, with a brief overview of the historical development of the theology of freedom from the fourth century through to the post-Reformation era (Chapter One), before turning to the portrayal of freedom in *Paradise Lost*. In the first two books of *Paradise Lost*,

---

53 Augustus H. Strong, *The Great Poets and Their Theology* (Philadelphia, 1897), 253–55.
54 Edwin Greenlaw, "A Better Teacher Than Aquinas," *Studies in Philology* 14 (1917), 199.
55 Regina M. Schwartz, "Milton on the Bible," in *A Companion to Milton*, 37. Milton himself claimed that poetry is a more powerful didactic medium than prose: thus in *Areopagitica* he states that Spenser is "a better teacher" than Thomas Aquinas (*CPW* 2:516).
56 As observed by Philip Dixon, *"Nice and Hot Disputes": The Doctrine of the Trinity in the Seventeenth Century* (London: T&T Clark, 2003), 24.

an anti-Calvinist view of freedom is immediately but subtly asserted by placing parodic, quasi-Calvinist sentiments in the mouth of the arch-heretic, Satan (Chapter Two). But in the heavenly colloquy, God corrects the Satanic theology of the first two books by articulating both the universality of predestining grace and the decisive autonomy of human freedom (Chapter Three). Chapter Four explores the poem's depiction of the contingent freedom of God, and the grounding of creaturely freedom in the deeper reality of this divine freedom. The contingent freedom of creatures comes to light most vividly in *Paradise Lost*'s portrayal of the fall of Adam and Eve (Chapter Five). The poem depicts human nature as universally enslaved through the fall, but also as universally liberated through the operation of prevenient grace. The final chapter of this study (Chapter Six) thus highlights the poem's pronounced universalism of grace, and its emphasis on the decisive role of the freed human will in obtaining salvation.

1. The Theology of Freedom: A Short History

Before turning to *Paradise Lost*, it is necessary to sketch the historical background of the seventeenth-century discussion of freedom. The account that follows begins with Augustine, not of course because the theological discussion of freedom began with him, but because Augustine is the decisive thinker who processed existing theological insights and creatively synthesised Christian ideas of grace and freedom in a way that established the fundamental terms of debate for the ensuing course of Western theology. In the eleventh century, one of Augustine's most influential medieval disciples, Anselm of Canterbury, developed a distinctive approach to the harmonisation of divine and human freedom, and attempted in part to revise the Augustinian view. In the thirteenth and fourteenth centuries, Christian theology was dominated by three thinkers and their respective schools: Thomas Aquinas, Duns Scotus and William of Ockham. These late medieval doctors worked with very diverse metaphysical and epistemological assumptions, and some of their most significant points of difference centred on their understanding of divine and human freedom. In many respects, their treatment of the idea of freedom exceeded in philosophical precision and sophistication the theologising both of their predecessors and of their Reformation and post-Reformation successors. Then in the sixteenth century, the reforming thought of Luther placed utmost emphasis on the relationship between freedom and salvation, while the later theology of Calvin was influential in its assertion of the sovereign freedom of God in predestination. The academic theology of post-Reformation Reformed orthodoxy combined the reformers' soteriological approach to freedom with a more scholastic and philosophical analysis of free agency. Following Calvin, this Reformed scholasticism strongly affirmed the freedom of God, especially in relation to the decree of predestination, while also placing significant restrictions on the scope of fallen human freedom. Reacting against the perceived imbalances of Reformed orthodoxy, the movements of Arminianism and Amyraldism sought to redefine ideas of grace, predestination and freedom in ways that allowed the significance of human choice to emerge more clearly. After outlining these major theological traditions, the historical sketch in this chapter will conclude with Milton's *De Doctrina*

Christiana, a treatise which draws on several theological traditions in order to develop its own independent and distinctive account of freedom.

Augustine

Augustine of Hippo (354–430 CE) developed the Christian tradition's first fully systematised account of freedom, and the influence of this account has been unsurpassed in the development of Western theology. Augustine's theology of freedom was worked out in the context of a sustained polemic against the British monk Pelagius, who had taught that human beings possess the free will (*liberum arbitrium*) and ability to keep God's commandments without the need of any special divine aid, and that the human will has no necessary or natural inclination to evil. For Pelagius, while the ability to obey comes from God, both the will to obey and the act of obedience arise from human nature itself.

Augustine systematically countered this Pelagian understanding of freedom.[1] On the basis of a literal interpretation of the Genesis fall-story, he argued that Adam and Eve were created with the natural endowments of reason and free will.[2] Their freedom consisted not in the fact that they were "unable to sin" (*non posse peccare*), but rather in the fact that they were both "able to sin" (*posse peccare*) and "able not to sin" (*posse non peccare*).[3] Augustine further argued that, in addition to these natural endowments, God gave Adam and Eve the supernatural gifts of immortality and integrity, which preserved them both from death and from concupiscence. The first human beings thus enjoyed a state of holiness in which they remained free to choose between good and evil. By remaining obedient to God and by eating of the Tree of Life, they would have eventually achieved a state of incorporeal, heavenly perfection.

Just as Augustine emphasised the happiness of humanity's original condition, so too he placed special emphasis on the great tragedy of the fall and its consequences. When Eve and Adam used their freedom to eat the forbidden fruit, they forfeited their supernatural gifts, and their natural ability to choose freely was perverted. By misusing their free-

---

1   On the relationship between Augustine's theology and Pelagianism, see Wolf-Dieter Hauschild, "Gnade: IV," *TRE*, 13:480–83.

2   Augustine, *De correptione et gratia*, 28; citations are from the Latin text in *PL* 44, and the translation in *NPNF* 5.

3   Augustine, *De correptione et gratia*, 29–33.

dom, their wills became inclined to concupiscence (*concupiscentia*)[4] and enslaved to evil: "it was by the bad use of his free will (*libero arbitrio male utens*) that man destroyed both it and himself."[5] As a consequence, human nature has lost its ability not to sin, and it is now left only with a miserable inability not to sin: "when man by his own free will sinned, sin was victorious over him and the freedom of his will was lost."[6] In this fallen state, all movements of the will, all choices, are necessarily sinful. According to Augustine, this is not because human nature has lost the freedom of spontaneous and unconstrained choice;[7] this kind of "free will" remains an essential aspect of human nature.[8] But all true "freedom" (*libertas*) — freedom to choose the right — has been lost.[9]

Thus in Augustine's view, human nature has subjected itself to a state of volitional slavery. Further, Augustine argued that all human beings were present in the historical person Adam: "we were all in that one man"[10] and so have inherited original sin, which includes both the guilt (*reatus*) and the corruption (*corruptio*) of human nature. Therefore, "from the bad use of [Adam's] free will (*a liberi arbitrii malo usu*)," the entire human race has become enslaved and condemned.[11] With their freedom vitiated even from birth, all human beings are now volitionally powerless to help themselves.

It was on the basis of this austere vision of human corruption and enslavement that Augustine developed his theology of grace and predestination.[12] Augustine argued that God has eternally decided to save a fixed number of human beings from the condemned mass (*massa*

---

4   See J. N. D. Kelly, *Early Christian Doctrines* (New York: HarperCollins, 1978), 364–65: "In Augustine's vocabulary concupiscence stands, in a general way, for every inclination making man turn from God to find satisfaction in material things which are intrinsically evanescent" — the most common form of which is sexual desire.

5   Augustine, *Enchiridion de fide, spe et charitate*, 30; citations are from the Latin text in *PL* 40, and the translation in *NPNF* 3.

6   Augustine, *Enchiridion*, 30.

7   Augustine, *De spiritu et littera*, 58; citations are from the Latin text in *PL* 44, and the translation in *NPNF* 5.

8   Augustine, *De gratia Christi et de peccato originali contra Pelagium, ad Albinam, Pinianum, et Melaniam*, 1.18; citations are from the Latin text in *PL* 44, and the translation in *NPNF* 5.

9   Augustine, *In evangelium Ioannis tractatus*, 5.1; citations are from the Latin text in *PL* 35, and the translation in *NPNF* 7.

10 Augustine, *De civitate Dei contra paganos*, 13.14; citations are from the Latin text in *PL* 41, and the translation in *NPNF* 2.

11 Augustine, *De civitate Dei*, 13.14.

12 On Augustine's theology of predestination, see James Wetzel, "Predestination, Pelagianism, and Foreknowledge," in *The Cambridge Companion to Augustine*, ed. Eleonore Stump and Norman Kretzmann (Cambridge: Cambridge University Press, 2001), 49–58.

perditionis) of humanity, on the basis of his sheer mercy,[13] and without any regard to foreseen faith or merit.[14] These elect individuals receive not only the gift of grace, but also the free gift of faith. Even the faith by which grace is received is itself a gift,[15] since any desire for grace must already arise from the operation of prevenient grace. Far from compelling or negating the human will, grace's "internal, secret, wonderful and ineffable power" (*interna et occulta, mirabili ac ineffabili potestate*) frees the will from its slavery to sin, creating "good dispositions" and thus enabling the will spontaneously to choose the good.[16] Grace changes the will's inclination, and so renders it free to move in the right direction—free to obey.[17]

With this systematic understanding of freedom, Augustine provided the basic framework within which the theology of freedom continued to evolve in the centuries that followed.

Anselm of Canterbury

Writing in the late eleventh century, Anselm of Canterbury (1033–1109) took up the theological problem of freedom as defined by Augustine, and introduced his own creative elaborations and developments, concentrating especially on the relationship between divine and human freedoms.

Using a more refined philosophical conceptuality than had been available to Augustine, Anselm set out to prove the compatibility of human freedom with divine foreknowledge, predestination and grace.[18] Positing the harmony between these divine and human realities,[19] Anselm searched for "agreements at every level."[20] He argued that divine foreknowledge does not entail a necessitation of human

---

13   Augustine, *De praedestinatione sanctorum ad Prosperum et Hilarium*, 11; citations are from the Latin text in *PL* 44, and the translation in *NPNF* 5.

14   Augustine, *De praedestinatione sanctorum*, 34–38.

15   Augustine, *De praedestinatione sanctorum*, 3.

16   Augustine, *De gratia Christi et de peccato originali*, 1.25.

17   Augustine, *De gratia et libero arbitrio*, 31; citations are from the Latin text in *PL* 44, and the translation in *NPNF* 5.

18   This is the argument of his treatise *De concordia praescientiae et praedestinationis et gratiae dei cum libero arbitrio*; citations are from the Latin text in *Opera omnia*, 6 vols. (Edinburgh: Thomas Nelson, 1938–61), 2:243–88; and the translation in Anselm, *Trinity, Incarnation, and Redemption: Theological Treatises*, ed. and trans. J. Hopkins and H. Richardson (New York: Harper & Row, 1970), 152–99.

19   See Anselm, *De concordia*, 1.1; 1.7; 2.1; 3.1.

20   G. R. Evans, *Anselm and Talking About God* (Oxford: Clarendon, 1978), 93.

choice, since God foreknows the freedom of free choices: "whether you sin or do not sin, it will not be by necessity, because God foreknows that whatever you do will be done without necessity (*sine necessitate*)."[21] To strengthen his denial of necessity, Anselm distinguished between subsequent necessity, in which "a thing that is to occur (*futura*) will occur necessarily," and antecedent necessity, in which "an event will occur because it must necessarily occur."[22] The former kind of necessity is really nothing more than certainty (for instance, tomorrow's revolt will certainly occur because it is foreknown), while the latter is a strict and proper necessity (for instance, tomorrow's sunrise is not merely certain, but intrinsically necessary).[23] Although whatever is going to happen in the future will happen certainly in as much as it has been foreknown by God,[24] this foreknowledge does not impose any necessity on future events. In fact, God foreknows that some things will occur "by necessity" and that others will occur "through the free choice of rational creatures."[25] He foreknows things, in other words, according to their own proper natures—necessary events are foreknown as necessary, and free events as free—so that foreknowledge itself does not influence the proper nature of an event.[26]

Anselm's demonstration of the harmony between predestination and freedom follows similar lines. There is "no contradiction in saying that some things are predestined to occur through free choice,"[27] for God predestines a free agent precisely by "leaving the will to its own power."[28] Thus the person who acts does so by "will alone" (*sola voluntate*) and not by any necessity.[29]

In exploring the harmony between grace and human freedom, Anselm argued that the usual dichotomy between salvation by "grace alone" (*sola gratia*) and salvation by "free choice alone" (*solum liberum arbitrium*) is misleading.[30] Far from being incompatible, grace and freedom must "work together for the justification and salvation of man."[31] Nevertheless, Anselm did not propose a symmetrical synergism, in which salvation is attributed partly to grace and partly to human choice.

21   Anselm, *De concordia*, 1.1.
22   Anselm, *De concordia*, 1.3.
23   The examples are from Anselm, *De concordia*, 1.3.
24   Anselm, *De concordia*, 1.2.
25   Anselm, *De concordia*, 1.3.
26   See G. R. Evans, *Anselm and a New Generation* (Oxford: Clarendon, 1980), 129–30.
27   Anselm, *De concordia*, 2.3.
28   Anselm, *De concordia*, 2.3.
29   Anselm, *De concordia*, 2.3.
30   Anselm, *De concordia*, 3.5.
31   Anselm, *De concordia*, 3.5.

Rather, he grounded the human power of choice itself in divine grace, so that salvation is achieved primarily through grace alone, and secondarily through the human will alone. All those who are born in original sin are "not able" to accept the saving word of God, "unless grace directs their wills"; but those individuals who subsequently reject the word of God must still be blamed for that rejection, since their lack of ability is itself the result of their own free choice.[32] On the other hand, "when God gives the ability to will" to certain people, this ability is to be attributed entirely to grace, even though such people in fact attain salvation through the exercise of their own wills.[33]

In all this, Anselm remained a creative but faithful disciple of Augustine. In his technical account of the nature of human agency, however, Anselm took issue with the Augustinian definition of freedom as "the ability to sin or not to sin" (*potentiam peccandi et non peccandi*).[34] For Anselm, freedom must be defined as the power to choose the good, the ability to preserve a "rectitude of will" (*rectitudinem voluntatis*),[35] since "nothing is more free than a right will."[36] True freedom of will consists in the will's "ability *not* to sin and *not* to serve sin."[37] Freedom is, in other words, "indistinguishable from obedience."[38] As a result, it is clear that the will that is not able to sin—the will of God himself, for instance—is "more free than the will that can desert its rectitude."[39] In the beginning, Adam possessed the ability to enslave himself and to become unfree; paradoxically, Adam's choice to relinquish his freedom was itself a free choice, even though his freedom did not consist in the ability to sin.[40] Adam simply possessed the ability to preserve rectitude of will, but he was also able to turn away from this rectitude. In his primal act of transgression, Adam was therefore "like a man who freely chooses to become another's slave; he made his choice freely, but in abdicating his freedom he did not act like a free man."[41] Through this original abdication of freedom, all human beings have

---

32   Anselm, *De concordia*, 3.7.

33   Anselm, *De concordia*, 3.5.

34   Anselm, *De libertate arbitrii*, 1; citations are from Anselm, *Opera omnia*, 1:201–26; and the translation in Anselm, *Truth, Freedom, and Evil: Three Philosophical Dialogues*, ed. and trans. J. Hopkins and H. Richardson (New York: Harper & Row, 1967), 121–44.

35   Anselm, *De libertate arbitrii*, 3.

36   Anselm, *De libertate arbitrii*, 9.

37   Anselm, *De libertate arbitrii*, 2; emphases added.

38   R. W. Southern, *Saint Anselm and His Biographer: A Study in Monastic Life and Thought, 1059–c.1130* (Cambridge: Cambridge University Press, 1963), 105.

39   Anselm, *De libertate arbitrii*, 1.

40   Anselm, *De libertate arbitrii*, 2.

41   Armand A. Maurer, *Medieval Philosophy* (New York: Random House, 1962), 57.

become "the slaves of sin."[42] Nevertheless, Anselm argued that the fall into servitude has not itself brought about a loss of free will. Since freedom is the *ability* to preserve rectitude, the fallen will—even the will of Satan—remains free, for it always retains this inherent ability, even when it has become merely a formal possibility that can no longer be actualised.[43] Even "in the absence of rectitude," then, nothing prevents a human being from possessing "the *ability* to preserve rectitude"[44]— and freedom is nothing other than this ability.

This subtle definition of freedom allowed Anselm, more than Augustine, to depict freedom as an unqualifiedly good gift from God, a gift that was not already tainted from the outset by the dark possibility of the fall. Further, Anselm's account of freedom sought to clarify the sense in which God is more free than other beings: God alone possesses an uncreated, unoriginated (*a se*) freedom,[45] an immutable freedom to maintain his own perfect rectitude. At the same time, Anselm preserved the most important feature of Augustine's theology of freedom: fallen human beings who have become enslaved to sin can never autonomously regain their rectitude, for they can no longer exercise their true freedom; they can thus be turned away from their slavery "only by another."[46] The rectitude that is necessary for salvation can be received as a free gift "only by the grace of God," although it must subsequently be preserved "by free will."[47] In this way, "grace works harmoniously with free will for the salvation of human beings."[48]

Thomas Aquinas

The thirteenth-century Dominican Thomas Aquinas (ca.1225–74) was the greatest of the late medieval doctors, and, like Anselm, he was above all a disciple of Augustinian theology. Partly through his creative use of the conceptual forms of Aristotelian thought, Thomas was able to explore the psychological aspects of freedom in a more subtle way than his predecessors had done, and also to develop a sophisticated and highly influential synthesis between divine and human freedoms.

---

42   Anselm, *De libertate arbitrii*, 2.
43   Anselm, *De libertate arbitrii*, 3–4; 10–12.
44   Anselm, *De libertate arbitrii*, 4; emphasis added.
45   Anselm, *De libertate arbitrii*, 14.
46   Anselm, *De libertate arbitrii*, 11.
47   Anselm, *De concordia*, 3.3.
48   Anselm, *De concordia*, 3.3.

Building on the intellectualism of Aristotle, Thomas taught that the will follows the dictates of reason, and that reason is of the very essence of freedom. This means that freedom cannot be defined simply as a spontaneous determination of the will,[49] or merely as the absence of coercion.[50] Freedom lies not in the will as such, but in the intellect's clear perception of the good, and in its judgment between differing objects: "wherever there is intellect (*intellectus*), there is free will (*liberum arbitrium*)."[51] According to Thomas, the intellect necessarily tends towards the good; and to know the good is necessarily to choose it. The good, "as soon as known, must also be willed."[52] Although it is therefore an exaggeration to describe the Thomist will merely as "a blind power,"[53] it is true that for Thomas the will can only follow the judgment of reason. Thomas argued that the will "is definable in terms of tending to ... the good as perceived," and, further, that a perception of the good always entails a volitional attraction to it.[54] He even affirmed that every inclination of the will is to some good, although the primacy of the intellect means that an object of volition need not be "good in very truth," but only that it be "apprehended as good" by the intellect (*apprehendatur in ratione boni*).[55] Thus the unfreedom of fallen humanity, for instance, lies not so much in the will itself, but in the intellect. Through sin, the intellect has become darkened by ignorance and clouded by passions, so that its judgment of the good is often mistaken. Even in such cases of mistaken judgment, however, the will acts according to its nature, choosing what the intellect deems to be good.

According to Thomas, the will of God, like the human will, necessarily knows and therefore chooses the good. God, however, chooses his own goodness, and the perfection of this goodness is such that God

---

49   Thomas, *Summa Theologiae*, 1a.83.1; citations are from the Latin text in *Summa Theologiae*, 60 vols. (London: Blackfriars, 1964–76); and the translation in Thomas Aquinas, *Summa Theologica*, trans. Fathers of the English Dominican Province, 3 vols. (New York: Benziger Brothers, 1947–48).

50   For Thomas, the absence of coercion from willing is simply self-evident, since it is the nature of the will to choose voluntarily without coercion. See Thomas, *Summa Theologiae*, 1a.82.1: "necessity of coercion is altogether repugnant to the will," since "it is impossible for a thing to be [both] absolutely coerced ... and voluntary"; that is to say, a coerced will would no longer be a will.

51   Thomas, *Summa Theologiae*, 1a.59.3.

52   Étienne Gilson, *The Philosophy of St. Thomas Aquinas*, trans. G. A. Elrington (New York: Arno Press, 1979), 120.

53   This misleading term is used by John A. Driscoll, "On Human Acts," an essay printed in the English edition of the *Summa Theologica*, 3:3204.

54   Brian Davies, *The Thought of Thomas Aquinas* (Oxford: Clarendon, 1992), 142.

55   Thomas, *Summa Theologiae*, 1a2ae.8.1.

has no need to will anything outside himself.[56] Nevertheless, precisely because of the divine goodness, there is in God also "an infinitely powerful tendency to diffuse and communicate Himself outside Himself,"[57] although this tendency does not necessitate God's creative act. God may choose between opposite possible ways of actualising his goodness, and he can therefore choose to create or not to create any given possibility, just as "we ourselves ... can will to sit down, and not will to sit down."[58] On the other hand, creation cannot be necessitated by anything outside God, since God is himself the cause of everything else,[59] and since all other things are willed ultimately for the purpose of the divine goodness.[60] Creation can therefore be ascribed only to a free and contingent choice of God, which as such is "nothing but a free gift and nothing even remotely resembling a necessity."[61] In short, then, "if we were to ask for God's reason in creating, all that could be said is that it lies in his goodness."[62] The existence of anything at all—and more concretely the existence of this particular world—is thus in Thomas's theology "an instance of what we are talking about when we say that God is loving."[63]

Thomas argued also that God's creation of all that exists implies his providential control over everything outside himself.[64] God's providence is his causal ordering of each thing towards its given end.[65] The natural necessity by which the will wills happiness as its final end is thus grounded in God as the first cause (*prima causa*) of the will's nature, and as the one who providentially orders the will towards its proper end. The divine causality has effected the initial movement of will, so that in this fundamental respect the will is determined and not autonomous.[66] Nevertheless, this causation does not compromise the freedom of the human will or imply that God is the efficient cause of all creaturely acts. Rather, by "the abundance of his goodness" he allows "the dignity of causality" (*dignitatem causalitatis*) to be imparted "even to creatures."[67] There is therefore a synthesis between the divine move-

---

56   Thomas, *Summa Theologiae*, 1a.19.2.
57   Gilson, *The Philosophy of St. Thomas Aquinas*, 141.
58   Thomas, *Summa Theologiae*, 1a.19.10.
59   Davies, *The Thought of Thomas Aquinas*, 145–46.
60   Thomas, *Summa Theologiae*, 1a.19.2.
61   Gilson, *The Philosophy of St. Thomas Aquinas*, 142.
62   Davies, *The Thought of Thomas Aquinas*, 149.
63   Davies, *The Thought of Thomas Aquinas*, 149.
64   Thomas, *Summa Theologiae*, 1a.22.1.
65   Thomas, *Summa Theologiae*, 1a.22.2.
66   Thomas, *Summa Theologiae*, 1a2ae.9.6.
67   Thomas, *Summa Theologiae*, 1a.22.3.

ment of the human will and the freedom of that will, for God moves the will only according to its own proper nature, which consists in an indeterminate freedom of choice.[68] "The divine will extends not only to the doing of something by the thing that he moves, but also to its being done in a way that is fitting to the nature (*congruit naturae*) of that thing."[69] And "just as by moving natural causes [God] does not prevent their acts being natural, so by moving voluntary causes he does not deprive their actions of being voluntary: but rather is he the cause of this very thing in them."[70] In this way, God wills that the human will should function *as* a will—as an indeterminate, contingent potency by which the soul directs itself freely towards the good.

More creatively and more effectively than his predecessors, Thomas thus forged a powerful synthesis of the dual realities of divine will and human will, a synthesis in which human freedom was grounded wholly in the primal freedom of the will of God.

John Duns Scotus

Seeking to provide an alternative to the Thomist system, John Duns Scotus (1265/6–1308) developed an anti-Aristotelian theology of freedom based on the idea of God's sheer freedom, and centred on the concept of radical contingence.

Scotus's highest concern was the freedom of God, and he affirmed consequently the contingent freedom of all creaturely being. By contingence, Scotus meant simply anything the opposite of which might have occurred.[71] According to Scotus, creaturely freedom is grounded in the contingence of the divine creative act. Because God might have acted differently, all his actual works are contingent,[72] and there is no intrinsic reason why created things should be as they are.[73] The nature of creatures thus depends not on any necessity, but on the gracious choice

---

68   Thomas, *Summa Theologiae*, 1a2ae.10.4.

69   Thomas, *Summa Theologiae*, 1a2ae.10.4.

70   Thomas, *Summa Theologiae*, 1a.83.1.

71   See James F. Ross and Todd Bates, "Duns Scotus on Natural Theology," in *The Cambridge Companion to Duns Scotus*, ed. Thomas Williams (Cambridge: Cambridge University Press, 2003), 221.

72   See Josef Pieper, *Scholasticism: Personalities and Problems of Medieval Philosophy*, trans. R. Winston and C. Winston (London: Faber, 1960), 140.

73   See Efrem Bettoni, *Duns Scotus: The Basic Principles of His Philosophy*, trans. Bernardino M. Bonansea (Westport: Greenwood Press, 1978), 153: "In showing how created beings proceed from God, Duns Scotus' main preoccupation is to emphasise both God's freedom and the radical contingency of things."

of God—that is, on the will with which God freely loves and chooses the existence of the creature.[74] Further, Scotus maintained both the divine causation and the volitional contingence of human freedom. Since the human will is a creature, it is causally related to its creator; but God has a causal relationship only to the faculty of the human will as such, not to any specific act of that will. Thus "while God causes any given human will, God does not cause the willing of that will."[75] The only efficient cause of an act of human will is the will itself.

Opposing Thomas's Aristotelian view of the primacy of the intellect, Scotus developed a thoroughgoing voluntarism, maintaining the primacy of the will both in human nature and in the nature of God.[76] At least in this respect, Scotus was a closer follower of Augustine than Thomas had been. Whereas for Thomas the will was said to be determined by the intellect's perception of the good, Scotus claimed that perception of the good is a condition, but not a cause, of choice. Rather the will is entirely self-caused: although the act of the intellect precedes the act of willing, it is not the intellect but only the will that determines its own willing. For Scotus, then, "the principal efficient cause of the volitional act is the will itself, while the act of the intellect is only a necessary condition ... or, at most, a partial cause of it."[77] The will is always free from any external determination, so that freedom is "wholly centred in the radical indetermination of the will, whose unforeseeable decisions spring from within."[78] According to Scotus, freedom therefore consists not in the power for rectitude as Anselm had argued, but in the "self-determining power for opposites."[79] The will is free in so far as it can choose between alternative possibilities.

Analysing the will of God, Scotus emphasised three main features of freedom: neutrality, contingence and spontaneity.[80] First, the power to choose between alternative possibilities (*potestas ad opposita*) is neu-

74 See Bettoni, *Duns Scotus*, 158–59; and Scotus, *Ordinatio*, 4.46.1; in *Duns Scotus on the Will and Morality*, ed. and trans. Allan B. Wolter (Washington: Catholic University Press of America, 1986).

75 Calvin G. Normore, "Duns Scotus's Modal Theory," in *The Cambridge Companion to Duns Scotus*, 144.

76 In this paragraph I have closely followed the discussion of Bettoni, *Duns Scotus*, 81–86.

77 Bettoni, *Duns Scotus*, 83.

78 Étienne Gilson, *The Spirit of Mediaeval Philosophy*, trans. A. H. C. Downes (London: Sheed & Ward, 1950), 310.

79 Marilyn McCord Adams, "Ockham on Will, Nature, and Morality," in *The Cambridge Companion to Ockham*, ed. Paul Vincent Spade (Cambridge: Cambridge University Press, 1999), 252–54.

80 Here I closely follow the summary of the three "focal features" of Scotus's view of freedom in Ross and Bates, "Duns Scotus on Natural Theology," 220–22.

tral to the possibilities, so that nothing in the will itself determines its choice. Second, at the moment of choice the will remains able to choose the opposite, so that the opposite of any given choice remains possible, and every actual choice remains contingent. It is always possible for the divine will "to will the opposite of the thing willed";[81] its choice is never determined by the object of choice.[82] Third, a choice arises only from the ability to choose, and it is never caused by anything outside the will (including the intellect), so that all choices are purely spontaneous.

Scotus's twofold emphasis on divine freedom and the primacy of the will also formed the basis of his ethical thought. He argued that the will of God alone "is the rule and ground (*regula et origo*) of justice,"[83] and that obedience to God is right not by virtue of anything intrinsic in certain acts, but purely by virtue of the divine command. Similarly, Scotus's innovative theology of predestination was grounded in his voluntaristic understanding of divine freedom. Not only did he affirm the contingence of the divine decree, but he also insisted that God's freedom to act in the present is not circumscribed by any decree in the eternal past, since predestination is not an act of the past but a present act "in the eternal now,"[84] and therefore an act that is always free. Scotus also brought his voluntarism to bear on the traditional problem of the divine foreknowledge of future contingents. He admitted that foreknowledge, as an act of the divine intellect, entails the certainty of foreseen events. But he observed that this certainty is not causally related to the future, since only the divine will, not the divine intellect, causes things to be.[85] Thus the future remains contingent regardless of God's foreknowledge.

Scotus's influential reformulation of the medieval problem of the relationship between faith (*fides*) and reason (*ratio*) similarly rested on his understanding of the freedom of God. While Anselm had sought rationally to demonstrate the mysteries of faith, for Scotus the freedom of God meant that things need not be as they are, and that things might have been and might still be other than they are. Thus for him it followed that human reason cannot search out the mysteries of divine freedom—these mysteries can be disclosed only by revelation and ac-

---

81   Bettoni, *Duns Scotus*, 158.

82   See Scotus, *Ordinatio*, 1.39.1; in Richard N. Bosley and Martin Tweedale, eds., *Basic Issues in Medieval Philosophy: Selected Readings Presenting the Interactive Discourses among the Major Figures* (Peterborough: Broadview Press, 1997).

83   Scotus, *Opera omnia*, ed. Luke Wadding, 26 vols. (Paris, 1891–95), 24:205.

84   Scotus, *Opera omnia*, 10:680–81.

85   Scotus, *Opera omnia*, 26:200.

cepted only by faith. At this point, Scotus's theological concentration on freedom profoundly undermined the very basis of theological rationalism and necessitarianism alike. This aspect of his thought would later be developed even more radically by William of Ockham.

William of Ockham

With his wholesale repudiation of metaphysics, the fourteenth-century theologian William of Ockham (ca.1285–ca.1349) departed sharply from both the Platonic realism of Duns Scotus and the Aristotelian realism of Thomas Aquinas,[86] offering instead one of the most creative accounts of freedom in the history of Christian thought.

Ockham asserted the primacy of the will more radically than Scotus had done, affirming even the will's freedom to choose against reason. Ockham believed that the perceptions of the intellect are determined by their object, so that there is no freedom in intellection as such. Thus to affirm with Thomas that the will is governed by the intellect would be to eliminate freedom altogether. For Ockham, freedom of will is precisely the will's power to choose for or against the dictates of the intellect.[87] Freedom thus consists in a neutral and indifferent (*indifferens*) potency of the will to act or not to act under any given set of circumstances. Thus while Thomas had claimed that the will is necessarily inclined towards the goal of happiness, Ockham argued that the will is formally indifferent even in this respect. It remains "free to will or not to will happiness, the last end."[88] Ockham did not deny that the will is subject to certain dispositions and habits; he admitted, for instance, that the will is strongly inclined not to will an object that will result in pain or death. Nevertheless, by its very nature the will remains free vis-à-vis all such inclinations. It always retains the power to choose against even the strongest habit.[89]

---

86 For Ockham's repudiation of realism, see for instance Ockham, *Scriptum in librum primum sententiarum ordinatio*, ed. Girard J. Itzkorn (St Bonaventure: St Bonaventure University, 1979), 1.2.6.

87 Since Ockham's view of freedom is so commonly criticised for threatening ethical responsibility, it is ironic that he denies the primacy of reason precisely on ethical grounds: if a choice is determined by the dictates of reason, then the will is passive and, consequently, not ethically responsible. See Adams, "Ockham on Will, Nature, and Morality," 254–55.

88 Frederick C. Copleston, *A History of Philosophy*, 9 vols. (Westminster: Newman Press, 1946–74), 3:102.

89 Copleston, *History of Philosophy*, 3:102–3.

For Ockham, the notion that the will is free from any subjection to reason led directly to the doctrine of the will's "liberty of indifference" (*libertas indifferentiae*).[90] Deeply influenced by Scotus's view of self-determining contingent freedom, Ockham affirmed that, in spite of the judgment of reason and the influence of various habits and inclinations, the will by its own intrinsic liberty and without any determination can choose either of two contrary possibilities.[91] He defined freedom as "the power by which I can indifferently and contingently posit diverse things, in such a way that I am both able to cause and able not to cause the same effect."[92] The ability to choose is therefore intrinsically neutral and indifferent with respect to the object of choice; in any choice, the will possesses the "capacity for ... the opposite."[93] In contrast to both Platonic and Aristotelian theories of volition, Ockham insisted that even the supreme good (*summum bonum*), when presented to the will by the intellect, may be rejected by a free act of will. Further, Ockham also repudiated the Thomist notion that the will chooses an evil object only because reason mistakenly discerns some good in the object. Ethical responsibility, according to Ockham, depends on the fact that evil is willed *as* evil, not merely under the guise of good.[94]

Scotus's view of the freedom of God became in Ockham's thought a fundamental controlling principle. Criticising Scotus for placing too much emphasis on reason and too little emphasis on the freedom of God's absolute power (*potentia absoluta*), Ockham argued that divine freedom is to be understood essentially "as unlimited freedom in the exercise of power."[95] Thus in response to the scholastic question whether God could have redeemed the human race by means other than the incarnation, Ockham insisted, in contrast to Anselm, that God could just as properly have chosen to redeem humanity by becoming a stone, a tree or an ass.[96]

Emphasising still further the divine freedom, Ockham maintained that, by virtue of the ontological dependence of human beings on their creator, the human will is obligated to obey the moral dictates of the

---

90   See for instance Ockham, *Scriptum in librum primum sententiarum ordinatio*, 1.1.6.

91   William of Ockham, *Quaestiones in librum quartum sententiarum*, ed. R. Wood and G. Gál (St Bonaventure: St Bonaventure University, 1984), 4.16.

92   Ockham, *Quodlibeta septem*, 1.16; from the text in *Quodlibetal Questions*, trans. A J. Freddoso and F. E. Kelley, 2 vols. (New Haven: Yale University Press, 1991).

93   William of Ockham, *Predestination, God's Foreknowledge, and Future Contingents*, ed. and trans. Marilyn McCord Adams and Norman Kretzmann (New York: Appleton, 1969), 86.

94   See Adams, "Ockham on Will, Nature, and Morality," 257–62.

95   Pieper, *Scholasticism*, 148.

96   See Pieper, *Scholasticism*, 148.

divine will. While Thomas had regarded morality as intrinsic to human acts and had viewed the divine commands as expressions of the divine nature, Ockham, like Scotus, sought to ground morality solely in the divine will. In this view, an act is evil only because it is forbidden by God, not because of anything intrinsic in the act or in the divine nature. In Ockham's thought, the freedom of God therefore stands even above good and evil. Although God has in fact forbidden acts such as adultery, theft and hatred of God, these same acts would be meritorious if God were to command rather than forbid them[97] — and the freedom of God means that God could in fact do this without contradicting his own nature. Thus every particular divine command is morally contingent. The only moral necessity is the obligation of the human will to obey the absolute authority of the divine will.

Ockham's thoroughgoing emphasis on the freedom of God led, in the nominalist tradition that followed him, to the concept of "an unknowable and absolutely free God,"[98] a rationally unpredictable deity who could no longer be submitted to theological and philosophical analysis. The influence of the Ockhamist theology of freedom was thus to a significant extent responsible for the collapse of the medieval synthesis.

Martin Luther

In the early sixteenth century, under the influence of Augustine, the German theologian Martin Luther (1483–1546) opposed the theological trends of the Ockhamist *via moderna* and radically reformulated the ideas of human freedom and divine grace. In contrast to the speculative, psychological and metaphysical approaches to freedom which the medieval doctors had developed, Luther's approach to the problem of freedom was pastorally and soteriologically oriented. The human will interested Luther only in so far as it related to God, grace and salvation — that is, it interested him to the extent that it shed light on what he regarded as the central and all-embracing doctrine of justification (*iustificatio*).

Luther's view of the human will was most fully developed in his *De servo arbitrio* (1525),[99] written in polemic against the *De libero arbitrio*

---

97   Ockham, *Quaestiones in librum quartum sententiarum*, 2.19.

98   David Knowles, *The Evolution of Medieval Thought* (London: Longman, 1962), 329.

99   Citations are from the translation in Martin Luther, *Luther's Works*, ed. J. Pelikan and H. T. Lehmann, 55 vols. (St Louis and Philadelphia: Concordia and Fortress, 1958–86), vol. 33; and the Latin text in *D. Martin Luthers Werke: Kritische Gesamtausgabe*, 66

(1524) of Erasmus of Rotterdam.[100] Luther readily acknowledged that free will is "the most excellent thing in human beings";[101] but the universal corruption of sin means that even in the best person free will "neither possesses nor is capable of anything, and does not even know what is righteous in the sight of God."[102] Because of Adam's fall, the human will has been left "with an inability to do anything except sin and be damned."[103] Human nature has become "misdirected"—inclined away from God and towards evil—so that the will cannot do or even attempt what is good.[104] Even those who obey God's law outwardly do not keep it inwardly, and hence the most "splendid, holy, and exalted" of human works "are nothing else than damnable."[105] In short, the human will is "not free, nor is it under its own control";[106] it is "nothing but a slave of sin, death, and Satan, not doing and not able to do ... anything but evil."[107] Luther sums all this up in the uncompromising statement that "free will is nothing."[108]

This severe view of the human will's enslavement may appear to lean towards a metaphysical or psychological determinism, in which the will's power of choice is simply negated. But in asserting the enslavement of the will (*servo arbitrio*), Luther was interested only in the human will as it stands before God (*coram Deo*), not in any psychological faculty of volition. Thus he did not deny the will's power of spontaneous, alternative choice in relation to "moral and civil" matters,[109] or in relation to the sphere of ordinary psychological decisions.[110] In Luther's words: "We are not disputing about nature but about grace, and we are not asking what we are on earth, but what we are in heaven before God.... What we are asking is whether [the human person] has

---

vols. (Weimar: Hermann Böhlaus Nachfolger, 1883–1987), 18:600–787. I will provide references only to the English edition, since this text includes references to the Weimar edition.

100 A translation of the work is in Desiderius Erasmus, *Collected Works of Erasmus*, 86 vols. (Toronto: University of Toronto Press, 1974–93), vol. 76.
101 Luther, *Works*, 33:249.
102 Luther, *Works*, 33:249.
103 Luther, *Works*, 33:272.
104 Luther, *Works*, 33:255.
105 Luther, *Works*, 33:260.
106 Luther, *Works*, 33:238.
107 Luther, *Works*, 33:275.
108 Luther, *Works*, 33:109.
109 Luther, *Works*, 33:270.
110 See E. Gordon Rupp, *The Righteousness of God: Luther Studies* (London: Hodder & Stoughton, 1953), 274–75.

free will in relation to God."[111] And "in relation to God, or in matters pertaining to salvation or damnation, a human being has no free will."[112] Before God and in relation to God, the human will has no freedom. It is enslaved by its own inclination to sin, and is therefore incapable of turning to God for salvation.

The relationship between human freedom and divine grace was central to Luther's theology of the enslaved will. According to Luther, the proclamation of "the help of grace" necessarily entails a simultaneous proclamation of "the impotence of free will."[113] The will's "impotence" was, in other words, asserted only in order to magnify both humanity's need for grace and the freedom of that grace. Luther thus insisted that he was "contending against free will on behalf of the grace of God."[114] Because human beings lack the ability to help themselves, because not even the law of God can help them, "[t]here is need of another light to reveal the remedy," and this light is "the voice of the gospel, revealing Christ as the deliverer."[115] For Luther, those who think that they can contribute "even the least thing" to their own salvation through the exercise of free will cannot receive the grace of God: "no person can be thoroughly humbled until he knows that his salvation is utterly beyond his own powers, devices, endeavours, will and works, and depends entirely on the choice, will and work of another, namely, of God alone."[116] And since God alone brings salvation by his own free will, divine grace is, according to Luther, predestining grace. In the work of salvation, God is utterly free, so that "free will" is properly "a divine term, and can be properly applied to none but the Divine Majesty alone."[117] The fundamental orientation of Luther's theology of freedom and predestining grace was thus not metaphysical, but soteriological: salvation comes from God alone.

---

111 Luther, *Works*, 33:284–85. See Gerhard Ebeling, *Luther: An Introduction to His Thought*, trans. R. A. Wilson (Philadelphia: Fortress, 1970), 218–19.

112 Luther, *Works*, 33:70.

113 Luther, *Works*, 33:244–45.

114 Luther, *Works*, 33:102. See also Luther's argument in *Works*, 33:244–45, that the proclamation of "the help of grace" necessarily entails the simultaneous proclamation of "the impotence of free choice."

115 Luther, *Works*, 33:262.

116 Luther, *Works*, 33:62.

117 Luther, *Works*, 33:68.

John Calvin

The reforming insights of Luther were taken up and developed by the French theologian John Calvin (1509–64), whose thought would prove to be a decisive influence on the future shape of Protestant theology.

Adopting a traditional faculty psychology, Calvin regarded the human soul as comprising both intellect (*intellectus*) and will (*voluntas*).[118] Like Luther, Calvin highlighted the corrupting power of original sin, arguing that "everything that is in a person, from the intellect to the will," is "utterly devoid of goodness."[119] The intellect has been "immersed in darkness," and the will has become "so enslaved by depraved lusts as to be incapable of one righteous desire."[120] Since no part of the soul remains exempt from sin, whatever proceeds from human nature is sinful.[121] Good works, therefore, are impossible for the human will to perform:[122] the will is "bound with the closest chains" of sin.[123]

In what sense, then, may the will be described as "free"? Calvin spoke approvingly of the medieval distinction between three kinds of freedom: "first, from necessity (*a necessitate*); second, from sin (*a peccato*); and third, from misery (*a miseria*): the first is naturally so inherent in humanity that it cannot possibly be lost, while through sin the other two have been lost."[124] Thus according to Calvin, only a freedom from necessity remains to fallen humanity: "a human person is said to have free will not because he has a free choice between good and evil, but only because he acts voluntarily, and not by compulsion (*coactione*)."[125] The freedom of the fallen will, in other words, amounts to nothing more than the fact "that a person is not forced to be the servant of sin,"

---

118 The question whether Calvin was, like Thomas Aquinas, an intellectualist, or, like Scotus, a voluntarist, has provoked considerable debate. See for instance the discussion of Richard A. Muller, *The Unaccommodated Calvin: Studies in the Foundation of a Theological Tradition* (Oxford: Oxford University Press, 2000), 159–73. Although this debate carries significant implications for the interpretation of Calvin's understanding of freedom, it is important not to distort the soteriological character of Calvin's thought by too intensive a philosophical analysis.

119 Calvin, *Institutes*, 2.1.8; citations are from the Latin text in *Institutio christianae religionis* (Geneva, 1563); and the translation in *Institutes of the Christian Religion*, trans. Henry Beveridge, 2 vols. (Grand Rapids: Eerdmans, 1989).

120 Calvin, *Institutes*, 2.2.12.

121 Calvin, *Institutes*, 2.1.9.

122 Calvin, *Institutes*, 2.2.6.

123 Calvin, *Institutes*, 2.2.27.

124 Calvin, *Institutes*, 2.2.5. Calvin takes the distinction from Peter Lombard, *Sententiae in IV libris distinctae* (Rome: Editiones Collegii S. Bonaventurae ad Claras Aquas, 1971–81), 2.25.

125 Calvin, *Institutes*, 2.2.7.

but is instead "a voluntary slave" whose will is firmly bound by an inclination towards sin.[126] Except through regeneration, "the human will is not free, in as much as it is subject to lusts that chain and master it";[127] it "cannot make a movement towards goodness, far less steadily pursue it."[128] Indeed, Calvin emphasised the will's enslavement to such an extent that he even advised the total abolition of the term "free will" from theological discourse.[129]

Calvin's view of human enslavement was, like Luther's, primarily oriented to soteriological concerns. In depriving humanity of every glimmer of self-confidence, Calvin was able to assert the total sovereignty of the grace of God. It is "the Lord" who "supplies us with what is lacking."[130] When the will lies chained by its own evil inclinations, God produces a "conversion in the will": his grace excites "a desire, a love, and a study of righteousness" in the human heart, thus "turning, training, and guiding our hearts to righteousness."[131] The fallen and enslaved will is thus liberated by grace, and "converted solely by the Lord's power (*sola Domini virtute converti*)."[132] Further, Calvin insisted that the liberating action of grace always produces its effect. God does not move the will in such a way that the recipient of grace is left with "the choice to obey or resist"; rather, grace "affects us efficaciously."[133] According to Calvin, this does not mean that the human will is simply inactive, or that it is constrained or compelled by the power of grace, but rather that "we proceed voluntarily, and are inclined to follow the movement of grace," since grace itself has produced a new inclination in the will.[134] Conversion thus consists in an irresistible work of grace that produces a voluntary response from the liberated human will. Following conversion, the entire Christian life is characterised by a

---

126 Calvin, *Institutes*, 2.2.7.
127 Calvin, *Institutes*, 2.2.8. Here Calvin is summarising the position of Augustine, but simultaneously stating his own view.
128 Calvin, *Institutes*, 2.3.5.
129 Calvin, *Institutes*, 2.2.8. Luther, *Works*, 33:70, had already suggested, although less emphatically, that "to let this term go altogether" would be "the safest and most God-fearing thing to do."
130 Calvin, *Institutes*, 2.3.6.
131 Calvin, *Institutes*, 2.3.6.
132 Calvin, *Institutes*, 2.3.7.
133 Calvin, *Institutes*, 2.3.10.
134 Calvin, *Institutes*, 2.3.11. On the will's active involvement in the renewal of human nature, see Susan E. Schreiner, *The Theatre of His Glory: Nature and Natural Order in the Thought of John Calvin* (Grand Rapids: Baker, 1991), 101–3.

liberty in which the believer "cheerfully and alertly" chooses to obey God.[135]

Closely related to Calvin's view of the will's enslavement and sub-sequent liberation was his theology of predestination. Here too, Calvin was motivated by the priority of grace,[136] seeking "to make it appear that our salvation flows entirely from the good mercy of God."[137] The substance of Calvin's predestinarian theology was that "God saves whom he wills of his mere good pleasure (*Deum mero beneplacito*) and does not pay a debt, a debt that never can be due."[138] God cannot be in debt to humanity, since in its corrupted and enslaved state humanity can do nothing to merit the divine favour. In bestowing grace, God thus remains utterly free and therefore utterly gracious. And in eter-nally decreeing to be gracious, God "considered nothing external to himself";[139] he did not ground his decision in any foreseen faith or merit, but only in his own "sovereign pleasure."[140] This strong accent on God's free choice as the ultimate ground of human salvation was, however, counterbalanced in Calvin's thought by the idea of reproba-tion (*reprobatio*), according to which some members of the human race have been "preordained ... to eternal damnation."[141] Again, Calvin could appeal here only to the freedom of God's will: "if we cannot as-sign any reason for [God's] bestowing mercy on his people, but just that it so pleases him, neither can we have any reason for his reprobat-ing others but his will."[142]

The theology of Calvin, with its striking depiction of an eternally active divine freedom as the backdrop to the temporal sphere of human choice, was to exert profound influence on Continental and British theological thought for the next 150 years.

---

135 Calvin, *Institutes*, 3.19.5.
136 This fact sharply qualifies claims that Calvin's view of predestination is simply a form of causal determinism.
137 Calvin, *Institutes*, 3.21.1.
138 Calvin, *Institutes*, 3.21.1.
139 Calvin, *Institutes*, 3.22.3.
140 Calvin, *Institutes*, 3.22.6.
141 Calvin, *Institutes*, 3.21.5.
142 Calvin, *Institutes*, 3.22.11.

Reformed Orthodoxy

The late sixteenth and early seventeenth centuries witnessed the dramatic evolution of Protestant theology in England and Europe.[143] The theology of the Calvinist Reformation gave way to what is usually termed Reformed "orthodoxy" or "scholasticism."[144] This was no longer a theology of reform, but of establishment. The period of Reformed orthodoxy extended roughly from the late sixteenth to the end of the seventeenth century, and in this period there developed both in England and on the Continent "a single but variegated Reformed tradition, bounded by a series of fairly uniform confessional concerns."[145] While early Reformation theology had been mainly oriented towards preaching, pastoral concerns and personal faith, the growing institutionalisation of Protestantism entailed the development of Protestant theology into a formal discipline that could be taught and studied in the universities. The increasing sophistication of philosophy and logic in the university curriculum around the beginning of the seventeenth century also led to more systematic and philosophical approaches to theology, while the humanist advances in philology, lexicography and textual criticism led to a more refined and scholarly engagement with the biblical texts. Thus the "hortatory" and "discursive" style of Reformation theology gave way to a more scholastic, "dialectical" form of theological reflection.[146] Further, as the Roman Catholic Church developed its increasingly sophisticated counter-Reformation polemics,[147] Protestant writers responded by refining and systematising their theology, bringing to their aid the conceptuality of late medieval scholasticism[148] and attempting to demonstrate the catholicity of Protestant dogma by engaging deeply with patristic and medieval traditions.[149]

---

143 For a summary of the social factors that contributed to the rise of Reformed orthodoxy, see Philip Benedict, *Christ's Churches Purely Reformed: A Social History of Calvinism* (New Haven: Yale University Press, 2002), 298–300.

144 The designation of this as the period of orthodoxy is conventional, and the validity of the term "orthodoxy" has been established by recent studies. See especially Muller, *PRRD*, 1:27–84.

145 Richard A. Muller, *After Calvin: Studies in the Development of a Theological Tradition* (Oxford: Oxford University Press, 2003), 7–8. This is, Muller notes, "a major methodological point that influences the historiography of the movement of Reformed thought" (8).

146 Muller, *PRRD*, 1:61.

147 The most important work of Roman polemics was Robert Bellarmine, *Disputationes de controversiis christianae fidei, adversus hujus temporis haereticos*, 4 vols. (Rome, 1586–93).

148 Muller, *PRRD*, 1:63–64.

The differences between Reformation and post-Reformation thought were thus more formal than material: the theology of the Reformation was adapted by later generations of thinkers in response to the intellectual demands imposed by a changing social and religious milieu.

The Reformed orthodox account of the fall of humanity contrasted the perfect freedom of the prelapsarian state with the corruption and enslavement brought about by sin. The Reformed writers viewed human freedom not as an Ockhamist liberty of indifference, in which the will is able to choose between two alternative possibilities, but rather as a positive ability to choose the good.[150] Reformed theologians argued that the prelapsarian freedom of Adam and Eve did not consist in an indifferent ability to sin or not to sin, since a will that was equally capable of good and evil would have already been an evil will;[151] an indifference between good an evil would be "a flaw in the creature" and even the "origin of sin."[152] Thus according to Reformed orthodoxy, the prelapsarian will was "directed and naturally inclin'd to God and Goodness,"[153] and it possessed no "irregular bias or inclination" towards anything except the good.[154] But in spite of the will's perfection, it was also "subject unto change"[155] and was "moveable to Evil" by "Man himself."[156] Thus the Reformed writers argued not that Adam became sinful when he ate the forbidden fruit, but that he was "a sinner before he did the eating," since he must have already inclined his own will towards evil before actually transgressing.[157] This self-determination towards evil was not so much an exercise of human freedom as an abdication of it.

According to Reformed orthodoxy, when Adam sinned, he relinquished his true freedom. Through the abuse of his freedom he "wilfully subjected himself to sin,"[158] bringing on himself "blindness of

---

149 Richard A. Muller, "The Problem of Protestant Scholasticism: A Review and Definition," in *Reformation and Scholasticism: An Ecumenical Enterprise*, ed. Willem J. van Asselt and Eef Dekker (Grand Rapids: Baker, 2001), 63.

150 See Muller, *PRRD*, 3:447.

151 Thomas Boston, *Human nature in its four-fold state* (Edinburgh, 1720), 7.

152 Johann Heinrich Heidegger, *Corpus theologiae* (Zurich, 1700), 6.99; cited in Heppe, 243.

153 Boston, *Human nature in its four-fold state*, 7.

154 Thomas Boston, *Commentary on the Shorter Catechism*, 2 vols. (Aberdeen, 1853), 1:182.

155 Westminster Confession of Faith, 4.2; in Schaff, 3:611.

156 Boston, *Human nature in its four-fold state*, 12.

157 William Ames, *The Marrow of Theology*, ed. and trans. John D. Eusden (Grand Rapids: Baker, 1968), 1.11.6.

158 *Confessio Belgica*, 14; in Schaff, 3:398.

mind, horrible darkness, vanity, and perverseness of judgment."[159] Deriving their corruption from Adam through original sin (*peccatum originale*), human beings are now "incapable of all saving good, prone to evil, dead in sin, and in bondage."[160] Thus the human will is characterised by both "Averseness to Good"[161] and a "woeful *Bent* towards Sin."[162] Because the will is enslaved in this way, those who are converted by grace cannot ascribe any merit to their own free will, but only to the freely acting God who "gives them faith and repentance, and rescues them from the power of darkness."[163] God softens the heart, quickens the will and infuses it with new qualities so that it becomes a good will, liberated from its enslavement to evil desires.[164] And Reformed orthodox writers insisted that the fallen will's enslavement is so great that this liberating work of grace is nothing less than "miraculous and supernaturall":[165] it is just as powerful as "creation or the resurrection of the dead."[166]

While Reformed orthodoxy did not understand human freedom in terms of an indifference between alternative possibilities, it nevertheless viewed the freedom of God as including a contingent liberty of indifference. In this respect, as in many others, Reformed orthodox theology exhibited significant continuity with Scotist thought. Reformed writers argued that God might have chosen not to will what he has actually willed; in particular, he might have chosen not to create the world.[167] God in fact "wills all things such that he is able not to will them,"[168] and, having willed them, they exist always as things that "he might not have willed."[169] This "indifference of the divine will" is, indeed, "the greatest proof of his perfection who, as an independent being, needs nothing out of himself."[170] The will of God is thus contin-

---

159 *Canones synodi Dordrechtanae*, 3/4.1; in Schaff, 3:564.

160 *Canones synodi Dordrechtanae*, 3/4.3; in Schaff, 3:564.

161 Boston, *Human nature in its four-fold state*, 82.

162 Boston, *Human nature in its four-fold state*, 86.

163 *Canones synodi Dordrechtanae*, 3/4.10; in Schaff, 3:566.

164 *Canones synodi Dordrechtanae*, 3/4.11; in Schaff, 3:566.

165 William Perkins, *A golden chaine: or, The description of theologie* (Cambridge, 1592), 272.

166 *Canones synodi Dordrechtanae*, 3/4.12; in Schaff, 3:567.

167 Francis Turretin, *Institutes of Elenctic Theology*, ed. James T. Dennison, trans. George Musgrave Giger, 3 vols. (Phillipsburg: P&R, 1992–97), 3.14.6.

168 Turretin, *Institutes*, 3.14.5.

169 Leonhardus Rijssen, *Francisci Turretini compendium theologiae didactico–elencticae ex theologorum nostrorum institutionibus auctum et illustratum* (Amsterdam, 1695), 3.28; cited in Heppe, 84.

170 Turretin, *Institutes*, 3.14.7.

gent, and there is "no necessary connection" between the divine nature and the acts of the divine will.[171]

This emphasis on divine freedom was particularly pronounced in the Reformed orthodox conception of an absolute decree (*decretum absolutum*) that stands behind all temporal events. The decree of God was described as "an internal act of the divine will, by which God determines, from eternity, freely, with absolute certainty, those matters which shall happen in time."[172] The decreeing will of God "is most free, completely and absolutely free, depending on nothing else."[173] And God's eternal decree is completely effectual in bringing about all things: God "hath most certainely decreed every thing and action, whether past, present, or to come."[174] God's will cannot be thwarted or frustrated, for "if [God] should properly will anything and not attain it he would not be wholly perfect."[175] But while the will of God is always effectual, it is not always an immediate or efficient cause of temporal events.[176] In particular, Reformed writers insisted that the divine will is only the permissive cause, never the efficient cause, of evil. Both good and evil "result from the decree and will of God; the former by efficient, the latter by permissive decree."[177] Thus the decree and will of God "are in no sense the cause of evil or sin, even though whatever God has decreed necessarily happens."[178]

In its account of the divine decree, Reformed orthodoxy was especially concerned with the predestination of human beings to salvation or damnation. Like Calvin, Reformed theology divided the human race into the two classes of elect (*electi*) and reprobate (*reprobi*): "some men and angels are predestinated unto everlasting life, and others foreordained to everlasting death."[179] This double predestination (*praedestinatio gemina*) serves the ultimate goal of God's glory, the "manifesting of the praise and excellencie of [his] glorious grace" in the election of some,[180] and the "manifestation of his justice" in the rejection of the rest.[181]

---

171 Ames, *Marrow of Theology*, 1.7.36.

172 Johannes Wollebius, *Compendium theologiae christianae*; in *Reformed Dogmatics*, ed. and trans. John W. Beardslee (Oxford: Oxford University Press, 1965), 1.3.3.

173 Ames, *Marrow of Theology*, 1.7.35.

174 Perkins, *A golden chain*, 19.

175 Ames, *Marrow of Theology*, 1.7.48.

176 Turretin, *Institutes*, 3.14.16.

177 Wollebius, *Compendium theologiae christianae*, 1.3.3.

178 Wollebius, *Compendium theologiae christianae*, 1.3.3.

179 Westminster Confession of Faith, 3.3; in Schaff, 3:608–9.

180 William Perkins, *An exposition of the symbole or creed of the apostles* (Cambridge, 1595), 436.

181 Perkins, *An exposition of the symbole or creed*, 448.

Further, God's predestining decision is based solely on his "absolutely free will," and not on any foreseen merit or demerit in his creatures.[182] Indeed, for the Reformed writers "there is no cause of God's will";[183] or rather, the sole cause is "the good pleasure of God" (*beneplacitum Dei*),[184] that is, the will of God itself. There can therefore be "no cause, or condition, or reason ... in man, upon the consideration of which God chose this rather than another one."[185] Here Reformed orthodox theology sought, as Luther and Calvin had done, to highlight the gratuitous character of grace—"the freedom and glory of sovereign grace"[186]—by removing any hint of creaturely influence from the will of God. If God's decisions were logically subsequent to the decisions of human beings, then the will of God would be "mutable and dependent upon the act of the creature";[187] and it is "absurd for the creator to depend upon the creature, God upon man and the will of God (the first cause of all things) upon the things themselves."[188]

Within Reformed orthodoxy there was, however, division over the question of the object of predestination (*obiectum praedestinationis*). According to the infralapsarian party, God's decree to create humanity and permit the fall logically precedes the decree to elect and reprobate, so that the object of predestination is "the human person created and fallen" (*homo creatus et lapsus*).[189] In contrast, according to the supralapsarians, the decree to create and permit the fall logically follows the decree to elect and reprobate, so that the object of predestination is "the creatable and lapsable person" (*homo creabilis et labilis*).[190] The supralapsarian view thus represents a more severe form of Reformed theology, in which God is depicted as creating a certain number of human beings for the specific purpose of reprobating and destroying them.[191] Still, in both the infra- and supralapsarian views, the accent on

---

182 Wollebius, *Compendium theologiae christianae*, 1.4.2.

183 Ames, *Marrow of Theology*, 1.7.39–40.

184 *Canones synodi Dordrechtanae*, 1.10; in Schaff, 3:554.

185 Turretin, *Institutes*, 4.11.9.

186 Boston, *Commentary on the Shorter Catechism*, 1:311.

187 Ames, *Marrow of Theology*, 1.7.43.

188 Turretin, *Institutes*, 4.3.4. See also Amandus Polanus, *Syntagma theologiae christianae* (Geneva, 1617), 4.6.

189 For a detailed presentation of the infralapsarian position, see Turretin, *Institutes*, 4.9.1–31.

190 By far the most elaborate defence of supralapsarianism is the massive work of William Twisse, *Riches of Gods love unto the vessells of mercy, consistent with his absolute hatred or reprobation of the vessels of wrath*, 2 vols. (Oxford, 1653).

191 Supralapsarianism could, however, also be presented in more moderate forms. See Guy M. Richard, "Samuel Rutherford's Supralapsarianism Revealed: A Key to the

divine freedom is pronounced. The controversy illustrates the manner in which Reformed orthodox theologians could employ refined scholastic forms of reasoning in their attempt to define precisely the free decision of God that stands behind all human history.

Arminianism

Reacting against the Reformed orthodox views of grace, predestination and freedom, the Dutch theologian Jacobus Arminius (1560–1609) developed a reformulation of Protestant theology that gave rise to bitter controversy in both England and Europe.

In the late sixteenth century, Arminius, who had studied under Calvin's disciple Theodore Beza, was asked to refute a polemical treatise that had been penned against Beza's strict supralapsarianism. But instead of refuting this anti-Calvinist treatise, Arminius had occasion to articulate his own distinctive view of grace and predestination. In doing so, he entered into sharp conflict with the Reformed orthodox establishment.[192] Arminius's appointment to the chair of theology at Leiden in 1603 initiated one of the most heated and far-reaching theological controversies of the post-Reformation era, with Arminius's followers pitted against the Reformed orthodox theologians. In response to this socially and politically intense theological controversy, the Dutch state called the international Synod of Dort in 1618–19; the Synod condemned Arminianism and affirmed a strictly Reformed theology of predestination, grace and freedom.[193] The temporary suppression of Arminian theology in The Netherlands coincided, however, with the growing influence of Arminianism elsewhere in Europe and England.[194]

Lapsarian Position of the Westminster Confession of Faith?" *Scottish Journal of Theology* 59:1 (2006), 27–44.

192 Older scholarship tended to perpetuate the legend that Arminius was at first a zealous Calvinist. It is, however, historically more probable that Arminius had never been a convinced Calvinist. The story of Arminius' conversion from Calvinism seems to have originated in the biographical account of Petrus Bertius, *The life and death of James Arminius and Simon Episcopius, professors of divinity in the University of Leyden in Holland* (London, 1672), 13–14, which depicts Arminius, after a painful struggle, being "overcome by the truth" through "the guidance of the holy Ghost."

193 The articles of the Arminian Remonstrance, entitled *Articuli Arminiani sive remonstrantia*, are reproduced in Schaff, 3:545–49; and the orthodox canons, entitled *Canones synodi Dordrechtanae*, are reproduced in Schaff, 3:550–97.

194 This account of theological Arminianism is not concerned with the English Laudian movement. In his important study, Nicholas Tyacke, *Anti-Calvinists: The Rise of English Arminianism, c.1590–1640* (Oxford: Clarendon, 1987), describes Laudianism as "Arminian." Tyacke uses the term not theologically, but as a label for a particular ec-

Formally, Arminian theology remained close to Reformed orthodoxy; but materially, it made a decisive break with the orthodox conceptions of freedom and grace. Following orthodoxy, Arminius divided
human history into a series of distinct "states": the state of innocence,
the state of corruption, and the state of renewed righteousness.[195] In the
state of innocence, human nature was characterised by a clear intellect
and a will that was holy yet mutable, being able by a "spontaneous as
well as free motion" to turn away from God.[196] By freely turning away
from the "Chief Good" towards an "inferior good," human nature enslaved itself.[197] In this state of corruption, then, the "free will of man" is
"not only wounded, maimed, infirm, bent, and weakened; but it is also
imprisoned (captivatum), destroyed, and lost."[198] With Reformed orthodoxy, Arminianism affirmed that the will is enslaved to such an extent
that it can do nothing spiritually good: "Man ... in the state of apostasy
and sin, can of and by himself neither think, will nor do anything that
is truly good."[199] Arminius insisted that the fallen intellect is "dark"
and "destitute"; the fallen will "loves" evil but "hates and has an aver-
sion to that which is truly good"; and the entire soul is characterised by
"utter weakness" (impotentia).[200] In short, the fallen human being is
"under the power of sin and Satan, reduced to the condition of a
slave."[201]

Arminian theology therefore emphasised the necessity of grace. A
person must be "regenerated and renovated in understanding, inclination, or will, and in all his powers" in order to "understand, think, will
and effect what is truly good."[202] The grace of God excites "new affections, inclinations and motions" in the human heart; it generates "new

---

clesiastical approach. Other studies have, however, confused these two distinct uses
of the term "Arminian," thus mistakenly assuming certain connections between ec-
clesiastical Laudianism and theological Arminianism. In such cases, the designation
of the Laudians as "Arminian" would be misleading, since these churchmen in general were concerned not with the theology of grace but with liturgical and ecclesiasti-
cal reform. On this confusion of terms, see Benedict, *Christ's Churches Purely Reformed*, 386. In the present study, "Arminian" is used only as a theological term,
without any reference to Laudian ecclesiology.

195 Jacobus Arminius, *The Works of James Arminius*, trans. James Nichols and William
Nichols, 3 vols. (Grand Rapids: Baker, 1986), 2:191.
196 Arminius, *Works*, 2:191–92.
197 Arminius, *Works*, 2:192.
198 Arminius, *Works*, 2:192.
199 *Articuli Arminiani sive remonstrantia*, 3; in Schaff, 3:546–47.
200 Arminius, *Works*, 2:192–94.
201 Arminius, *Works*, 2:194.
202 *Articuli Arminiani*, 3; in Schaff, 3:546–47.

powers" to enable the will to choose the good.[203] Grace applies a "gentle persuasion adapted to move the will,"[204] and thus "bends the will" towards the good.[205] In this way, the human will is "liberated" from its former captivity.[206] According to Arminianism, grace is therefore "the beginning, continuance and accomplishment of all good,"[207] so that "without this preceding, or preventing, exciting, following and co-operating Grace," no one can "think, will, or perform any thing that is savingly good."[208]

Having gone this far with Reformed orthodoxy, Arminian theology nevertheless also argued that "the mode of the operation of this grace" is "not irresistible."[209] In spite of the power of divine grace, the human will is able to "despise and reject the Grace of God, and resist the operation of it,"[210] through "the wickedness and hardness of the human heart."[211] While according to Reformed orthodoxy regenerating grace is given only to the elect, Arminian theology asserted that such grace "is granted even to those who do not comply."[212] This grace is therefore a "sufficient grace" (*gratia sufficiens*), but not an "efficacious grace" (*gratia efficax*).[213] Sufficient grace makes regeneration possible, but not yet actual; it is "sufficient to beget Faith,"[214] but it "does not always obtain its effect."[215] Those who obtain salvation "freely yield their assent to grace" — they can, of course, yield this assent only because they have been "previously excited, impelled, drawn and assisted by grace" — but "in the very moment in which they actually assent, they possess the capability of not assenting."[216] The point here is a subtle one, but it was at the heart of the Arminian critique of Reformed orthodoxy. According to Arminianism, the fallen will remains free in one decisive respect. Enabled by grace, it retains the power either to choose or to reject the

---

203 Arminius, *Works*, 2:194.
204 Arminius, *Works*, 3:454.
205 Arminius, *Works*, 2:700.
206 Arminius, *Works*, 2:194.
207 *Articuli Arminiani*, 4; in Schaff, 3:547.
208 Simon Episcopius, *The confession or declaration of the ministers or pastors which in the United Provinces are called Remonstrants, concerning the chief points of Christian religion* (London, 1676), 204.
209 *Articuli Arminiani*, 4; in Schaff, 3:547.
210 Episcopius, *The confession or declaration*, 205.
211 Arminius, *Works*, 2:397.
212 Arminius, *Works*, 2:721.
213 Arminius, *Works*, 2:721–22.
214 Episcopius, *The confession or declaration*, 207.
215 Arminius, *Works*, 2:722.
216 Arminius, *Works*, 2:722.

offer of salvation. Grace itself does not secure the conversion of any specific person; it makes conversion possible, but ultimately it is the human will that casts the deciding vote.[217]

The Arminian theology of predestination similarly gave greater prominence to the role of human choice, without departing from the basic conceptual categories of Reformed orthodox doctrine. Following Reformed orthodoxy, the Arminian theologians viewed predestination as "an eternal and immutable decree" that God has "determined" from "before the foundation of the world."[218] The cause of this decree is simply the "good pleasure of God."[219] Further, Arminianism also affirmed reprobation as the logical opposite of election: "Election necessarily implies Reprobation."[220] In reprobation, God has "resolved from all eternity to condemn to eternal death unbelievers,"[221] and thus "to leave the contumacious and unbelieving under sin and wrath."[222] The difference between Arminianism and Reformed theology at this point lay not in the conception of predestination itself, but in the understanding of the ground (*fundamentum*) and object (*obiectum*) of predestination. In contrast to Reformed orthodoxy, Arminianism grounded both election and reprobation in the divine foreknowledge: God decrees "to receive into favour (*gratiam*) those who repent and believe," but "to leave under sin and wrath those who are impenitent and unbelievers."[223] God's decree to accept and reject these believers and unbelievers therefore "rests or depends on the prescience and foresight of God, by which he foreknew from all eternity" those persons who would respond to grace,

---

217 Arminius taught that the fallen will, unaided by grace, possesses a negative ability (the power to reject grace), but that it lacks any positive ability (the power to accept grace). Without the prior assistance of prevenient grace, the fallen will is not capable of accepting grace; but the operation of prevenient grace also gives the will this positive ability. At issue here was not simply a precise understanding of the capacities of the fallen will, but the whole theological understanding of grace itself. From the Reformed perspective, Arminius's position removed the *sola* from *sola gratia*, since grace becomes something that does not secure conversion purely by its own action.

218 *Articuli Arminiani*, 1; in Schaff, 3:545.

219 Arminius, *Works*, 2:392.

220 Arminius, *Works*, 2:228. This feature of Arminian theology is often overlooked in the scholarly literature. Even a historian as accomplished as Nicholas Tyacke, "Puritanism, Arminianism and Counter-Revolution," in *The Origins of the English Civil War*, ed. Conrad Russell (London: Macmillan, 1973), 119, can describe the "essence of Arminianism" in these terms: "Arminians rejected the teaching of Calvinism that the world was divided into elect and reprobate whom God had ... predestinated, the one to Heaven and the other to Hell."

221 Arminius, *Works*, 2:228.

222 *Articuli Arminiani*, 1; in Schaff, 3:545.

223 Arminius, *Works*, 2:719.

and those who would reject it.[224] In this way, the Arminians grounded predestination in God's foreknowledge of the human response to grace. According to Reformed orthodoxy, individuals believe because they have been elected; according to Arminianism, they are elected because they will believe. Thus in Arminianism, the object of predestination was thought to be not creatable human beings (as in Reformed supra-lapsarianism) or fallen human beings (as in infralapsarianism), but *believing* human beings. God has eternally decreed to save "believers,"[225] that is, all those who in the future "shall believe" and who are thus foreseen to be believers.[226] This view of foreseen faith (*praevisa fides*) illustrates the underlying concern of Arminianism to assign greater importance and autonomy to the human will, and to prevent the decisive role of human freedom being undermined or negated by the absolute and inscrutable will of God.

Amyraldism

Attempting to find a middle way between the entrenched positions of Reformed orthodoxy and Arminianism, a creative new theological account of grace and freedom emerged in the Academy of Saumur in seventeenth-century France. This theological tradition, usually referred to as Saumur theology or Amyraldism, originated in the thought of John Cameron (1579–1625), a Scotsman who taught theology at Saumur from 1618 to 1621; and it was then more fully and more influentially developed by Moïse Amyraut (1596–1664), a French theologian at Saumur from 1626 until 1664.

Amyraldism's most distinctive contribution to post-Reformation theology was its theory of "hypothetical universalism" (*l'universalisme hypothétique*). Amyraut argued that God has replaced the legal covenant of the Old Testament with a covenant of grace, in which God displays "grace in favour of all people indifferently" through Christ.[227] Never-

---

224 Arminius, *Works*, 2:719. Further, Arminius's theology of divine providence adopts the Molinist concept of middle knowledge (*scientia media*) in order to emphasise the contingent freedom of the foreknown acts of human will. Thus when God foresees a person's response to grace (and on the basis of this foreknowledge predestines that person to salvation), he is not merely foreseeing an effect of his own providential work, but a genuinely contingent act of the human will.

225 Arminius, *Works*, 2:226.

226 *Articuli Arminiani*, 1; in Schaff, 3:545.

227 Moïse Amyraut, *Paraphrases sur les epistres de l'apostre s. Paul au Galates, Ephesiens, Philippiens, Colossiens, I Thessaloniciens, II Thessaloniciens* (Saumur, 1645), 151; cited in Brian G. Armstrong, *Calvinism and the Amyraut Heresy: Protestant Scholasticism and*

theless, this covenant of grace does not convey salvation automatically, but only on the basis of the fulfilment of the condition of faith. According to Amyraut the grace of salvation is thus universal, but also conditional. It was this emphasis on universality that evoked particularly bitter opposition from the Reformed orthodox establishment, leading to the controversy over universal grace that continued until the end of the seventeenth century.

In contrast to Reformed orthodoxy's pronounced emphasis on particularism, the Amyraldian theologians described grace as both universal and particular. This soteriological dualism was especially expressed in the Amyraldian view of predestination. In contrast both to supralapsarianism, which placed the election and rejection of specific individuals at the head of God's decree, and to infralapsarianism, which placed creation but not grace at the head of the decree, Amyraut's theology of predestination began with God's general benevolence towards the whole human race: God foresaw that his gracious plan to perfect humanity would be ruined by the fall, and so he ordained Christ to be the redeemer of the whole human race. All human beings are elected to partake of salvation through Christ on the condition that they exercise faith in Christ: "these words, *God wills the salvation of all people*, necessarily meet this limitation, *provided that they believe*.... [God's] will to make the grace of salvation universal and common to all people is conditional in such a way that, without the accomplishment of the condition, it is entirely ineffective."[228] Amyraut thus insisted that everything depends on this condition: salvation "is destined equally for all" in so far as they are willing to receive it.[229] And yet he agreed with the Reformed orthodox view of the spiritual enslavement of the will: no fallen human being can exercise faith, and hence no one is in fact able to fulfil the condition of predestination to salvation.

The Amyraldian system therefore introduced a second decree of predestination. Foreseeing that no one could fulfil the necessary condition of predestination to salvation, God elected to grant the gift of faith to some particular human beings, thereby graciously enabling them to meet the condition of faith. There is thus both a general "predestination to salvation" and a particular "predestination to faith,"[230] both a conditional decree and an absolute decree; or, in other words, both the uni-

---

Humanism in Seventeenth-Century France (Madison: University of Wisconsin Press, 1969), 152 n. 98.

228 Moïse Amyraut, *Brief traitté de la predestination et de ses principales dependances* (Saumur, 1634), 89–90.

229 Amyraut, *Brief traitté de la predestination*, 78.

230 Amyraut, *Brief traitté de la predestination*, 163.

versalism of Arminianism and the particularism of Reformed orthodoxy. With this formulation, Amyraldism maintained a sharp focus on
the human role in salvation, as well as an emphasis on the ultimate
impossibility of salvation apart from the gift of irresistible grace.[231]

Further, in contrast to the voluntarism of Reformed orthodoxy,
Amyraut developed a faculty psychology closer to that of Arminianism, regarding the intellect as "the governor" of the soul.[232] For Amyraut, "[t]he power of choice resides in the understanding, and whatever
choice it makes the will must follow."[233] It is "natural" for the intellect
both to perceive and "to love ardently" the true and the good.[234] As in
Thomism, then, the intellect possesses a "natural and necessary" tendency towards the supreme good.[235] Original sin has not corrupted this
tendency, but has only brought a "thick darkness" upon the intellect so
that it fails rightly to perceive and approve of the good.[236] As a result,
the will is misled and so fails to choose what is good. Thus while Reformed orthodoxy affirmed the direct enslavement of the will, and
consequently the need for the direct influence of regenerative grace, in
Amyraldism the will is enslaved only indirectly, in as much as it is
governed by a fallen intellect.

This intellectualist account of human freedom, and of the effect of
sin on freedom, formed the basis of Amyraut's theology of conversion.
Cameron had taught that the will is converted indirectly, through the
enlightenment and persuasion (*persuasio*) of the intellect by grace.
Similarly, Amyraut believed that the fallen will is always essentially
free. Because of the darkening of the intellect, the will has lost its
"moral" ability to choose the good; but its "natural" ability remains
intact as an inherent aspect of human nature.[237] Conversion, then, does
not require any direct regeneration of the will, but only an enlighten-

---

231 On Amyraut's doctrine of predestination, see Jürgen Moltmann, "Prädestination
     und Heilsgeschichte bei Moyse Amyraut," *Zeitschrift für Kirchengeschichte* 65 (1953–
     54), 270–303.
232 Moïse Amyraut, *Sermons sur divers textes de la sainte ecriture* (Saumur, 1653), 269; cited
     in Armstrong, *Calvinism and the Amyraut Heresy*, 243 n. 4.
233 Armstrong, *Calvinism and the Amyraut Heresy*, 243.
234 Amyraut, *Brief traitté de la predestination*, 157.
235 Amyraut, *Sermons sur divers textes*, 274; cited in Armstrong, *Calvinism and the Amy-
     raut Heresy*, 245–46 n. 17.
236 Amyraut, *Brief traitté de la predestination*, 48, 98–99. See also John Cameron, *An exami-
     nation of those plausible appearances which seeme most to commend the Romish Church, and
     to prejudice the Reformed* (Oxford, 1626), 4–5.
237 In the eighteenth century, the same distinction between "moral" and "natural"
     ability was taken up and developed by the American theologian Jonathan Edwards:
     see Jonathan Edwards, *A careful and strict enquiry into the modern prevailing notions of
     ... freedom of will* (London, 1762).

ment of the intellect, which in turn directs the will towards God. Even in conversion, divine grace operates "according to the natural processes of human psychology."[238]

The Amyraldian insistence on the goodness of God, coupled with its emphasis on human freedom and integrity, resulted in a more circumscribed view of divine freedom than that of Reformed orthodoxy. While Reformed orthodoxy distinguished between the necessary justice by which God condemns sinners and the unnecessitated mercy by which God saves sinners, Amyraldism sought to make goodness rather than justice the supreme divine attribute. Cameron thus asserted that the exercise of mercy is even more necessary than the exercise of justice, and Amyraut argued that all God's actions are subordinated to the divine character.[239] Because of his goodness, God "cannot but love" unfallen human beings; and he is "unable not to love" those who are fallen but repentant.[240] In Amyraldian theology, universal grace was therefore said to be grounded in a moral necessity of the divine nature: God is gracious to all because he is by nature inclined to be gracious. Such a conception of the divine nature—the antithesis of the "absolute power" of Ockham's God—constituted a bold attempt to integrate the universalism of Arminianism with the predestinarianism of Reformed orthodoxy, while excluding any shadow of arbitrariness from God's relationship to humanity.

De Doctrina Christiana

The treatise now known as the *De Doctrina Christiana* was discovered, as a "complicated mess of manuscript,"[241] among John Milton's state papers in 1823.[242] In the treatise, Milton adopts a highly biblicist theological

---

238 G. Michael Thomas, *The Extent of the Atonement: A Dilemma for Reformed Theology from Calvin to the Consensus, 1536–1675* (Carlisle: Paternoster, 1997), 198.

239 See Thomas, *The Extent of the Atonement*, 198.

240 Moïse Amyraut, *Mosis Amyraldi dissertationes theologicae quatuor* (Saumur, 1645), 30–31, 36–39; cited in Thomas, *The Extent of the Atonement*, 198.

241 Roy Flannagan, *John Milton: A Short Introduction* (Oxford: Blackwell, 2002), 74. For a brief account of the manuscript and its history, see Thomas N. Corns, *John Milton: The Prose Works* (New York: Twayne, 1998), 136–39. The Columbia edition of Milton's works (*CM*) includes a Latin transcription of the *De Doctrina* with an English translation by Charles R. Sumner; and the Yale edition of Milton's works (*CPW*) includes an English translation by John Carey with extensive annotations by Maurice Kelley. John K. Hale is currently transcribing and translating the treatise for a new critical edition, to be published by Oxford University Press.

242 The treatise is generally thought to have been completed some time shortly before 1660. James Holly Hanford, "The Date of Milton's *De Doctrina Christiana," Studies in*

method, seeking "to cram my pages even to overflowing (*ingerentibus redundare*) with quotations from Scripture, and to leave as little space as possible for my own words."[243] Indeed, the pages of the treatise are filled with over nine thousand biblical quotations, so that the whole work is more biblicist than perhaps any other post-Reformation systematic theology.[244] Although the treatise's authorship was challenged in recent years, the emerging scholarly consensus is that it can rightly be described as "Miltonic," even though it is an uneven and unfinished work, and even though no full reconstruction of the various stages of its composition and revision has been possible. In spite of the remaining questions surrounding the *De Doctrina's* textual history and its relationship to the rest of the Miltonic corpus, the treatise remains a highly significant feature of the theological context within which *Paradise Lost* must be situated.

The *De Doctrina* argues forcefully against the Reformed orthodox notion of an absolute decree.[245] It is "beyond dispute" that God "has not decreed all things absolutely" but has rather decreed things "in a non-absolute (*non absoluta*) way."[246] This denial of the absoluteness of predestination is grounded in the treatise's commitment to human freedom: if the decree were absolute, "we [should] have to jettison entirely all human freedom of action, all endeavour or desire to do right."[247] According to the treatise, God "has not decreed everything absolutely";[248] if he had done so, or if divine foreknowledge necessitated the

---

Philology 17 (1920), 309–19, dates the composition from 1655 to 1660. William Riley Parker, *Milton: A Biography*, 2 vols. (Oxford: Clarendon, 1968), 2:1052–57, guesses that Milton composed the entire work between May 1655 and May 1658. Although there is no substantive internal evidence for dating the treatise, Parker points out that a comment on the former practice of bishops was "almost certainly dictated before 1660, when the bishops returned to power." But with the number of hands and stages of revision involved, the dating of one statement reveals little about the period of the whole work's composition. For a discussion of the problems of dating the treatise, see Maurice Kelley, *This Great Argument: A Study of Milton's De Doctrina Christiana as a Gloss Upon Paradise Lost* (Princeton: Princeton University Press, 1941), 8–24.

243 *CPW* 6:122; *CM* 14:10.

244 For this point, see Michael Bauman, *A Scripture Index to John Milton's De Doctrina Christiana* (Binghamton: Medieval and Renaissance Texts and Studies, 1989), 9. Bauman's index lists some 9350 biblical citations in the *De Doctrina*: see 173–79.

245 On the relationship between the treatise and the Reformed orthodox tradition, see William B. Hunter, "The Theological Context of Milton's *Christian Doctrine*," in *Achievements of the Left Hand: Essays on the Prose of John Milton*, ed. Michael Lieb and John T. Shawcross (Amherst: University of Massachusetts Press, 1974), 269–87.

246 *CPW* 6:156; *CM* 14:68.

247 *CPW* 6:157; *CM* 14:70.

248 *CPW* 6:164; *CM* 14:84.

future, God would be "the cause (*causam*) and author (*auctorem*) of sin."[249]

In its account of predestination, the *De Doctrina*'s main emphasis is on the universality of grace. Predestination is defined as God's mercy "ON THE HUMAN RACE," given "BEFORE THE FOUNDATIONS OF THE WORLD," when, foreseeing the fall, God planned to display his glorious mercy in Christ.[250] The treatise adds, in continuity with Arminianism, that God predestined in Christ "THOSE WHO WOULD IN THE FUTURE BELIEVE AND CONTINUE IN THE FAITH."[251] But in contrast to Arminianism, the *De Doctrina* goes on to argue that God predestined the salvation of all human beings on the condition of faith and perseverance.[252] Here the *De Doctrina*'s theology is closer to Amyraldism than to Arminianism: God's decree is "not particular but only general": "Peter is not predestined or elected as Peter, or John as John, but each only insofar as he believes and persists in his belief." The "general decree of election" (*generale electionis decretum*) thus applies to specific individuals only on the condition of faith.[253]

The *De Doctrina*'s most striking departure from the Reformed orthodox and Arminian views of predestination lies in its repudiation of the idea of reprobation. The logical deduction of reprobation from election, common to Reformed orthodoxy and Arminianism alike, is emphatically denied in the treatise.[254] In scripture, the term predestination refers "always to election alone."[255] There is no decree of reprobation,[256] and reprobation "is no part of divine predestination,"[257] for God "desires the salvation of all (*omnium salutem*) and the death of none ...

---

249 *CPW* 6:166; *CM* 14:88.
250 *CPW* 6:168; *CM* 14:90. Here the treatise differentiates its position from that of Reformed orthodoxy, in which God predestines in order to display both his mercy and his justice.
251 *CPW* 6:168; *CM* 14:90.
252 Barbara K. Lewalski, *The Life of John Milton: A Critical Biography* (Oxford: Blackwell, 2000), 423, is one of the few scholars to observe that this account of general election differs significantly from Arminianism's theology of particular election. Similarly, Christopher Hill, *Milton and the English Revolution* (London: Faber, 1977), 276, suggests that the author of the treatise "knew Dutch Remonstrant theology but press[ed] a good deal further."
253 *CPW* 6:176; *CM* 14:106.
254 Although the *De Doctrina* is still often described simply as Arminian, Barbara K. Lewalski, "Milton and *De Doctrina Christiana*: Evidences of Authorship," *Milton Studies* 36 (1998), 216–19, observes that the treatise departs from Arminius's view of an absolute, double decree, and she rightly suggests that Milton argues "toward his own distinctive position." See also Richard Luckett, "Milton," *TRE*, 22:757–58.
255 *CPW* 6:169; *CM* 14:92.
256 *CPW* 6:168–75; *CM* 14:90–102.
257 *CPW* 6:173; *CM* 14:100.

and has omitted nothing that might suffice for the salvation of all (*salutem omnium sufficeret*)."[258] Admittedly, certain persons may be "predestined to destruction ... through their own fault and, in a sense, *per accidens*"; but such reprobation is determined purely by the individual's own sin, and it is therefore only a temporary and provisional reprobation, which can always be "rescinded by repentance."[259] The treatise thus speaks of the "sufficient grace" that God "bestows on all":[260] the only ones who are excluded from salvation are those who consistently "reject and despise the offer of grace sufficient for salvation, until it is too late."[261] While the election of grace rests solely on the divine will, the cause of reprobation must therefore be "human sin alone, not God's will."[262] Reprobation is grounded in the obstinacy of those who refuse God's grace, and so "it is not the decree of God, but rather of the reprobate themselves, resulting from their refusal to repent while it is in their power."[263]

Taking up the question of the "matter or object of predestination" (*materia seu obiectum praedestinationis*), the *De Doctrina* argues, against supralapsarianism, that the object of predestination is not creatable humanity (*homo creandus*) but humanity as a self-fallen (*sponte lapsurus*) creature.[264] The fall was foreseen by God but was in no sense decreed by God, so that human beings could have avoided falling if they wished. Although all post-Reformation theologians agreed that hypothetically the first human beings could have avoided falling, the treatise offers an independent conclusion: predestination itself "was not an absolute decree (*decretum absolutum*) before the fall of humanity (*ante lapsum hominis*)."[265] The divine decree is thus radically contingent on the free acts of human beings.

In its view of the fallen human will, the theology of the *De Doctrina* remains close to Reformed orthodoxy.[266] According to the treatise, original sin involves the "darkening of ... right reason" and the "extinction of righteousness and of the liberty to do good," so that the human will

---

258 *CPW* 6:174–75; *CM* 14:102.
259 *CPW* 6:190–92; *CM* 14:142–44.
260 *CPW* 6:192–93; *CM* 14:146.
261 *CPW* 6:194; *CM* 14:152.
262 *CPW* 6:195; *CM* 14:154.
263 *CPW* 6:195; *CM* 14:154.
264 *CPW* 6:173–74; *CM* 14:100.
265 *CPW* 6:174; *CM* 14:102.
266 William Poole, *Milton and the Idea of the Fall* (Cambridge: Cambridge University Press, 2005), 145, rightly notes that in this respect the treatise "clearly follows broadly Calvinist lines, with Arminian qualifications."

suffers from a "slavish subjection to sin."[267] The treatise thus speaks even of "the death of the will, as it were."[268] Corresponding to this view of the enslavement of the will is a theology of universal grace, in which grace liberates the fallen will and enables it to turn to God in faith and repentance. God "gives us the power to act freely, of which we have been incapable since the fall";[269] and through regeneration God "restores the person's natural faculties of right judgment and of free will more completely than before."[270] In regeneration, the will is thus restored "to its former liberty."[271] Here the *De Doctrina* articulates a theology of universal and resistible prevenient grace. The minds and wills of all human beings are partially enlightened and liberated, making it possible for all to obtain salvation. In regeneration, we are "given the ability to obtain salvation if we desire it";[272] for even in the work of salvation, human beings "always use their free will."[273]

In the theology of the treatise, salvation thus depends on the liberating grace of God, but also on the decisive act of the human will. Regeneration "is not the work of God alone (*non opus unius Dei*)."[274] The *De Doctrina* asserts even that some people are "well or moderately disposed or affected" to salvation, and are thus "more suitable, and as it were, more properly disposed for the kingdom of God."[275] And in a sharp departure from Reformed orthodox and Arminian theology alike, the treatise suggests that "some cause ... should be sought in human nature itself why some persons embrace and others reject this divine grace."[276] Moreover, in spite of its own insistence on human depravity, the treatise adds that "the gift of reason has been implanted in all, by which they may of themselves resist depraved (*pravis*) desires, so that no one can complain of ... the depravity (*pravitatem*) of his own nature."[277]

---

267 *CPW* 6:395; *CM* 15:206.
268 *CPW* 6:395; *CM* 15:206.
269 *CPW* 6:457; *CM* 15:356.
270 *CPW* 6:461; *CM* 15:366.
271 *CPW* 6:462; *CM* 15:370.
272 *CPW* 6:463; *CM* 15:370.
273 *CPW* 6:189; *CM* 14:138.
274 *CPW* 6:395; *CM* 15:204.
275 *CPW* 6:185; *CM* 14:128. The counter-Reformation theology of the Council of Trent similarly speaks of people being "disposed" to obtaining justification, and it defines this disposing as itself a work of grace: see *Canones et decreta Concilii Tridentini*, 6.4; in Tanner, 2:679.
276 *CPW* 6:186; *CM* 14:128.
277 *CPW* 6:186; *CM* 14:130.

Underlying the theology of the *De Doctrina*, then, is a deep commitment to the idea of freedom. The treatise itself cannot accurately be said to belong to any specific theological tradition, but it draws eclectically on various concepts and traditions, and presses toward its own unique theological position.

The reading of *Paradise Lost* in the chapters that follow is situated against the backdrop of these complex and variegated theological contexts. Although the historical account in this chapter has necessarily been summary and concise, throughout my engagement with *Paradise Lost* I will explore pertinent features of the poem's theological context in greater detail. Having set the stage for an interpretation of *Paradise Lost*'s theology, it is now time to follow the complex portrayal of freedom as it unfolds throughout the poem's narrative.

2. The Satanic Theology of Freedom

It is fitting that an investigation of the theology of *Paradise Lost* should begin where the epic itself begins: in hell. As a stated attempt to "justifie the wayes of God to men" (1.26), *Paradise Lost* is prejudiced in God's favour from the outset; but the poem also allows the *need* for such a justification of God to emerge profoundly from the very start. Readers of the poem first meet God not directly, but indirectly, through the medium of theology—that is, they get to know what God is like by hearing others talk about him. And in the poem's first two books, readers hear not the theologising of saints and angels, but the persuasive theological rhetoric of Satan and his fallen followers, all of whom can lay claim to first-hand knowledge of what God is like. Indeed, the strength of "Satanist" readings of *Paradise Lost* derives, in part, from the mere fact that Satan gets the first word in the poem.[1] "It is from Hell ... that we get our first ideas about Heaven in the poem."[2] This does not of course mean, as Marjorie Hope Nicolson has rather mischievously suggested, that Satanist critics have never read beyond the epic's first two books.[3] Rather, such critics have been acutely sensitive to the fact that, from the mouths of fallen angels—Satanic theologians—*Paradise Lost* really does call into question the goodness of God, and only then does it attempt to justify it.[4]

Within the overall narrative structure of *Paradise Lost*, the first two books serve two basic purposes: they paint the pre-temporal backdrop to the fall of Adam and Eve; and they depict the complex reality of evil, a reality that is sometimes alluring, sometimes repulsive, but always

---

1   On Satanist readings of the poem, see R. J. Zwi Werblowsky, *Lucifer and Prometheus: A Study of Milton's Satan* (London: Routledge & Kegan Paul, 1952), 1–26; and Neil Forsyth, *The Satanic Epic* (Princeton: Princeton University Press, 2003), 64–76. See also John Carey, "Milton's Satan," in *The Cambridge Companion to Milton*, ed. Dennis R. Danielson (Cambridge: Cambridge University Press, 1999), 160–74.

2   Michael Wilding, *Milton's Paradise Lost* (Sydney: Sydney University Press, 1969), 44.

3   Marjorie Hope Nicolson, *John Milton: A Reader's Guide to His Poetry* (New York: Thames & Hudson, 1964), 186.

4   In this respect, there is truth in the pointed remark of Douglas Bush, *Paradise Lost in Our Time: Some Comments* (Gloucester: Peter Smith, 1957), 43: "A good many modern critics, in their comments on Milton's Deity, only echo the most unreliable of theologians, Satan."

intensely fascinating. And within the structure of the poem's theodicy, the most important function of Books 1 and 2 is to offer an uncompromising portrayal of the kind of God whom one might feel the need to justify. Such a need simply might not emerge if the poem were to start, as Genesis does, with an account of creation, or if it were to start, *in medias res*, in the prelapsarian paradise. Instead, readers of *Paradise Lost* immediately hear about God from the perspective of fallen angels. In this way, they encounter a God whose character is at once called into question, and whose goodness therefore cannot simply be taken for granted.[5]

Satan as Heretic

It is uncontroversial to assume that Satan should not be trusted, and to assert that most readers of *Paradise Lost* will make this assumption, even if they have to be taught to make it through the recurring interposition of narratorial comment.[6] But the fact that Satan should not be trusted when he speaks of God does not mean that his portrayal of God cannot be taken seriously, or that it should be regarded as merely comical or absurd. Satan is not an "ass";[7] and there is no need to perform, out of some quasi-religious anxiety, what William Empson called "the modern duty of catching Satan out wherever possible."[8]

Satan's portrayal of God in fact constitutes a highly important aspect of the theology of *Paradise Lost*.[9] In a discussion of the Genesis fall-story, Karl Barth has facetiously but perceptively remarked that the serpent is the world's first theologian: the serpent's speech, beginning

---

5   John S. Diekhoff, *Milton's Paradise Lost: A Commentary on the Argument* (New York: Columbia University Press, 1946), 82–83, thinks that the argument of *Paradise Lost* is "circular," since the goodness of God is simply assumed at the outset, "not merely as an hypothesis to be tested, but as a premise on which to build an argument." But this interpretation of the poem's theodicy overlooks one of the basic narrative functions of the first two books: namely, not to assume the goodness of God, but to call it in question.

6   On the didactic role of narratorial interposition, see Stanley E. Fish, *Surprised by Sin: The Reader in Paradise Lost* (London: Macmillan, 1967), 1–56; and Anne Davidson Ferry, *Milton's Epic Voice: The Narrator in Paradise Lost* (Cambridge, Mass.: Harvard University Press, 1963), 44–66.

7   As suggested by S. Musgrove, "Is the Devil an Ass?" *Review of English Studies* 21 (1945), 302–15.

8   William Empson, *Milton's God* (London: Chatto & Windus, 1961), 74.

9   In a different connection, Forsyth, *The Satanic Epic*, 17, rightly observes that Satan "has an extremely important role to play in the philosophical or theological structure of *Paradise Lost*."

with the question, "Yea, hath God said ..." is "the original" of "all bad theology."[10] The attribution of "bad theology" to Satan has been common in Christian tradition. Already in the early centuries of Christianity, as Neil Forsyth notes, Satan began to serve "a vital theological function": "As the prince of error and the father of lies, he became the arch-heretic, the name under which rival teachers were denounced."[11] Justin Martyr and Irenaeus attributed all heresies to Satanic influence,[12] while Tertullian ascribed heretical interpretations of scripture to "the devil, of course, to whom pertain those wiles to pervert the truth."[13] Thus heretics were viewed as "apostates, following the one great and original Apostate," Satan.[14] According to Augustine, too, heresies within the church were inspired by the devil;[15] and Luther regarded the temptation to heresy as central to Satan's work.[16] Such identifications of Satan as the instigator of theological error and controversy persisted also in the post-Reformation era, not least among English Protestants.[17] Even into the eighteenth century, Satan was still being described by English writers as "the Arch-Heretic."[18] In an account of a seventeenth-century exorcism, Samuel Clarke describes the way the devil "quoted many scriptures out of the Old and New Testament, both in Hebrew and Greek, cavilled and played the critick, and backed his allegations with sayings out of the fathers." In this account, Satan is portrayed as a subtle theologian, a master of "sophistry."[19] In more academic seven-

---

10 Karl Barth, *Church Dogmatics*, ed. Geoffrey W. Bromiley and T. F. Torrance (Edinburgh: T&T Clark, 1956–77), IV/1, 420; referring to the serpent's speech in Genesis 3:1.

11 Neil Forsyth, *The Old Enemy: Satan and the Combat Myth* (Princeton: Princeton University Press, 1987), 310. See also Gregory C. Jenks, *The Origins and Early Development of the Antichrist Myth* (Berlin: Walter de Gruyter, 1991), 60–64.

12 Justin Martyr, *First Apology*, 58; in *ANF* 1; and Irenaeus, *Against Heresies*, 1.21; in *ANF* 1.

13 Tertullian, *De praescriptionibus adversus haereticos*, 40; in *PL* 2 and *ANF* 3. See also Tertullian, *Adversus Praxeam*, 1; in *PL* 2 and *ANF* 3.

14 Forsyth, *The Satanic Epic*, 45.

15 Augustine, *De civitate Dei contra paganos*, 18.51; in *PL* 41 and *NPNF* 2.

16 See the comment on Luther in Darren Oldridge, "Protestant Conceptions of the Devil in Early Stuart England," *History* 85 (2000), 234: "For Luther, Satan's primary work in the world was to create illusions in the mind, 'printing in the heart a false opinion of Christ and against Christ.' It was his ceaseless mission to tempt people into heresy by infecting their minds with superstitious thoughts."

17 See Michael P. Winship, *Making Heretics: Militant Protestantism and Free Grace in Massachusetts, 1636–1641* (Princeton: Princeton University Press, 2002), 106–7.

18 John Taylor, *A narrative of Mr. Joseph Rawson's case* (London, 1742), 74.

19 Samuel Clarke, *A generall martyrologie ... whereunto are added, the lives of sundry modern divines* (London, 1651), 458–61. On seventeenth-century encounters with the devil, see Philip C. Almond, ed., *Demonic Possession and Exorcism in Early Modern England: Contemporary Texts and Their Cultural Contexts* (Cambridge: Cambridge University Press, 2004), 1–42.

teenth-century works, Archbishop Ussher speaks of "the Devils sophistry,"[20] while John Downham adduces the serpent's "Equivocations
and Sophisticall Elenches" as proof that Satan is "the father" of all subtle scholasticism[21]—he is, in other words, the first bad theologian, and
the author of all ensuing bad theology.

Similarly, in *Paradise Lost*, Satan is the first theologian (θεολόγος)—
the first to speak words (λόγοι) concerning God (θεός). And as the first
theologian, Satan is also the first heretic—the first to use bad theology
as an instrument of blasphemy; or, as the narrative voice says, the "Ar-
tificer of fraud," and "the first / That practisd falshood under saintly
shew" (4.121–22).[22] When Satan speaks about God he does, of course,
express himself in predominantly political terms; nevertheless, he also
frequently employs the language of post-Reformation theological controversy, so that it is appropriate to regard Satan not only as a political
orator but also as a theologian. Indeed, Satan's chronologically earliest
public speeches are markedly theological in tone and content. He
speaks of the "Decree" of God (5.774), the freedom of the angels (5.787–
92), and the fact that "Orders and Degrees" among diverse beings cohere with the intrinsic "liberty" of those beings (5.792–93). And when
Abdiel points out that God created the angels through the agency of the
Son, Satan responds like a cunning scholastic theologian:

> That we were formd then saist thou? and the work
> Of secondarie hands, by task transferrd
> From Father to his Son? strange point and new!
> Doctrin which we would know whence learnt... (5.853–56)

---

20   James Ussher, *A body of divinitie, or the summe and substance of Christian religion* (London, 1653), 130.

21   John Downham, *The summe of sacred divinitie first briefly and methodically propounded,
and then more largly and cleerly handled and explained* (London, 1620), 235.

22   The fact that in *Paradise Lost* Satan is a heretical theologian has often been noted, but
not explored in detail. William B. Hunter, "The Heresies of Satan," in *Th' Upright
Heart and Pure: Essays on John Milton Commemorating the Tercentenary of the Publication
of Paradise Lost*, ed. Peter A. Fiore (Pittsburgh: Duquesne University Press, 1967), 25–
34, has interpreted Satan as an anti-trinitarian heretic; and Paul M. Zall, "Heresies,
Milton's," in *A Milton Encyclopedia*, ed. William B. Hunter et al., 9 vols. (Lewisburg:
Bucknell University Press, 1978–83), 3:175, notes that Milton's portrayal of Satan employs "heresies for dramatic purposes." In his recent study, *The Satanic Epic*, Forsyth
describes Satan as "heretic and hater" (1), and he argues that Milton's Satan drama-
tises the fact that Christianity is "a religion of controversy" in which fundamental
doctrines arise "from the quarrel with ... heresy" (74). And while not specifically
speaking of Satan as a heretic, Michael Bryson, *The Tyranny of Heaven: Milton's Rejection of God as King* (Newark: University of Delaware Press, 2004), has raised the important question: "Why does Milton write his Satan to sound so much like Calvin"?
(107).

Here Satan draws on the assumption, common in post-Reformation theology, that antiquity is a sign of truth and novelty a sign of error. In the words of John Cameron, "Antiquity ... is Divine and venerable; novelty, on the other side, damnable and devillish."[23] Ironically, Satan claims to be wary of unproven doctrinal innovations even while himself becoming the first theological innovator, the first heretic to deny traditional heavenly "Doctrin."

In exploring the theology of *Paradise Lost*, due attention must be given to the heretical "Doctrin" propounded by Satan and his fallen hosts. Nothing could be clearer in the first two books than the fallen angels' preoccupation, even obsession, with God. Again and again, in different ways, the fallen angels theologise: they talk about God. In the discussion that follows, I will argue that in particular this "Satanic theology" takes the form of a parodic exaggeration of Calvinism, in which God appears as an ethically arbitrary tyrant whose absolute power undermines both his own goodness and the freedom of his creatures. The God of this Satanic theology is a projection of the Satanic consciousness, and as such he is virtually indistinguishable from the devil. This Satanic theology provides a heretical foil against which the epic then proceeds, from Book 3 onwards, to offer its own positive theological account of the goodness of God.[24]

Divine Tyranny

Throughout the first two books of *Paradise Lost* the fallen angels repeatedly describe God's omnipotence as a morally indifferent exercise of power that amounts to a kind of demonic tyranny. This view of God

---

23 John Cameron, *An examination of those plausible appearances which seeme most to commend the Romish Church, and to prejudice the Reformed* (Oxford, 1626), 58. This view of antiquity and novelty was most often invoked, as in the present instance, in Catholic–Protestant debate, with each party claiming its own correspondence to Christian antiquity.

24 Arthur Sewell, *A Study in Milton's Christian Doctrine* (London: Oxford University Press, 1939), 134–40, argues that *Paradise Lost* presents a Calvinist view of divine sovereignty in Books 1 and 2, and a milder view throughout the remainder of the poem. Sewell sees this as evidence that Milton's theological thought had developed between the writing of the first two books and the rest of the epic. Although Sewell is right to notice the Calvinist portrayal of God in Books 1 and 2, his reading fails to take account of the fact that God himself does not enter the poem until Book 3, so that the reader first learns about God only from Satan and his followers. The contrast between the theology of Books 1 and 2 and that of Book 3, then, is not a contrast between an earlier and later Milton, but between Satanic theology and heavenly theology, between darkness and light.

parodies Calvinist theology, and presents a quasi-Calvinist Satanic theology in which creaturely freedom is negated and the divine goodness is undermined by absolute sovereignty.

In the early lines of Book 1, the narrative voice allows Satan's questioning of creaturely freedom and divine goodness to arise, by designating God only with titles such as "Monarchy" (1.42), "Almighty Power" (1.44), and "Eternal Justice" (1.70), and with adjectives like "Omnipotent" (1.49). These titles and descriptions cohere with the poem's account of God in Book 3 and elsewhere,[25] but the one-sided emphasis on such terms at the start of the narration, and the corresponding lack of any mention of divine "Grace" (3.142), "love" (3.267), or "goodness" (12.469), set the stage for the Satanic attempt to undermine God's goodness throughout the first major section of the epic.

The portrayal of God as an omnipotent tyrant begins almost as soon as the fallen angels begin to speak, in the opening moments of *Paradise Lost*. Breaking the "horrid silence" of hell (1.83), Satan acknowledges God's supreme power. God is the "Potent Victor" (1.95), "the Conquerour" (1.323) and "Monarch" (1.638), who by the "force" of his "dire Arms" (1.94) has triumphed over his rebellious subjects. Beelzebub, too, calls God "our Conquerour" (1.143), and "th' Omnipotent" (1.273). But the fallen angels acknowledge God's power only in order profoundly to undermine the divine goodness.[26] According to Satan, God is the "Potent Victor" who "in his rage" will "inflict" misery and ruin on his foes (1.95–96). Hell is thus described as a "dungeon" (2.317) in which God will hold his enemies "In strictest bondage" (2.321). God is full of "vengeful ire" (1.148), willing to grant his enemies continuing existence only in order to force them to bear greater suffering, and thus to satisfy his own lust for revenge:

> But what if hee our Conquerour (whom I now
> Of force believe Almighty, since no less
> Then such could have orepow'rd such force as ours)
> Have left us this our spirit and strength intire
> Strongly to suffer and support our pains,
> That we may so suffice his vengeful ire. (1.143–48)

Indeed, God is said to experience a sadistic "excess of joy" in subduing and oppressing his enemies (1.123). He is "the Torturer" (2.64). Later,

---

25   The most consistent title of the Father in the poem is simply "th' Almighty."

26   As Dennis R. Danielson, *Milton's Good God: A Study in Literary Theodicy* (Cambridge: Cambridge University Press, 1982), 116, argues in a different connection, Satan reveals "only part of the truth," in order "to raise questions concerning the goodness of God."

Belial parodies the theological idea of salvation by claiming that God's "anger saves" his foes, only in order to extend their punishment and misery (2.158–59).[27]

This God whom the fallen angels describe—a sadistic deity who takes joy in torturing his subjects—has been vigorously condemned by William Empson.[28] But as Michael Wilding has pointed out, the hell of *Paradise Lost* "is not well furnished with tortures";[29] only from the mouths of the fallen angels themselves does the reader hear that God is a vengeful torturer. In fact, in contrast to traditional portrayals of hell,[30] the hell of *Paradise Lost* is characterised by silence and absence; Matthew Steggle has described this as "Milton's almost unique presentation of hell."[31] One need only compare Milton's hell with the horrors that surround Lucifer in Dante's *Inferno*,[32] or with the depictions of hell in English Renaissance tragedies, to realise how little the God of *Paradise Lost* is truly a "Torturer."[33] In Thomas Kyd's *Spanish Tragedy* (1592), for instance, an array of tortures is invoked in the portrayal of hell:

> deepest hell,
> Where bloody furies shakes their whips of steele,
> And poor Ixion turns an endless wheele:
> Where usurers are chok'd with melting gold,
> And wantons are embrac'd with ugly snakes,
> And murderers groan with never-killing wounds,

---

27 Similarly, commenting on Satan's Mount Niphates speech, Keith W. F. Stavely, "Satan and Arminianism in *Paradise Lost*," *Milton Studies* 25 (1989), 135, notes that Satan "deludes himself with the convenient fiction that God is a grim Calvinist 'punisher' who would never grant pardon even if Satan should be so untrue to himself as to beg for it."

28 Empson, *Milton's God*.

29 Wilding, *Milton's Paradise Lost*, 40. Wilding observes that the poem's emphasis "is not on God's vengeance ... but on the goodness God will produce from evil."

30 For a characteristic example, see the Reformed orthodox portrayal of hell in Isaac Ambrose, *The compleat works of that eminent minister of God's word, Mr. Isaac Ambrose* (London, 1701), 284, in which the writer depicts the "furious despair," the "horrour of mind," the "tearing [of] hair and gnashing of teeth," and the "wailling, weeping, roaring, yelling" of the damned—which tortures not only fill hell, but also overflow into "heaven and earth."

31 Matthew Steggle, "*Paradise Lost* and the Acoustics of Hell," *Early Modern Literary Studies* 7:1 (2001), 13 <http://purl.oclc.org/emls/07-1/stegmil2.htm>.

32 See Dante Alighieri, *Inferno*, 34; in *The Divine Comedy*, ed. and trans. Charles S. Singleton, 6 vols. (Princeton: Princeton University Press, 1970–75), 1:360–69.

33 Seventeenth-century theologians also spoke graphically of the torments of hell. See Philip C. Almond, *Heaven and Hell in Enlightenment England* (Cambridge: Cambridge University Press, 1994), 81–100.

> And perjur'd wights scalded in boiling lead,
> And all foul sins with torments overwhelm'd.[34]

If there is a God behind these hellish torments, he might justly be described as a torturer, for he has—rather intimately, one might say—
designed specific tortures perfectly adapted to each individual sufferer.
The Reformed orthodox theologian Ezekiel Hopkins similarly writes
that "God doth use several Instruments of Torture in Hell";[35] while
Isaac Ambrose speaks of hell's "torments ... past imagination."[36] But in
contrast, within the silent void of hell in *Paradise Lost* the fallen angels
are free to build a palace, to conduct parliamentary debate, and even to
create music. Their hell is peculiarly characterised by a *lack* of torture.[37]
Further, Satan himself acknowledges that the hell he inhabits is not so
much a region created by God as a creation of his own "mind" (1.253–
55). Hell is in fact Satan's own self-confinement and self-torture, not
merely a location in which he is subjected to divine tortures: "Which
way I flie is Hell; my self am Hell" (4.75).[38] Wilding is right, then, to
remark that the God of vengeance and torture is really "the God the
devils 'create' for us in their comments."[39]

---

34 Thomas Kyd, *The Spanish Tragedy*, ed. Philip Edwards (London: Methuen, 1959),
    1.1.64–71. In citing *The Spanish Tragedy* in this connection, I have followed Steggle,
    "*Paradise Lost* and the Acoustics of Hell," n. 9.

35 Ezekiel Hopkins, *The works of the Right Reverend and learned Ezekiel Hopkins* (London,
    1701), 406.

36 Ambrose, *Compleat works*, 284.

37 A. J. A. Waldock, "*Paradise Lost*" and Its Critics (Cambridge: Cambridge University
    Press, 1947), 92–96, has argued that this lack of torture is a flaw in *Paradise Lost*'s
    portrayal of hell. According to Waldock, Milton was trying "to accomplish two in-
    compatible things at the same time": to present both a hell of torture, and a dramati-
    cally interesting hell (94). Waldock is right to observe that the punishment of hell is
    "meagre," that Books 1 and 2 show "how little the rebels are inconvenienced by their
    situation" (93), and, indeed, that "the chief un-hell-like characteristic of Milton's Hell
    is simply the atmosphere of busy planning, of life nearly as lively as ever, of energies
    unquenched" (94). But Waldock's argument that these characteristics conflict with
    the torturous hell that Milton was trying to create rests on the mistaken assumption
    that Milton wanted simply to portray the hell of traditional theology and of Dante's
    Inferno, and that only such a hell could be "legitimate" in *Paradise Lost* (92–94). On
    the contrary, instead of contrasting the hell Milton *actually* created with the hell he
    allegedly *wanted* to create, it is more illuminating to contrast the hell the devils *ac-
    tually* inhabit with the hell they *claim* to inhabit.

38 Thus I think that Grant McColley, "*Paradise Lost*," *Harvard Theological Review* 32:4
    (1939), 206, is mistaken to view this self-hell concept simply as an intensification of
    Satan's tortures. According to McColley, the fallen angels undergo "perpetual tortu-
    re" because they "always carr[y] hell and its excruciating tortures within them."

39 Wilding, *Milton's Paradise Lost*, 40.

This God whom the fallen angels "create" is a grim parody of the Calvinist deity, an omnipotent being who arbitrarily exercises absolute power (*potentia absoluta*).[40] As the one who "holds the Tyranny of Heav'n" (1.124), God is "Heav'ns high Arbitrator," reigning by sheer "strength" (2.359–60). Beelzebub's description of God as "Arbitrator"[41] refers to God's deciding victory in war but also, and more importantly, calls up the image of a Calvinistic God who ordains the fates of others "by the mere pleasure of his own will."[42] Earlier in the same speech, Beelzebub had spoken of the "arbitrary punishment / Inflicted" on God's foes (2.334). God's triumph over the rebel angels is not conceived of as ethically motivated, but as "arbitrary," and in the same way God himself is regarded as nothing other than a supreme "Arbitrator" who inflicts his will on those who lack the power to resist. Reformed orthodoxy always faced the risk of portraying God in such terms of absolute power, a "power before whose completely inscrutable arbitrariness man has no choice but to bend."[43] Calvin had sought explicitly to distance his own theology from any notion of "arbitrary power"[44] that would suggest that God is "a tyrant" who "acts without a reason" and who resolves "to do what he pleases, not by justice, but through caprice."[45] But such an arbitrary "tyrant" was exactly the God whom Arminian theologians claimed to find in Reformed orthodoxy. The charge of moral arbitrariness was consistently brought against the Reformed conception of divine sovereignty, in which God predestines all things on the sole basis of "his meere pleasure."[46] While Reformed orthodox theologians did not concede that their view entailed divine arbitrari-

---

40 On the theological concept of absolute power, see Heiko A. Oberman, *The Harvest of Medieval Theology: Gabriel Biel and Late Medieval Nominalism* (Cambridge, Mass.: Harvard University Press, 1963), 30–56.

41 For this distinction, see *OED* "arbitrator," 1 and 3.

42 This formula was frequently used by Reformed orthodox writers. See for example Johannes Wollebius, *Compendium theologiae christianae*; in *Reformed Dogmatics*, ed. and trans. John W. Beardslee (Oxford: Oxford University Press, 1965), 1.3.3; Lucas Trelcatius, *A briefe institution of the common places of sacred divinitie* (London, 1610), 82; and David Dickson, *Truths victory over error* (Edinburgh, 1684), 32–37.

43 G. C. Berkouwer, *Divine Election*, trans. Hugo Bekker (Grand Rapids: Eerdmans, 1960), 53.

44 John Calvin, *Commentaries on the Epistle of Paul the Apostle to the Romans*, trans. John Owen (Edinburgh, 1849), 366. On Calvin's relationship to the doctrine of *potentia absoluta*, see David C. Steinmetz, *Calvin in Context* (Oxford: Oxford University Press, 1995), 40–52.

45 John Calvin, *Commentary on the Book of the Prophet Isaiah*, trans. William Pringle, 4 vols. (Edinburgh, 1850), 2:152.

46 William Perkins, *A golden chaine: or, The description of theologie* (Cambridge, 1592), 409.

ness,[47] the God portrayed by Beelzebub fully fits the description of the God depicted in the rhetoric of seventeenth-century anti-Calvinist polemics.[48] He is a being of naked will, of ethically arbitrary power, the exercise of which constitutes an all-inclusive and inescapable "tyranny."[49]

The accusation that God's exercise of power is ethically arbitrary is further advanced by Satan's claim that God is himself directly responsible for the fall of the angels: God deceitfully "conceald" his true strength, and in this way "tempted our attempt, and wrought our fall" (1.641–42). As Stephen Fallon observes, Satan and his followers invoke "an infernal version of the Calvinist doctrine of absolute predestination, blaming God for their choices, and suggesting that the system was rigged. For the devils, God, like the Calvinist deity ... is the author of sin."[50] This deity of whom the fallen angels speak is thus both cause and punisher of sin; he rules by arbitrary omnipotence, like a Nietzschean tyrant whose ethically arbitrary "will to power" subdues and controls those who are weaker. Or, more precisely, he is a parodic, Satanic version of the Calvinist God, standing in absolute control over his creatures, causing sin and then condemning the sinner.[51]

Beelzebub further speculates whether God might have preserved the fallen angels' existence not simply as a means to torture, but also so that God's enemies might

> do him mightier service as his thralls
> By right of Warr, what e're his business be,
> Here in the heart of Hell to work in Fire,
> Or do his Errands in the gloomy Deep. (1.149–52)

---

47   There were, however, isolated exceptions. For example, in discussing predestination, John Edwards, *Veritas redux: Evangelical truths restored*, 2 vols. (London, 1707), 1:177, writes: "It is from the mere Arbitrary Will of God that he chose those rather than these, and rejected these rather than those."

48   In this connection, the remark of David Loewenstein, *Milton: Paradise Lost* (Cambridge: Cambridge University Press, 1993), 29, is apposite: the theodicy of *Paradise Lost* is Milton's attempt "to differentiate his God from the Calvinist God of arbitrary power."

49   In modern theology, Karl Barth has argued that absolute power is by definition demonic power. See for example Karl Barth, *The Humanity of God*, trans. John Newton Thomas and Thomas Wieser (Richmond: John Knox Press, 1960), 71: "God's freedom is not merely unlimited possibility or formal majesty and omnipotence, that is to say empty, naked sovereignty.... God Himself, if conceived of as unconditioned power, would be a demon and as such His own prisoner."

50   Stephen M. Fallon, "*Paradise Lost* in Intellectual History," in *A Companion to Milton*, ed. Thomas N. Corns (Oxford: Blackwell, 2001), 333.

51   That the God of Calvinism was the "cause of evil" (*causa mali*) or the "author of evil" (*auctor mali*) was one of the most persistent criticisms brought against Reformed orthodoxy. For a discussion of the Reformed response, see Heppe, 276–80.

It is strange that commentators like Verity, Hughes and Fowler should gloss these lines with a reference to the *De Doctrina Christiana*'s assertion that the evil angels are sometimes permitted "to carry out God's judgments"[52]—as though here the devils of *Paradise Lost* are offering a pious theological reflection on divine providence. Rather Beelzebub's speculation involves a characteristically perverse and Satanic portrayal of God. Beelzebub claims that hell is part of God's "Empire" (2.327); he portrays God as a distant monarch whose business occasionally requires the running of shady errands by sinister servants. In a similar way, employing typical Reformed orthodox rhetoric, Sin informs her offspring and its father, Satan, that they are "ordaind" God's "drudge[s]," and that they exist only "to execute / What e're his wrauth, which he calls Justice, bids" (2.732–33). According to Sin, the divine wrath is nothing other than an arbitrary exercise of superior power, which God euphemistically "calls Justice." Further, Sin emphasises the evil nature of God's will with her pun on "execute": God's darker subjects serve as his executioners, and in this way they execute his angry judgments. These accounts, in which evil characters claim to be slaves or servants of God's sovereign "Empire," are vivid theological expressions of a quasi-Calvinist Satanic theology. The deity of this Satanic theology thus parodies the God of Reformed orthodoxy who controls "[b]oth good and evil" alike.[53] He is, in short, a distinctly devilish deity.

Fatalism

The Satanic theology of the fallen angels continues to find expression throughout the council of Pandemonium. Moloch's despairing view is, in the words of Belial, that "we are decreed, / Reserv'd and destind to Eternal woe" (2.160–61). Each of these verbs—most importantly, "decreed"—is drawn from the standard rhetoric of Reformed orthodox theology.[54] The particular kind of predestination to which Moloch re-

---

52 Verity, 374; Hughes, 148; and Fowler, 53; citing *CPW* 6:348. Similarly, according to Downham, *The summe of sacred divinitie*, 103, God carries out his will "also in *Hell*: for even the *Devils* themselves, struggle they never so much, are forced to be subject to him, and to runne at his commandement."

53 Wollebius, *Compendium theologiae christianae*, 1.6.1. See also Francis Turretin, *Institutes of Elenctic Theology*, ed. James T. Dennison, trans. George Musgrave Giger, 3 vols. (Phillipsburg: P&R, 1992–97), 1.7.1–35.

54 On the term "decree," see the discussion and citations in Heppe, 133–49; and Barth, *Church Dogmatics* II/1, 519–22. The term was confessionally sanctioned in the Thirty-nine Articles (Schaff, 3:497) and the Irish Articles of Religion (Schaff, 3:528), and

fers is the Reformed orthodox decree of reprobation (*reprobatio*), according to which God "hath determined to reject certaine men unto eternall destruction, and miserie."[55] Disagreeing with Moloch, Belial does not attempt to refute Moloch's fatalism, but only the despairing course of action that he proposes. Belial himself is no less a theological fatalist, when he claims:

> Fate inevitable
> Subdues us, and Omnipotent Decree,
> The Victors will. (2.197–99)

Reformed orthodox theologians insisted that their predestinarianism did not amount to fatalism;[56] but Arminian writers consistently accused Reformed orthodoxy of an "iron" necessity,[57] an "absolute necessity,"[58] and a "fatal necessity."[59] Thus in defence against such criticisms, the Reformed theologian Francis Turretin seeks to free "our doctrine" from "the calumnies" of those who "continually oppose to it the tables of the fates and the fatal and Stoical necessity of all things and events."[60] In *Paradise Lost*, Belial's expression draws on the admittedly distorted rhetoric of such Arminian criticisms; the ancient pagan concept of "Fate inevitable" and the Reformed concept of an "Omnipotent Decree" are linked and virtually equated. This theological fatalism is attributed, in typical Reformed language, to the divine "will."[61] And like all the fallen

---

above all in the Westminster Confession of Faith, 3 (Schaff, 3:608). Like the systematic theologies of Wollebius and most other Reformed orthodox writers, the *De Doctrina Christiana* includes an early chapter *de divino decreto*.

55 Perkins, *A golden chaine*, 391.

56 See for example Turretin, *Institutes*, 6.2.1–7; and, earlier, John Calvin, *Institutes of the Christian Religion*, trans. Henry Beveridge, 2 vols. (Grand Rapids: Eerdmans, 1989), 1.16.8. Calvin's successor in Geneva, Theodore Beza, had leaned further towards necessitarianism: see Richard A. Muller, *Christ and the Decree: Christology and Predestination in Reformed Theology from Calvin to Perkins* (Grand Rapids: Baker, 1986), 81, 87–89.

57 Simon Episcopius, *The confession or declaration of the ministers or pastors which in the United Provinces are called Remonstrants, concerning the chief points of Christian religion* (London, 1676), 115–16.

58 John Goodwin, *Confidence dismounted* (London, 1651),10.

59 John Sharp, *Fifteen sermons preached on several occasions* (London, 1701), 291. For the accusation of Stoic fatalism, see also Jacobus Arminius, *The Works of James Arminius*, trans. James Nichols and William Nichols, 3 vols. (Grand Rapids: Baker, 1986), 3:358–88.

60 Turretin, *Institutes*, 6.2.1. Similarly, the Reformed theologian John Edwards, *Theologia reformata, or the body and substance of the Christian religion* (London, 1713), iv, insists that no Calvinists "hold that the Decrees lay any Force or Necessity on any Man."

61 For a comparable Reformed orthodox reference to the divine "will," see the Westminster Confession of Faith, 3.1 (Schaff, 3:608): "God from all eternity did, by the most wise and holy counsel of his own will, freely and unchangeably ordain whatsoever comes to pass."

angels, Belial understands this divine will purely in terms of power. As the stronger party, the "Victor," God's prerogative is to "Subdue" those who are weaker than himself. The "Decree" of his "will" is an exercise of sheer power.

During the consult, Moloch speaks of the "abhorred Deep" (2.87) of hell as "this dark opprobrious Den of shame, / The Prison of his Tyranny" (2.58–59). Moloch claims that hell is a confining prison, a sphere in which all freedom is negated. Further, like Beelzebub, who claims that the fallen angels are "determined" (2.330), Moloch speaks of the "compulsion" with which the rebelling spirits "sank thus low" into hell (2.80–81), so that they are now no more than slaves of divine wrath (2.90–92). Moloch's reference to "compulsion" here is of special theological significance. The notion that creatures are forcibly compelled by the divine will constitutes the most extreme form of necessitarianism. Even some of the ancient fatalists insisted that the will is not compelled. Cicero affirmed the general control of fate, but nevertheless claimed that the free will is not subject to fate;[62] and fundamental to the Stoic ethic was the conviction that the individual disposition and will remain free vis-à-vis the control of fate.[63] Reformed orthodox theologians, always sensitive to accusations of fatalism, insisted that their understanding of the sovereignty of God did not entail a compulsion (*coactio*) of creaturely choice. Thus John Flavel writes that "Compulsion" is "none of God's Way and Method,"[64] while John Owen insists that God "offers no Violence or Compulsion unto the Will" of human beings.[65] When Moloch describes God as a tyrant who compels, constrains and enslaves those less powerful than himself, he therefore expresses a grotesquely parodied quasi-Calvinism—a theology in which creaturely freedom is utterly negated by the tyrannical rule of the divine will.

The idea of divine compulsion is also expressed by Mammon, who contemplates the Origenistic doctrine that God will provide grace even for the fallen angels:[66]

---

62 Cicero, *De fato*, 17–18; in Marcus Tullius Cicero, *De Oratore; De Fato; Paradoxa Stoicorum; De Partitione Oratoria* (Cambridge, Mass.: Harvard University Press, 1942). Cicero opposes this view to the all-inclusive fatalism of Democritus, Heraclitus, Empedocles and Aristotle.

63 See F. H. Sandbach, *The Stoics* (New York: Norton, 1975), 28–68.

64 John Flavel, *The whole works of the Reverend Mr. John Flavel*, 2 vols. (London, 1701), 1:272.

65 John Owen, *Pneumatologia: or, A discourse concerning the Holy Spirit* (London, 1674), 271.

66 See Origen, *De principiis*, 3.6.5; in *ANF* 4. See also the discussion of J. N. D. Kelly, *Early Christian Doctrines* (New York: HarperCollins, 1978), 473–74; and the detailed account of C. A. Patrides, "The Salvation of Satan," *Journal of the History of Ideas* 28

> Suppose he should relent
> And publish Grace to all, on promise made
> Of new Subjection; with what eyes could we
> Stand in his presence humble, and receive
> Strict Laws impos'd, to celebrate his Throne
> With warbl'd Hymns, and to his Godhead sing
> Forc't Halleluiah's. (2.237–43)

Mammon thus decides that the "Hard liberty" of hell is to be preferred over the "easie yoke / Of servil Pomp" in heaven (2.255–57). Mammon's radical misunderstanding of "Grace" is revealing. According to post-Reformation theology, divine grace effects a change of heart that allows the recipient of grace to come "freely" to God, having been "made willing by his grace";[67] but Mammon cannot think of grace except as a form of compulsion that brings about "Forc't" worship—in other words, he cannot think of grace at all. Even in speculating about the possibility of divine grace, Mammon portrays God as an utterly ungracious tyrant who extracts worship from his subjects by force. This Satanic theology of compulsion attempts to undermine one of the central emphases of the theodicy of *Paradise Lost*: that God desires only willing worship and obedience, and that for this reason he grants his creatures freedom to obey or disobey, to worship or rebel. Mammon's description of the "Forc't Halleluiah's" is thus later corrected by the Son, who tells the Father that the saints will sing "Unfained *Halleluiahs* to thee" (6.744). This contrast between "Forc't" and "Unfained" hallelujahs highlights the contrasts between the Satanic and the heavenly theologies of God and freedom. The fatalistic and tyrannical God of the Satanic theology stands in the sharpest possible contrast to the God whom heaven worships.

When the council of Pandemonium is dissolved and the fallen angels seek to "entertain / The irksom hours" (2.526–27) until Satan's return, their sad entertainments express their acute sense of theological fatalism. Some sing, like ancient poets, of the grandeur and misery of

---

(1967), 467–78. Stavely, "Satan and Arminianism in *Paradise Lost*," 125–39, argues that grace is in fact offered to and then rejected by Satan at several points in the poem. Satan thus inhabits "an Arminian universe" (136) in which he is free to accept or to refuse redeeming grace. Whether or not *Paradise Lost* does contain any such Origenistic–Arminian idea, Stavely's underlying thesis is correct: the poem's universe "is not Calvinistic with respect to Satan and Arminian with respect to everyone else" (125). But, more importantly, if the poem's universe *seems* Calvinistic with respect to Satan, it is only because Satan himself is a quasi-Calvinist theologian.

67   Westminster Confession of Faith, 10.1; in Schaff, 3:624. For a rhapsodic account of this view, see Stephen Charnock, *The Existence and Attributes of God* (London, 1797), 419–20.

the war in heaven, and "complain that Fate / Free Vertue should enthrall to Force or Chance" (2.550–51). According to this "partial" song
(2.552),[68] fate has enslaved the freedom and virtue of the heroic angels,
subjecting them to the divine power or merely to arbitrary chance.
Other fallen angels, seeking to charm not the senses but the soul, resort
to elevated theological discussion:

> and reasond high
> Of Providence, Foreknowledge, Will, and Fate,
> Fixt Fate, free Will, Foreknowledge absolute,
> And found no end, in wandring mazes lost. (2.558–61)

Although this form of intellectual entertainment is condemned by the
narrative voice as "Vain wisdom" and "false Philosophie" (2.565), it is a
mistake to find here only a parody of classical philosophy.[69] This entertainment above all calls to mind the theological reasoning associated
with Reformed orthodox scholasticism; it is a picture of devilish theologising, in which, as Verity points out, the narrative voice is "ridi-
culing the theological controversies" of the seventeenth century,[70] even
making "a kind of labyrinth in the very words that describe it."[71] These
devilish theologians are therefore lost "in the labyrinth of their own
language";[72] they "cannot get ... out of their textual Hell."[73] Most importantly, as Stephen Fallon observes, in this theologising "free will
disappears into the tight knot it shares with fixed fate and absolute
foreknowledge."[74]

Ironically, *Paradise Lost* is itself preoccupied with precisely the same
theological topics; indeed, "[t]he first subject ... to which the Satanic
philosophers turn is 'Providence,' the theme of *Paradise Lost*."[75] It is
therefore not so much the subject-matter that makes this theologising
distinctively Satanic, but rather the *form* of theologising: the "high"
reasoning of the devils leads them into endless subtleties and aimless

---

68 As Fowler notes, "partial" denotes both "polyphonic" and "prejudiced" (Fowler,
115).
69 For example, Bush's annotation observes only that this intellectual entertainment
refers to the "metaphysical and ethical philosophies of the Greeks and Romans"
(Bush, 244).
70 Verity, 413. Werblowsky, *Lucifer and Prometheus*, 87, shrewdly notes that the devils
are "discussing, in fact, the agenda of the Westminster Assembly."
71 Joseph Addison, *The Tatler* (Glasgow, 1754), 72.
72 Wilding, *Milton's Paradise Lost*, 37.
73 Forsyth, *The Satanic Epic*, 272.
74 Fallon, "*Paradise Lost* in Intellectual History," 334.
75 Dennis H. Burden, *The Logical Epic: A Study of the Argument of Paradise Lost* (London:
Routledge & Kegan Paul, 1967), 60.

labyrinths. The barb of this parody is thus directed against the scholastic form of theological inquiry, and especially against the scholasticism of those Reformed orthodox theologians who so closely scrutinised the concepts of providence, foreknowledge and free will.[76] These Reformed theologians were regularly criticised by their opponents for "wandring" too deeply into the inscrutable "mazes" of the divine counsel. The foreword to one Arminian work speaks of the "prickly Disputations" and "obscure intricacies" involved in the Calvinist–Arminian controversy,[77] while a moderate Lutheran like Martin Chemnitz warns against "[t]he labyrinth of arguments concerning the foreknowledge of God by which our minds are often greatly disturbed."[78] The Satanic theologians of *Paradise Lost*, with their excessive use of scholastic reasoning, thus parody the Reformed theologians against whom such criticisms were directed. The narrative voice's judgment that the reasoning of these theologians is "Vain" and "false" (2.565) warns the reader to distrust this Satanic theology, and to distrust the other instances of Satanic theologising that are encountered throughout the poem's first two books.

Devil Writ Large

In the opening books of *Paradise Lost*, then, the fallen angels theologise; and their theology depicts a devilish, tyrannical deity. The demonic character of this deity is perhaps most strikingly illustrated in Mammon's comparison between heaven and hell:

> This deep world
> Of darkness do we dread? How oft amidst
> Thick clouds and dark doth Heav'ns all-ruling Sire
> Choose to reside, his Glory unobscur'd,
> And with the Majesty of darkness round
> Covers his Throne; from whence deep thunders roar

---

76 For an indication of the elaborate detail with which Reformed scholastic theologians discussed such topics, see the extensive treatment of the Reformed orthodox understanding of the divine knowledge and will in Muller, *PRRD*, 3:384–475. According to Muller's account, Reformed orthodoxy posits no fewer than eighteen binary distinctions within the divine will alone (453–73).

77 Thomas Goad, *Stimulus orthodoxus, sive Goadus redivivus: A disputation partly theological, partly metaphysical, concerning the necessity and contingency of events in the world, in respect of Gods eternal decree* (London, 1661). The epistle "To the Reader," which is not paginated, is signed "F. G."

78 Martin Chemnitz, *Loci Theologici*, trans. J. A. O. Preus, 2 vols. (St Louis: Concordia, 1989), 1:211.

Must'ring thir rage, and Heav'n resembles Hell?
As hee our Darkness, cannot wee his Light
Imitate when we please? (2.262–70)

Here Mammon draws on the familiar Old Testament metaphor of the darkness surrounding God's self-manifestation. The function of this metaphor in the Old Testament is, of course, not to suggest a demonic or hell-like divine darkness, but rather to depict the divine majesty: as Walther Eichrodt notes, "the majestic phenomenon of the thunderstorm" is evoked in the Old Testament theophanies;[79] God is "Dark with excessive bright" (3.380). But in Mammon's account, the divine thunder expresses the hellish emotion of "rage," while the dark clouds express "our Darkness," that is, the Satanic darkness of hell. Roy Flannagan rightly points out that Mammon's image is thus "perverted," since "the Old Testament God uses darkness or clouds to set off his brilliance ..., not to make Heaven resemble Hell."[80] The God of whom Mammon speaks thus hides himself in a darkness that is indistinguishable from the blackness of evil and hell. Such a God—whatever else might be said about him—bears a striking resemblance to the devil.

According to the famous assessment of the nineteenth-century philosopher Ludwig Feuerbach, the Christian idea of God is simply a projection of human consciousness: "the knowledge of God [is] nothing else than a knowledge of man."[81] Similarly, in *Paradise Lost* the Satanic theology of God is essentially a projection of the Satanic consciousness. The God described by the fallen angels is devil writ large: knowledge of him is nothing other than knowledge of Satan. In this respect, *Paradise Lost* subtly invokes a characteristic seventeenth-century criticism of Reformed orthodox theology, according to which the God of Calvinism is indistinguishable from the devil.[82] Thomas Goad, for example, accuses the Calvinists of holding "this damnable doctrine ... which transformeth *God* into a *Devil*, to be most *accursed*";[83] while an anonymous

---

79 Walther Eichrodt, *Theology of the Old Testament*, trans. J. A. Baker, 2 vols. (London: SCM, 1961–67), 2:16.

80 Flannagan, 388. Colleen Donnelly, "The Syntactic Counterplot of the Devil's Debates and God's Council," *Language and Style* 19:1 (1986), 63, has it exactly backwards when she suggests that "[t]he flaw in Mammon's argument is that he does not see that hell cannot imitate or ever become heaven." Rather, Mammon simply draws the conclusion that hell can imitate heaven from his prior, and far more questionable, assumption that heaven often imitates hell.

81 Ludwig Feuerbach, *The Essence of Christianity*, trans. George Eliot (New York: Harper & Row, 1957), 207.

82 As noted by Barth, *Church Dogmatics* II/2, 140, it is especially the God of supralapsarian Calvinism who "threatens to take on the appearance of a demon."

83 Goad, *Stimluus orthodoxus, sive Goadus redivivus*, 5–6.

Arminian treatise asserts that Calvinist views "do make God seem worse to some Men than the Devil."[84] The Laudian theologian Thomas Jackson condemns Calvinism as "idolatrous and blasphemous,"[85] and John Goodwin speaks of Calvinism's "evil" and its "intolerable Blasphemies."[86] Similarly, Henry More remarks that the supralapsarian God "is the genuine *Idea* of a *Devil*."[87] In the same way, but even more pointedly, Milton's *De Doctrina Christiana* also accuses Calvinist theologians of blasphemy, stating: "If I should attempt to refute them, it would be like inventing a long argument to prove that God is not the Devil" (*prolixe disputem Deum non esse Diabolum*).[88] The need for such a "long argument" is precisely what the Satanic portrayal of God in the first two books of *Paradise Lost* provokes. By overhearing the Satanic theologising of hell, the reader's first impression of God is that he is indeed a good deal like the devil—that he is, in other words, exactly the kind of God who is in need of justification.

In *Paradise Lost*, then, the fallen angels are heretical theologians of a debased and distorted Calvinism. They depict God as an ethically arbitrary, tyrannical being who undermines the freedom of his creatures and whose own goodness is negated by naked sovereignty. The God of this quasi-Calvinist Satanic theology is a devilish deity, a dark projection of the Satanic consciousness. By portraying the theology of the fallen angels in this way, *Paradise Lost* subverts Calvinist theological

---

84 [Anon.], *An antidote against some principal errors of the predestinarians* (London, 1696), 11.

85 Thomas Jackson, *Works*, 12 vols. (Oxford, 1844), 11:209.

86 John Goodwin, *Redemption redeemed* (London, 1651), 515. See also Richard Burthogge, *Christianity a revealed mystery* (London, 1702), 41, who speaks of the Reformed orthodox idea of predestination as involving "the greatest Blasphemy."

87 Henry More, *Divine dialogues: containing sundry disquisitions and instructions concerning the attributes and providence of God* (London, 1668), 411.

88 *CPW* 6:166; *CM* 14:88. Similarly but more broadly, the underlying assumption of Empson, *Milton's God*, is that the Christian (not merely the Calvinistic) God is morally identical to the devil. Christians, according to Empson, "worship as the source of all goodness a God who, as soon as you are told the basic story about him, is evidently the Devil" (255). Literally, then, Empson's position cannot be refuted without "inventing a long argument to prove that God is not the Devil." More recently, in *The Satanic Epic*, Neil Forsyth has suggested that the *De Doctrina*'s statement is in fact a definition of exactly what *Paradise Lost* attempts to do: "to prove that God is not the devil." According to Forsyth, "Milton knew God may seem very like the Devil—and the poem shows how much" (9). So too, the central thesis of Michael Bryson's recent work, *The Tyranny of Heaven*, is that "Milton constructs"—on purpose—"a God who is nearly indistinguishable from Satan" (25), in order to show the evil of all (even divine) forms of monarchy.

tradition and challenges its "orthodoxy."[89] Ironically, in post-Reformation England Calvinism was itself the dominant theological orthodoxy that labelled competing theological discourses as heterodox. In the theological thought-world of *Paradise Lost*, however, Calvinist orthodoxy is subtly redefined as a heresy of Satanic ancestry.

The Satanic theology expressed in the first two books of *Paradise Lost* thus constitutes a heretical foil against which the poem's ensuing theological account of the goodness of God is then presented from Book 3 onwards. The God who is depicted in the theologising of the fallen angels is a God who needs to be justified; and the justification of the ways of God in *Paradise Lost* rests in part on the demonstration that God is not at all like this deity. As Thomas Kranidas has observed in a different connection, Satan in fact "helps us to know God, through a series of marvellously engineered inversions."[90] Far from portraying a God who negates creaturely freedom, the rest of the epic seeks to show that freedom is in fact God's own highest concern. It is the fundamental characteristic of his own being, and of all created being.

---

89 Behind this transformation of orthodox Calvinism into Satanic heresy lies Milton's distinctive understanding of "heresy." In *A Treatise of Civil Power*, he writes: "He then who to his best apprehension follows the scripture, though against any point of doctrine by the whole church receivd, is not the heretic; but he who follows the church against his conscience and perswasion grounded on the scripture" (*CPW* 7:248). Such a subjectivised view of heresy is of course appealing to those who find their own theology relegated to the heterodox fringes by the presiding establishment orthodoxy. In a similar way, the English Arminian Goodwin, *Confidence dismounted*, 14, accuses Reformed orthodox authorities of seeking "to bind what burthens of Faith they please upon the necks of men, without giving any why, or wherefore, but their own Authority"; and in contrast to such an orthodoxy, Goodwin advises that Christians should not believe "any thing, whether from me, or any other man, but what they see sufficient ground and reason why they should beleeve." On Milton's view of heresy, see Janel Mueller, "Milton on Heresy," in *Milton and Heresy*, ed. Stephen B. Dobranski and John P. Rumrich (Cambridge: Cambridge University Press, 1998), 21–38.

90 Thomas Kranidas, *The Fierce Equation: A Study of Milton's Decorum* (The Hague: Mouton, 1965), 129.

3. Predestination and Freedom

When the narrative of *Paradise Lost* shifts from Book 2 to Book 3, the Satanic theologians cease to occupy centre stage, and God himself becomes the focus of attention. Perhaps surprisingly, God is also portrayed as a theologian. As Roy Flannagan notes, in contrast to the "sensuously deceptive" speeches of Satan and his followers, God speaks with a stark, forthright simplicity; his speech is "plain, clear, unequivocal, dignified, and authoritative."[1] Many readers have been irritated by the portrayal of God as a theologian. Alexander Pope, for instance, famously intoned that "God the Father turns a School Divine" in *Paradise Lost*.[2] The depiction of God as a theologian can, however, be appreciated when viewed against the backdrop of the poem's post-Reformation context.[3] Reformed orthodox writers argued that the mind of God contains the highest form of theological knowledge. They thus spoke of "archetypal theology" (*theologia archetypa*) as the perfect and complete theology which exists in God's own mind, and they described the fragmented and incomplete theology of human beings as an "ectypal theology" (*theologia ectypa*) which partially and imperfectly reflects its divine archetype.[4] According to post-Reformation theology, and according to *Paradise Lost*, God is thus the ultimate theologian. No one, after all, could be more qualified to speak about God than God. In the words of Blaise Pascal, "God rightly speaks of God."[5]

In *Paradise Lost*, God's own theologising immediately contradicts the Satanic theology of the poem's first two books. While the Satanic theologians speak of a divine tyrant who negates the freedom of his creatures, God himself proclaims that he has eternally ordained creaturely freedom, and that he will never undermine or compromise the autonomy of his creatures. While the Satanic theologians speak of God

---

1   Roy Flannagan, *John Milton: A Short Introduction* (Oxford: Blackwell, 2002), 91.

2   Alexander Pope, *The first epistle of the second book of Horace, imitated* (London, 1737), 7.

3   Thus replying to Pope, Newton rightly remarked that "this sort of divinity was much more in fashion in Milton's days" (Newton, 2:278).

4   On the distinction between *theologia archetypa* and *theologia ectypa*, see Muller, *PRRD*, 1:225–38; and Sebastian Rehnman, *Divine Discourse: The Theological Methodology of John Owen* (Grand Rapids: Baker, 2002), 57–71.

5   Blaise Pascal, *Pensées*, trans. W. F. Trotter (London, 1908), 12.799.

as a cruel and loveless torturer, God himself declares the universality of his grace and goodness. And while the Satanic theologians fatalistically claim to be reprobated by divine predestination, God affirms that there is no reprobation of creatures, except the self-reprobation which some creatures freely choose and actualise for themselves.

The Satanic theology of Books 1 and 2 is thus the dark background against which Book 3 begins to offer a positive account of the theology of God and freedom. And while Satan and his fallen hosts are untrust-worthy theological witnesses, the poem expects its readers to regard God himself as the most reliable of all theologians.

Universal Election

The entire heavenly colloquy in the third book of *Paradise Lost* may be viewed as a dramatic portrayal of predestination. The world has just been created, and God the Father exercises his foreknowledge, bending "his eye" towards earth in order "to view" both "His own works and their works" (3.58–59). He looks upon "Our two first Parents," who are enjoying the "blissful solitude" of their "happie Garden," and reaping the "immortal fruits of joy and love" (3.64–69). Already this punning omen of "fruits" hints at God's foresight of the fall. Foreseeing Satan's strategy to visit earth and to attempt the destruction of Adam and Eve, God tells his Son:

> Man will heark'n to his glozing lyes,
> And easily transgress the sole Command,
> Sole pledge of his obedience: So will fall
> Hee and his faithless Progenie. (3.93–96)

Lest this foresight of the fall appear to entail the fall's necessitation, the Father adds that "Foreknowledge had no influence on thir fault" (3.118).

Having foreseen the fall, the Father immediately declares his gracious intent to restore humanity: "Man ... shall find Grace" (3.131). Reflecting the Father's will and character, the Son shines as a visible expression of the grace of God:

> Beyond compare the Son of God was seen
> Most glorious, in him all his Father shon
> Substantially exprest, and in his face
> Divine compassion visibly appeerd,
> Love without end, and without measure Grace. (3.138–42)

Praising the Father's "gracious" promise "that Man should find Grace" (3.144–45), the Son himself pleads with the Father for the salvation of humanity, described as God's "youngest Son" and his "lov'd" creature (3.151). The Father replies that the Son has perfectly expressed his own predestined plan:

> O Son, in whom my Soul hath chief delight,
> Son of my bosom, Son who art alone
> My Word, my wisdom, and effectual might,
> All hast thou spok'n as my thoughts are, all
> As my Eternal purpose hath decreed. (3.168–72)

The entire colloquy so far is, then, a depiction of the "Eternal purpose" that God has—in the language of post-Reformation theology—"decreed." Before human beings have any need of salvation, before they have fallen, God has already planned their salvation. This is the essential point of the idea of predestination (*praedestinatio*) as it was understood in post-Reformation theology: the grace of salvation is not an afterthought, but a gift of God that precedes even the need for salvation. The heavenly colloquy in *Paradise Lost* especially highlights the gracious character of God's decree for humanity.[6] God has eternally purposed to turn towards humanity, his "creature late so lov'd" (3.151), in grace. From the outset, predestination in the poem is thus an act of God's grace.

The gracious character of predestination is vividly expressed when the Father proceeds to explain in detail his predestined plan:

> Some I have chosen of peculiar grace
> Elect above the rest; so is my will:
> The rest shall hear me call, and oft be warnd
> Thir sinful state, and to appease betimes
> Th' incensed Deitie, while offerd Grace
> Invites; for I will cleer thir senses dark,
> What may suffice, and soft'n stonie hearts
> To pray, repent, and bring obedience due.
> To prayer, repentance, and obedience due,
> Though but endevord with sincere intent,
> Mine eare shall not be slow, mine eye not shut.
> And I will place within them as a guide

---

6   On the portrayal of God as gracious, see the annotation of Todd, 3:18: "Homer, and all who followed him, where they are representing the Deity speaking, describe a scene of terrour and awful consternation." But in contrast, Milton has "the words of the Almighty diffusing fragrance and delight to all around him," and in this way Milton depicts a distinctively "mild, merciful, and benevolent" deity.

My Umpire *Conscience*, whom if they will hear,
Light after light well us'd they shall attain,
And to the end persisting, safe arrive. (3.183–97)

This is, theologically, a remarkable passage. Most importantly, it emphasises the sheer universality of grace. When the Father says that "Some" are "Elect above the rest," he may appear to be asserting the common post-Reformation distinction between election and reprobation. Both Reformed orthodox and Arminian theologians agreed in affirming a notion of double predestination (*praedestinatio gemina*),[7] according to which God has eternally divided the human race into the elect (*electi*) on the one hand and the reprobate (*reprobi*) on the other.[8] The definition of William Ames is typical: "There are two kinds of predestination, election and reprobation."[9] In such a distinction between election and reprobation, the grace of God is restricted to a certain number of human beings, while the greater proportion of humanity is excluded from grace. This position lies behind John Bunyan's stark observation that only "one of a thousand ... Men" and "for Women, one of ten thousand" are saved.[10]

In *Paradise Lost*, however, the Father's reference to certain individuals as "Elect above the rest" cannot be regarded as a statement of dou-

---

7   Thus the supralapsarian theologian William Twisse, *Riches of Gods love unto the vessells of mercy, consistent with his absolute hatred or reprobation of the vessells of wrath*, 2 vols. (Oxford, 1653), 2:67, takes pleasure in observing that all Arminians affirm not only election but also reprobation.

8   The idea of double predestination had been expressed in different ways by Augustine, Isidore of Seville (ca. 560–636) and Gottschalk (ca. 805–ca. 868). The most influential Reformed accounts are John Calvin, *Institutes of the Christian Religion*, trans. Henry Beveridge, 2 vols. (Grand Rapids: Eerdmans, 1989), 3.21–24; Theodore Beza, *Tabula praedestinationis* (Geneva, 1555); and William Perkins, *A golden chaine: or, The description of theologie* (Cambridge, 1592).

9   William Ames, *The Marrow of Theology*, ed. and trans. John D. Eusden (Grand Rapids: Baker, 1968), 1.25.17. Reformed orthodox theologians often argued that election cannot exist without reprobation: see for example Pierre du Moulin, *The anatomy of Arminianisme* (London, 1620), 83: "Of ... predestination there are two parts; the one is election, the other is reprobation, whereof the first doth necessarily lay downe the second: For, as often as some are chosen out of many, the rest are necessarily reprobated." In the eighteenth century, this view was summed up by the Anglican Calvinist Augustus Toplady, *The Church of England vindicated from the charge of Arminianism* (London, 1769), 93: "Election, without Reprobation, cannot stand: it must have the other leg, or it will tumble down."

10 John Bunyan, *A holy life, the beauty of Christianity: or, An exhortation to Christians to be holy* (London, 1684), 44. Post-Reformation theologians often speculated that only a small minority of human beings is elect and that the majority is reprobate: see Philip C. Almond, *Heaven and Hell in Enlightenment England* (Cambridge: Cambridge University Press, 1994), 72–74.

ble predestination.[11] On the contrary, as Boyd Berry remarks, when the Father says that some are "Elect above the rest," he is asserting "that God extends election to all men," but that "[s]ome ... are more elect than others."[12] All human beings are eternally elected for salvation, but some individuals are "Elect above the rest." The universality of election is indicated by the way in which God describes "the rest": they hear his "call" to salvation (3.185); they are "invite[d]" by "offerd Grace" (3.187–88); their minds are enlightened and their hearts softened (3.188–90); they are brought by grace "To prayer, repentance and obedience due" (3.191); they receive "Light after light" to lead them to salvation (3.196); and if they follow this light and endure to the end, they will "safe arrive" in the kingdom of God (3.197). Saving grace is thus clearly predestined for all human beings alike. The Son echoes this theology of universal grace (*gratia universalis*) when, responding to the Father, he describes grace as "The speediest of thy winged messengers," which "visit[s] all thy creatures," and comes "to all" humanity (3.229–31).

The theological significance of this depiction of universal election can hardly be overstated. In resisting the division of predestination into election and reprobation, *Paradise Lost's* theology is sharply discontinuous with all the major post-Reformation theological traditions. The seventeenth-century predestinarian controversies among Reformed orthodox, Arminian and Amyraldian theologians centred on the question of the grounds of God's decision to elect some and reject others; but all such theologians shared the assumption that predestination formally consists of both a decree to elect and a decree to reject.[13] According to Arminius, for instance, scripture teaches that election "has

---

11　The notion of double predestination has been detected in this passage by Fowler, who suggests that here, as in the *De Doctrina Christiana*, "elect" means "no more than 'whoever believes and continues in the faith'" (Fowler, 153; citing *CPW* 6:168), so that, by implication, all "the rest" are simply unbelievers. An even sharper double-predestination reading is offered by Maurice Kelley, "The Theological Dogma of *Paradise Lost*, III, 173–202," *PMLA* 52 (1937), 75–79. Kelley views the "elect" as referring to generally elected believers, and "the rest" simply as the reprobate unbelievers: "'Some,' then, refers to the believers; and the 'rest' ... are the unbelievers" (79). In such an interpretation, God's gracious election is relegated to just two lines of the speech, with the following 18 lines speaking of "the rest," i.e., the unbelievers. In this reading the whole passage's emphasis on divine grace is thus undermined.

12　Boyd M. Berry, *Process of Speech: Puritan Religious Writing and Paradise Lost* (Baltimore: John Hopkins University Press, 1976), 255.

13　Thus as Richard A. Muller, *After Calvin: Studies in the Development of a Theological Tradition* (Oxford: Oxford University Press, 2003), 15, notes, even the hypothetical universalism of Amyraldism never claimed "that nonelect individuals might actually believe."

Reprobation as its opposite";[14] while a Reformed writer like William
Perkins speaks of predestination "either to salvation or condemnation."[15] Exploring the contours of the controversy between Reformed
orthodoxy and Arminianism, the Arminian theologian John Goodwin
notes that both parties agree that there is "both a Decree of Election,
and a Decree also of Reprobation," both decrees being eternal and "absolutely immutable."[16] In departing from the assumption that predestination must formally be twofold, *Paradise Lost*'s theology moves beyond the conceptual framework of post-Reformation predestinarian
theology, offering a radically universalised vision of God's gracious
election. Such a view of universal election stands in the sharpest possible contrast to the Satanic Calvinism propounded by the fallen angels
in the opening books of *Paradise Lost*, in which God is depicted as cruel
and graceless.

In thus affirming the universality of election, *Paradise Lost*'s theology moves toward the great nineteenth-century theologian Friedrich
Schleiermacher (1768–1834), who criticised the line of thought that "if
everything is to be neat and logical, we must admit a foreordination by
which some are predestined to damnation, as others to blessedness,"
and who argued instead for a "single divine foreordination to blessedness" that encompasses the entire human race.[17] For Schleiermacher, if
"the universality of redemption" is taken seriously, then election to
salvation must also be understood "quite universally."[18] In this
reformulation of predestinarian theology, the decree of predestination
is seen to be wholly and radically a decree of grace. In the same way,
the graciousness of predestination is radically asserted in *Paradise Lost*,
and this is one of the most significant features of the poem's theology of
predestination.

But in view of *Paradise Lost*'s account of the universality of God's
gracious election, what is to be made of the poem's assertion that certain individuals are more elect than others, "Elect above the rest"
(3.184)?[19] In the first place, as Dennis Danielson suggests, this may sim-

---

14 Jacobus Arminius, *The Works of James Arminius*, trans. James Nichols and William
    Nichols, 3 vols. (Grand Rapids: Baker, 1986), 2:226.
15 Perkins, *A golden chaine*, 23.
16 John Goodwin, *The agreement and distance of brethren* (London, 1652), 1.
17 Friedrich Daniel Ernst Schleiermacher, *The Christian Faith*, ed. H. R. Mackintosh and
    J. S. Stewart (Edinburgh: T&T Clark, 1928), 548–49. On Schleiermacher's theology of
    predestination, see Theodor Mahlmann, "Prädestination: V," *TRE*, 27:142–44.
18 Schleiermacher, *The Christian Faith*, 560.
19 On this complex feature of the poem's theology, see especially Newton, 1:178–79;
    Kelley, "The Theological Dogma of *Paradise Lost*," 75–79; William J. Grace, *Ideas in
    Milton* (Notre Dame: University of Notre Dame Press, 1968), 6; G. D. Hamilton,

ply be a reference to the notion that certain individuals are chosen to perform special tasks in God's kingdom.[20] Such a view of special election was affirmed in Arminian theology, which distinguished between the election of individuals "to perform some particular service," and the election of individuals "to be ... heirs of eternal life."[21] Moïse Amyraut, too, writes that "when God calls out some particular persons on some great and eminent employments ... he frequently confers [on them] more sensible influences of his grace and Spirit"; such influences of grace, he says, differ from the "ordinary methods of the divine Spirit."[22] In *Paradise Lost*, the specially elected individuals may likewise simply be those who are elected to "great and eminent employments"; indeed, Stephen Fallon has suggested that the poem's account of special election may reflect Milton's own self-understanding as an individual specially singled out by God.[23]

Alternatively, the description of some as "Elect above the rest" may refer to the differing degrees of grace (*gradus gratiae*) that God grants to different people. Such a notion of degrees of grace was by no means restricted to Reformed orthodox theology.[24] Anselm had written that

---

"Milton's Defensive God: A Reappraisal," *Studies in Philology* 69:1 (1972), 97–98; Berry, *Process of Speech*, 254–56; Dennis R. Danielson, *Milton's Good God: A Study in Literary Theodicy* (Cambridge: Cambridge University Press, 1982), 82–85; Thomas N. Corns, *Regaining Paradise Lost* (London: Longman, 1994), 82–83; and above all Stephen M. Fallon, "'Elect above the Rest': Theology as Self-Representation in Milton," in *Milton and Heresy*, ed. Stephen B. Dobranski and John P. Rumrich (Cambridge: Cambridge University Press, 1999), 93–116.

20   Danielson, *Milton's Good God*, 83.

21   H. O. Wiley, *Christian Theology*, 3 vols. (Kansas City: Beacon Hill, 1940–43), 2:339–40, summarising the traditional Arminian position.

22   Moïse Amyraut, *A treatise concerning religions, in refutation of the opinion which accounts all indifferent* (London, 1660), 21.

23   Fallon, "Elect above the Rest," 93–116. Throughout his essay, Fallon speaks of Milton's "desires," his "yearning," and his "need" to be recognised as outstanding. This view of Milton's psychological condition is common. It is an axiom for Denis Saurat, *Milton, Man and Thinker* (London: J. M. Dent, 1944), xii–xiii, who describes Milton's personality as consisting of a "powerful feeling of egotism and pride, in the fullest self-consciousness of a tremendous individuality"; and it has sometimes been hyperbolised, as, for instance, by Robert Graves, *Wife to Mr. Milton: The Story of Marie Powell* (New York: Octagon, 1943). But the emphasis on Milton's egotism should be balanced by a recognition of his own profound distrust of human pride. As Stanley E. Fish, *How Milton Works* (Cambridge, Mass.: Harvard University Press, 2001), 280, rightly points out, Milton's "fierce egotism is but one-half of his story."

24   For Reformed orthodox examples, see William Day, *Man's destruction, prov'd to be of himself: in which, the Antinomian and Arminian errors are confuted* (London, 1713), 16, who speaks of the "sev'ral Degrees" of divine grace; and du Moulin, *The anatomy of Arminianisme*, 83: "of them that are chosen, some are preferred before others." The idea of degrees of grace was occasionally linked explicitly to bourgeois sentiments. See for example Henry Whiston, *A short treatise of the great worth and best kind of nobi-*

God "does not have mercy equally on all those to whom he shows mercy";[25] and the same point was often made in Arminian theology. According to Arminius, God "does not equally effect the conversion and salvation of all," even though he "seriously will[s] the conversion and salvation of all";[26] and similarly Simon Episcopius speaks of "a very great disparity of Grace according ... to the most free dispensation of the divine will."[27] Moïse Amyraut, too, writes that all grace is sufficient "to bring salvation," but that grace may nevertheless "also differ in degrees."[28] In the same way, Milton's *De Doctrina Christiana* affirms that God "has not distributed grace equally" to all people.[29] According to the treatise, God "bestows grace on all, and if not equally upon each, at least sufficient to enable everyone to attain knowledge of the truth and final salvation."[30] *Paradise Lost*'s description of some people as "Elect above the rest" may be a similar reference to the differing degrees of grace that God freely bestows on different individuals. Such a concept of degrees of grace clearly does not undermine the universality or sufficiency of grace. All are elected by grace, but some are "super-elect."[31]

Again, it is possible that the poem's account of super-election refers not simply to differing degrees of grace, but to different *kinds* of saving grace. Some such notion was articulated by the counter-Reformation theologian Ambrosius Catharinus (ca.1484–1553), who taught that certain specially elected individuals, such as Mary and the Apostles, are saved by the operation of irresistible grace, while the rest of humanity is offered a sufficient grace that can be either accepted or rejected.[32]

---

lity (London, 1661), 46: "the Divine grace and blessing, though not tyed to any, doth most usually fall in some special manner upon those Families whose Ancestors have done worthily," so that "Birth and Breeding" concur with "special blessings from above."

25 Anselm, *De concordia*, 3.8; from the text in *Opera omnia*, 6 vols. (Edinburgh: Thomas Nelson, 1938–61), 2:243–88.

26 Arminius, *Works*, 3:442; see also 3:233.

27 Simon Episcopius, *The confession or declaration of the ministers or pastors which in the United Provinces are called Remonstrants, concerning the chief points of Christian religion* (London, 1676), 207.

28 Moïse Amyraut, *A discourse concerning the divine dreams mention'd in Scripture* (London, 1676), 20.

29 *CPW* 6:192; *CM* 14:146.

30 *CPW* 6:192; *CM* 14:146.

31 This expression is used by Berry, *Process of Speech*, 256; and Danielson, *Milton's Good God*, 83.

32 Here I have followed the summary of Catharinus's theology in the article, "Catharinus, Ambrosius," in *The Oxford Dictionary of the Christian Church*, ed. F. L. Cross (London: Oxford University Press, 1958), 247–48.

Similarly, the nineteenth-century Lutheran theologian Hans Larsen Martensen (1808–84) writes that "grace interests itself in an especial manner about some, whom it will make its personal subjects and instruments, while it interests itself about others only in a general way,"[33] so that even within the kingdom of God there is a great difference between "the chosen and the left."[34] Although such ideas of differing kinds of grace were almost unheard of in seventeenth-century theology, they may be close to *Paradise Lost*'s "Elect above the rest," in which a qualitative distinction seems to be made between those who are saved by the gospel through "sufficient grace" (3.99; 3.189), and those super-elect individuals who are saved in some other way through "peculiar grace" (3.183).

In any case, whether the super-elect differ from the elect in kind or only in degree, the theology of predestination in *Paradise Lost* strongly affirms both the universality of grace and the freedom of God to distinguish between individuals and to be more gracious to some than to others. The super-election of some persons in distinction from others thus does not reflect the Satanic Calvinists' assertion of divine arbitrariness in Books 1 and 2, nor does it qualify the sheer graciousness of God to all humanity. Rather, it accentuates the gracious character of God's election by offering an illustration of "Grace in her greatest super-abundancy."[35]

Reprobation

Notwithstanding this emphasis on the universality of electing grace, in *Paradise Lost* God the Father also adopts the theological language of reprobation, and affirms that some human beings will ultimately perish:

> This my long sufferance and my day of Grace
> They who neglect and scorn, shall never taste;
> But hard be hard'nd, blind be blinded more,
> That they may stumble on, and deeper fall;
> And none but such from mercy I exclude. (3.198–202)

---

33 H. L. Martensen, *Christian Dogmatics: A Compendium of the Doctrines of Christianity*, trans. William Urwick (Edinburgh, 1898), 374.

34 Martensen, *Christian Dogmatics*, 379.

35 This expression is used in a different connection by John Goodwin, *The banner of justification displayed* (London, 1659), 5.

In spite of the fact that all people are elected by grace, this election does not negate human freedom. Individuals retain the power to reject the grace of God, to "neglect and scorn" their own election, and in this way to choose their own reprobation. The fact that those who are wilfully "hard" and "blind" become increasingly "hard'nd" and "blinded" is due not to any reprobating divine agency, but to their own obstinate denial and rejection of God's gracious election.

The language of the "blinding" and "hardening" of sinners derives from scripture,[36] and was consistently used in post-Reformation accounts of reprobation (*reprobatio*). Most Reformed orthodox writers defined the divine hardening of sinners as God's "permission" (*permissio*), in which he simply "passes over" the reprobate, leaving them to their own devices.[37] Here Reformed orthodoxy followed the thought of the Reformation theologian Heinrich Bullinger, who had argued that the reprobation of some is grounded not in the will of God, "but in the man himself who rejects the grace of God and does not receive the heavenly gifts."[38] William Prynne expresses this position when he claims that the hardening of reprobate individuals "proceedes not primarilie from any peremptory Decree, or Act of God ... but from Reprobates themselves."[39] Similarly, Thomas Watson writes: "God doth not infuse Evil into Men, only he withdraws the Influence of his Graces, and then the Heart hardens of itself, even as Light being withdrawn, Darkness presently follows."[40] Other Reformed theologians, however, remained closer to Calvin, who had denied the distinction between the divine will and the divine permission,[41] and had attributed the "blind-

---

36   See, for example, Exodus 4:21; 7:13; 9:12; 14:17; John 9:39; 12:40; Romans 9:18; 11:7; 11:25. The Father's statement that the hardened and blinded will "stumble on, and deeper fall" (3.201) is perhaps verbally influenced by Romans 9:11: "Have they stumbled that they should fall?" And this question, like the Father's speech in *Paradise Lost*, is in fact part of a broader defence of the universality of divine mercy.

37   See for example Amandus Polanus, *Syntagma theologiae christianae* (Geneva, 1617), 4.10.

38   From the Latin cited in Cornelis P. Venema, *Heinrich Bullinger and the Doctrine of Predestination: Author of "the Other Reformed Tradition"?* (Grand Rapids: Baker, 2002), 67 n. 38. This had also been Anselm's position. See *De concordia*, 3.5: the one who "spurns" grace "continues in his hardness and iniquity" only by "his own fault, not God's."

39   William Prynne, *God, no impostor, nor deluder: or, An answer to a Popish and Arminian cavill, in the defence of the free-will, and universall grace* (London, 1630), 9. See also 6–7, where Prynne argues that God does not actively blind the reprobate, but that they blind themselves.

40   Thomas Watson, *A body of practical divinity* (London, 1692), 71.

41   See John Calvin, *Commentaries on the First Book of Moses, Called Genesis*, trans. John King, 2 vols. (Edinburgh, 1847), 1:144; and Calvin, *Institutes*, 3.23.8. See also Richard

ing" and "hardening" of the reprobate to the immediate will of God.[42] William Perkins, for instance, asserts that "God is not onely a bare permissive agent in an evill worke, but a powerfull effectour of the same."[43] In contrast, Arminian theologians sought to place the full responsibility for "blinding" and "hardening" on the wilful disobedience of the sinners themselves. According to Episcopius, for instance, the wilfully rebellious are "blind[ed]" and "harden[ed]" only when God delivers them "unto their own corrupt desires," so that they are really self-blinded and self-hardened.[44] And John Goodwin writes that "God never *hardneth* any man," but he withdraws his prevenient grace from those "who first voluntarily *harden* themselves, and are *obstinately* disobedient."[45] Milton's *De Doctrina Christiana* adopts a similar Arminian interpretation, emphasising the sufficiency and universality of grace: "God, to show the glory of his long-suffering and justice, excludes no one from the way of repentance and eternal salvation, unless that person has continued to reject and despise the offer of grace, and of grace sufficient for salvation, until it is too late."[46]

In the same way, *Paradise Lost*'s account of the blinding and hardening of those who reject grace is grounded in the poem's thoroughgoing commitment to both the universality of election and the freedom of human beings to determine their own futures. The decisiveness of the human will is especially highlighted by the contrasting wordplay between "cleer" and "soft'n" on the one hand (3.188–89), and "hard'nd" and "blinded" on the other (3.200). God is the subject of the former verbs—"I will cleer thir senses ... and soft'n stonie hearts"—so

---

A. Muller, *Christ and the Decree: Christology and Predestination in Reformed Theology From Calvin to Perkins* (Grand Rapids: Baker, 1986), 24–25.

42 See Calvin, *Institutes*, 3.23.1: "hardening is not less under the immediate hand of God than mercy." See also *Institutes*, 3.24.13–14. Luther's position was similar: see *Luther's Works*, ed. J. Pelikan and H. T. Lehmann, 55 vols. (St Louis and Philadelphia: Concordia and Fortress, 1958–86), 33:164–206. The late medieval theologian Thomas Bradwardine (ca.1290–1349) had also rejected the distinction between divine will and permission, advocating a thoroughgoing necessitarianism in which even evil constitutes a necessary part of the divine plan: see Gordon Leff, *Bradwardine and the Pelagians: A Study of His De Causa Dei and Its Opponents* (Cambridge: Cambridge University Press, 1957); and see also the brief discussion in Augustus Neander, *Lectures on the History of Christian Dogmas*, trans. J. E. Ryland, 2 vols. (London, 1858), 2:609.

43 Perkins, *A golden chaine*, 22.

44 Episcopius, *The confession or declaration*, 113.

45 John Goodwin, *An exposition of the nineth chapter of the Epistle to the Romans* (London, 1653), 214; on the withdrawal of prevenient grace, see 217: "God never withdraws that preventing or exciting grace, which is given unto every man, from any man, untill the man himself by voluntariness of sinning provoketh him to it."

46 *CPW* 6:194; *CM* 14:152.

that the illumining of the mind and the softening of the heart, which make salvation possible, are attributed solely to divine grace. But in contrast, the subjects of "hard'nd" and "blinded" are simply the "hard" and the "blind": "But hard be hard'nd, blind be blinded more." Divine action is thus grammatically excluded from this account of reprobation. The blinding of the mind and the hardening of the heart are solely the work of the human agents who choose and thereby actualise their own reprobation. God's grace is predestined for and bestowed on all people. But the individual always remains free to reject grace and so to perish.

Even in this context, then, where *Paradise Lost* speaks of the possibility of condemnation, its real emphasis is on the freely offered grace of God. Indeed, the whole divine colloquy in Book 3 is not even peripherally concerned with condemnation, but only with a positive statement of the way in which "Man should find Grace" (3.145). Even when the Father makes passing reference to the condemnation of some human beings, the subject-matter of his speech is still "my day of Grace" (3.198). Most importantly, the emphasis here is on the inclusiveness and universality of grace. Even the line, "none but such from mercy I exclude" (3.202), is a statement of the inclusiveness of mercy. No one is excluded from mercy, except those who wilfully refuse to be included, and thus exclude themselves. Their exclusion rests solely on their own act, and not on any divine decree.

In *Paradise Lost*, reprobation is therefore not an act of the divine will, but an act of the human will. It is not, as in Reformed orthodox theology, an eternal decree that statically fixes the fate of some human beings, but it is rather a temporal decision made by human beings, and as such it can never be a once-for-all, irreversible decision. Even those "hard'nd" and "blinded" individuals, who "stumble on, and deeper fall," are never in principle beyond the possibility of salvation.[47] As the *De Doctrina Christiana* says, reprobation can always be "rescinded by repentance" (*reprobationem resipiscentia rescindi*).[48] They are among the reprobate only to the extent that they persist in their stubborn self-reprobation, and in the rejection of God's electing grace. Once again, *Paradise Lost* here moves toward Schleiermacher's influential reformulation of the idea of predestination. In Schleiermacher's theology, the reprobate are understood simply as those who "at any par-

---

47   Such a position is flatly rejected by William Perkins, *A golden chaine: or, The description of theologie* (Cambridge, 1592), 350: "both the election and reprobation of God stand immutable, so that neither the Elect can become reprobates, nor the reprobates elect; and consequently neither these [can] be saved, nor they condemned."

48   *CPW* 6:191; *CM* 14:144.

ticular moment" are "not yet to be regarded as chosen."[49] In this conception, reprobation is taken down from a pre-temporal realm and is
instead grounded in the concrete sphere of human decision and history.[50] So also, in *Paradise Lost* the self-reprobation of certain individuals
is a process that takes place in history, and that remains in principle
always open to the possibility of the triumph of grace. Edward
Wagenknecht has thus rightly remarked that although *Paradise Lost*
does not advocate universal salvation, the poem's theology "obviously
trie[s] to make it as difficult as possible to be damned."[51] As those who
have been eternally elected by God, all the "hard'nd" and "blinded"
remain potentially among those who will, "to the end persisting, safe
arrive" (3.197).

Paradise Lost's account of temporal and dynamic reprobation thus
offers a powerful critique of the Reformed orthodox notion of a "fixed
number" of elect and reprobate individuals. Calvin had written: "God,
by an eternal decree, fixed the number of those whom he is pleased to
embrace in love, and [of those] on whom he is pleased to display his
wrath";[52] while for Lucas Trelactius, "[t]he number of the Elect, and
Reprobates ... is certaine."[53] According to the Westminster Confession,
all those who are "predestinated unto everlasting life" and "foreordained to everlasting death" are "particularly and unchangeably designed, and their number so certain and definite, that it cannot be either
increased or diminished."[54] In *Paradise Lost*, in contrast, God the Father

---

49 Schleiermacher, *The Christian Faith*, 548.

50 According to Wolfhart Pannenberg, *Systematic Theology*, trans. Geoffrey W. Bromiley,
    3 vols. (Grand Rapids: Eerdmans, 1991–98), 3:450, this development of "a historical
    reference to human history for the thought of election" constitutes "one of the most
    important and lasting achievements of Schleiermacher."

51 Edward Wagenknecht, *The Personality of Milton* (Normon: University of Oklahoma
    Press, 1970), 141. On the speech under consideration (3.183–202), see also the pene-
    trating observation of Berry, *Process of Speech*, 255: "The last five lines make it clear
    that not all men make the right choices and progress, yet in a sense the impact of all
    that precedes these lines suggests ... that all *will* safely arrive."

52 Calvin, *Institutes*, 3.24.17.

53 Lucas Trelcatius, *A briefe institution of the common places of sacred divinitie* (London,
    1610), 97.

54 Westminster Confession of Faith, 3.3–4; in Schaff, 3:608–9. See also the Lambeth
    Articles, 3; in Schaff, 3:523. The idea of a "fixed number" had already been asserted
    by Augustine, *De correptione et gratia*, 13; in *PL* 44 and *NPNF* 5: "The number of the
    predestined is fixed, and cannot be increased or diminished"; and Thomas Aquinas,
    Summa Theologiae, 60 vols. (London: Blackfriars, 1964–76), 1a.23.7: "the number of the
    predestined is certain to God; not only by way of knowledge, but also by way of a
    principal preordination." Arminius, *Works*, 2:719, had also continued to affirm the
    notion of a fixed number: "the number both of those who are to be saved, and of
    those who are to be damned, is certain and fixed." Arminius, however, sought to

denies the possibility of any such "certain and definite number" by locating reprobation in the fluid and temporal sphere of human choice. He thus negates the dark idea that a "fixed number" of reprobate individuals can, like the Satanic Calvinists in Book 1 and 2, only dread but not escape their certain condemnation.[55] According to *Paradise Lost*, because there is no such "fixed number," every person is potentially saveable. The Arminian divine John Goodwin had similarly insisted that all the reprobate "may very possibly be saved, any Decree of God notwithstanding."[56] So dynamic an approach to reprobation removes all numerical restrictions from grace, and highlights the universality of the plan of salvation—its *de jure* if not *de facto* universalism. In the twentieth century, a similar universalism of grace is emphasised by Emil Brunner, who writes: "Whoever excludes himself [from grace], is excluded; he who does not allow himself to be included, is not included. But he who allows himself to be included, he who believes, *is* 'elect.'"[57] In just this way, according to *Paradise Lost* all human beings are among the elect, but remain free to reject their own election and so to exclude themselves from the grace of God.

Predestined Freedom

I have argued that the theology of predestination in *Paradise Lost* is characterised both by an emphasis on the universality of grace, and by a corresponding emphasis on the decisive role of human freedom. But at certain points, the poem's portrayal of predestination presses human

---

soften the force of this concept by grounding the fixed number in the divine fore-knowledge of human responses to grace: individuals are "fixed" in one group or another not by the mere divine pleasure, but by their own (future and foreseen) response to sufficient grace.

55 Balachandra Rajan, *The Lofty Rhyme: A Study of Milton's Major Poetry* (Coral Gables: University of Miami Press, 1970), 76, notes that "the prolonged drama of temptation" in *Paradise Lost* "would not be very much of a drama if the man at the centre could only prefer what he was elected or condemned to prefer. Predestination may be grimly edifying but it has its deficiencies as a poetic spectacle."

56 John Goodwin, *The agreement and distance of brethren*, 2. Less emphatically, Thomas Aquinas, *Summa Theologiae*, 1a.23.3, distinguishes between "conditional" and "absolute" possibility: "Reprobation by God does not take anything away from the power of the person reprobated. Hence, when it is said that the reprobated cannot obtain grace, this must not be understood as implying absolute impossibility; but only conditional impossibility." To take up the same distinction: in *Paradise Lost* the reprobate possess the absolute, not merely the conditional, possibility of obtaining grace.

57 Emil Brunner, *Dogmatics*, trans. Olive Wyon et al., 3 vols. (London: Lutterworth, 1949–62), 1:320.

freedom into the foreground in a still more radical and creative way. During the heavenly colloquy in Book 3, the Father says of humanity:

> for so
> I formd them free, and free they must remain,
> Till they enthrall themselves: I else must change
> Thir nature, and revoke the high Decree
> Unchangeable, Eternal, which ordaind
> Thir freedom: they themselves ordaind thir fall. (3.123–28)

In describing the divine "decree" as "Eternal" and "Unchangeable," the Father uses language typical of both Reformed orthodox and Arminian theologians. The Arminian Articles, for instance, speak of predestination as God's "eternal and unchangeable decree" (*Deus aeterno et immutabili decreto*).[58] But while in post-Reformation theology the "eternal and unchangeable decree" refers to God's election of human beings to salvation, in *Paradise Lost* the Father refers to an eternal and unchangeable decree of *human* freedom. This freedom is the focus of the eternal, decreeing will of God. Human freedom is "formd" by God, and constituted by a "high Decree."[59] Its reality is grounded in an eternal, divine decision. In short, the Father makes human freedom, rather than human salvation, the object of predestination (*obiectum praedestinationis*).[60] As the object of the divine decree, human freedom is thus elevated to a status of eternal significance. It is depicted as the highest concern of the eternal will of God.

Further, while this freedom has been "ordaind" by God, according to *Paradise Lost* the human beings thus constituted as free agents "themselves ordaind thir fall." The term "ordained" was commonly used in post-Reformation predestinarian discourse; but in a striking appropriation of this term, the Father shifts its reference from a divine to a human context.[61] According to Reformed orthodoxy, the fall had

---

58 *Articuli Arminiani sive remonstrantia*, 1; in Schaff, 3:545. For an example of the same use of terminology in Reformed orthodoxy, see Francis Turretin, *Institutes of Elenctic Theology*, ed. James T. Dennison, trans. George Musgrave Giger, 3 vols. (Phillipsburg: P&R, 1992–97), 4.3.3.

59 See Richard Luckett, "Milton," *TRE*, 22:757.

60 In post-Reformation discourse, the term "object of predestination" was used especially in the controversy between the infra- and supralapsarian parties within Reformed orthodoxy. On the term and its context, see Karl Barth, *Church Dogmatics*, ed. Geoffrey W. Bromiley and T. F. Torrance (Edinburgh: T&T Clark, 1956–77), II/2, 127–45; Heppe, 157–62.

61 Here there is an important underlying continuity between the theology of *Paradise Lost* and Arminian theology. As Peter Harrison notes in *"Religion" and the Religions in the English Enlightenment* (Cambridge: Cambridge University Press, 1990), 24, the

been predetermined by the God who "unchangeably ordain[s] whatsoever comes to pass."[62] But according to the God of *Paradise Lost*, the fall
has not been divinely ordained, but rather "ordaind" by the freedom of
human beings.[63]

Earlier in the same speech, the theological term "decree" is similarly taken from its usual context in predestinarian theology and appropriated as a description of human freedom:

> As if Predestination over-rul'd
> Thir will, dispos'd by absolute Decree
> Or high foreknowledge; they themselves decreed
> Thir own revolt, not I: if I foreknew,
> Foreknowledge had no influence on thir fault,
> Which had no less prov'd certain unforeknown. (3.114–19)

By the seventeenth century, the concept of an absolute decree (*decretum
absolutum*) was widely associated with the Reformed orthodox view of
predestination.[64] The Father's words here thus stand in continuity with
anti-Calvinist polemic by asserting that no such "absolute Decree" has
compromised the freedom of Adam and Eve.[65] Rather, the only decree
that has any bearing on the fall is that of Adam and Eve themselves:
they "decreed" their own revolt from God. Here any notion of a divine
decree is deemed to be irrelevant to the fall, and the theological concept
of "decree" is shifted from the abstract realm of eternal mysteries to the
concrete realm of human action and decision. Using the same terminology of "decree," Milton's *De Doctrina Christiana* also suggests such a
reformulation of predestinarian theology, when it argues that the reprobation of the disobedient "lies not so much in the divine will, as in
the obstinacy of their own minds; nor is it the decree of God, but rather

---

Arminians took salvation down from "the inaccessible reaches of the inscrutable will
of God," and placed it instead in the ordinary realm of human affairs and objective
knowledge. The result was not merely a modified understanding of salvation, but a
new conception of religious truth.

62 Westminster Confession of Faith, 3.1; in Schaff, 3:308. For Calvin's influential and
uncompromising statement on the foreordination of the fall, see *Institutes*, 3.23.7.

63 Hamilton, "Milton's Defensive God," 94–95, thus notes that in this passage God "is
skillfully using high Calvinist language to deny high Calvinist conclusions."

64 On the important concept of *decretum absolutum* in Reformed orthodoxy, see Barth,
Church Dogmatics II/2, 68–76, 158–61. For use of the term by Reformed orthodox
theologians, see for example Polanus, *Syntagma theologiae christianae*, 4.6; and Turretin, *Institutes*, 4.3.2.

65 For examples of Arminian polemical use of the concept of *decretum absolutum*, see
Arminius, *Works*, 2:718; [Anon.], *An antidote against some principal errors of the prede-
stinarians* (London, 1696), 11; and Richard Burthogge, *Christianity a revealed mystery*
(London, 1702), 41.

of the reprobate themselves."[66] According to the treatise, the only "decree" of reprobation is the decree of the human will. In this conception, it is not God who stands behind history with an all-determining "absolute decree." Rather, human freedom itself has the power to decree and to render the future certain.

According to *Paradise Lost*, God's endowment of human beings with radical freedom and autonomy is, even from the divine standpoint, unchangeable. Adam and Eve "must remain" free, or else God himself "must change / Thir nature" (3.125–26). Here the inviolable integrity of human freedom is closely connected to the immutability of God's own character:[67] the enjambement—"I else must change / Thir nature"—implicitly suggests that changes in either divine or human nature are equally inconceivable. The integrity and autonomy of human nature are such that God himself, having decreed and created human freedom, cannot compromise or alter it.[68] With this freedom, this creaturely autonomy vis-à-vis God, human beings have "decreed / Thir own revolt," "ordaind thir fall," and predestined their own future.

God's remark that the fall would have been no less "certain" if it had been "unforeknown" may thus be taken to mean that, far from exercising any positive influence on the future, divine foreknowledge can only observe the "certain" outcome of the human "decree."[69] The same priority of human action over divine foreknowledge is suggested when God claims that Adam and Eve trespass "without least impulse or shadow of Fate, / Or aught by mee immutablie foreseen" (3.120–21). God's foresight is not logically prior to the fall.[70] The event of the fall, in so far as it is an event of human freedom, possesses a real autonomy that stands apart even from divine knowledge. Adam and Eve decree their fall and, as a result, God foresees the fall. Strictly speaking, then,

---

66 *CPW* 6:195; *CM* 14:154.

67 The divine immutability was an aspect of the doctrine of God carried over from patristic theology. On the patristic view, see G. L. Prestige, *God in Patristic Thought* (London: SPCK, 1959), 6–9. On divine immutability in post-Reformation theology, see Muller, *PRRD*, 3:308–21.

68 Even if God could alter the freedom of human nature, such an alteration would bring about, as Roland M. Frye, *God, Man, and Satan: Patterns of Christian Thought and Life in Paradise Lost, Pilgrim's Progress, and the Great Theologians* (Princeton: Princeton University Press, 1960), 43, observes, "a fall far more drastic than that which man ordains for himself."

69 See Luckett, "Milton," 757.

70 Similarly, see Arminius, *Works*, 2:368: "neither Prediction nor any Prescience induces a necessity of any thing that is afterwards to be (*futurae*); since they are posterior in nature and order to the thing that is future. For a thing does not come to pass because it has been foreknown or foretold; but it is foreknown and foretold because it is yet to come to pass."

the fall itself takes place "without" foreknowledge, "without" any shadow of divine influence. Adam and Eve are thus truly "Authors to themselves in all" (3.122). They are characterised by a staggering volitional autonomy that reaches back, as it were, even to the depths of eternity.

This account of foreknowledge (*praescientia*) stands in continuity with the theory of middle knowledge (*scientia media*) expounded by the Roman Catholic theologian Luis de Molina (1535–1600).[71] Seeking to uphold the liberty of human choice, Molina argued that between God's knowledge of the possible on the one hand and the necessary on the other there lies a middle knowledge of those events that are brought about by the freedom of creatures. Such events are not determined by the divine will or foreknowledge, but only by the freedom of human agents; God foreknows such events because they will happen, not because he has made them happen.[72] Molina's theory was at the centre of extensive controversy in the seventeenth century.[73] While Reformed orthodoxy rejected middle knowledge because it made the divine knowledge "uncertain and dependent on the Creature,"[74] Arminian theology appropriated Molinism in metaphysical support of its view of predestination and grace.[75] Not all Arminians, however, were comfortable attributing this kind of causal independence to human agents; Thomas Goad, for instance, anathematises the notion that events come to pass by "Casuality," that is, "*ex improviso*, beside the fore-thought."[76] Goad's polemical description of middle knowledge

---

71 Molina's major work, first published in 1588, is *Concordia liberi arbitrii cum gratiae donis, divina praescientia, providentia, praedestinatione et reprobatione*, ed. Johann Rabeneck (Onia: Collegium Maximum Societatis Jesu, 1953).

72 On middle knowledge, see William Lane Craig, *The Problem of Divine Foreknowledge and Future Contingents: Aristotle to Suárez* (Leiden: E. J. Brill, 1988), 169–206; Muller, *PRRD*, 3:417–32; and Thomas P. Flint, *Divine Providence: The Molinist Account* (Ithaca: Cornell University Press, 1998).

73 See Muller, *PRRD*, 3:419–20: "The extent of the seventeenth-century debate over middle knowledge was vast.... Nearly every theologian and exegete of the age touched on the problem and, with the exceptions of the Jesuits, Socinians, and Arminians, response was largely negative."

74 Edward Leigh, *A system or body of divinity* (London, 1662), 2.7.

75 On Arminius's appropriation of middle knowledge, see Eef Dekker, "Was Arminius a Molinist?" *Sixteenth Century Journal* 27:2 (1996), 337–52; Richard A. Muller, "Arminius and the Scholastic Tradition," *Calvin Theological Journal* 24:2 (1989), 263–77; and idem, "Grace, Election, and Contingent Choice: Arminius's Gambit and the Reformed Response," in *The Grace of God, the Bondage of the Will*, ed. Thomas R. Schreiner and Bruce A. Ware, 2 vols. (Grand Rapids: Baker, 1995), 2:251–78.

76 Thomas Goad, *Stimluus orthodoxus, sive Goadus redivivus: A disputation partly theological, partly metaphysical, concerning the necessity and contingency of events in the world, in respect of Gods eternal decree* (London, 1661), 13.

serves as a useful explication of *Paradise Lost*. In the poem, the acts of human beings come about "beside the fore-thought," independently of the divine knowledge and will. Indeed, in *Paradise Lost* the Father goes still further when he denies that human actions are "by mee immutablie foreseen" (3.121). Here the poem's theology leans even towards Socinianism, which used the theory of middle knowledge to deny that God possesses a full and certain knowledge of the future.[77] According to *Paradise Lost*, human freedom operates independently of the divine will to so great an extent that the divine knowledge of the future cannot even be described as "immutable." God's knowledge is subject to and influenced by the free actions of those creatures to whom he has granted freedom.[78]

In *Paradise Lost*, the freedom of Adam and Eve is thus a freedom that God himself has decreed, so that at the deepest level the freely predestining grace of God retains its primacy. The freedom of human beings is a created and bestowed freedom. Its ground is in the will of the God who has graciously "ordaind / Thir freedom" (3.127–28). Far from negating human freedom, as the Satanic Calvinists claim in the poem's opening books, God thus ordains and affirms the reality and the decisiveness of human choice.

According to *Paradise Lost*, God has elected all people to participate in the grace of salvation. But God has also predestined the freedom of all human beings, leaving them free to accept or to reject their own election. In continuity with Arminian theology, *Paradise Lost* thus depicts the free will of human beings as the deciding factor in salvation. But the poem's universalism of electing grace far exceeds the universalistic features of both the Arminian and Amyraldian theologies. While these traditions had carried over from Reformed orthodoxy the concept of an eternal distinction in God's decree between election and reprobation, in *Paradise Lost* this distinction is sharply undermined, so that election is depicted as fully universal, and reprobation is reformulated as the temporal decision of those human beings who wilfully reject the grace of God. Reprobation is, in other words, historically rather than eternally conditioned—it is determined by the human will, not by the will of God. In this way, the poem portrays the election of all persons as a divinely appointed actuality, and their reprobation as a self-appointed,

---

77   On the Socinian view of limited foreknowledge, see Muller, *PRRD*, 3:424–30.

78   Augustus H. Strong, *Systematic Theology: A Compendium* (Philadelphia, 1907), 284, also suggests that this passage of *Paradise Lost* is close to Socinianism in denying the certainty of God's knowledge of the free acts of creatures.

mutable possibility. This theology of predestination in *Paradise Lost* invests the whole plan of salvation with a more profound emphasis on universal grace than Arminianism or Amyraldism had been able to achieve with their respective concepts of "foreseen faith" and "hypothetical universalism"—concepts which had, in principle, done little to challenge the Reformed orthodox notion of an eternal decree that immutably fixes the condemnation of a certain number of human beings. The poem's creative reconstruction of the traditional idea of predestination thus moves beyond the entire framework of post-Reformation predestinarian controversy, and presses toward a more historical, more universal, and more anthropologically oriented vision of divine election.

Alongside the universality of grace, at the heart of *Paradise Lost's* predestinarian theology stands the "high mystery"[79] of the free human will, a will that decrees the future and authors its own fate. The poem's theology of predestination consistently presses the decisiveness of human freedom into the foreground, and views the human will as possessing, by the grace of God, an autonomy that allows it even to decree and to ordain its own future. In *Paradise Lost*, as I will argue in the following chapter, this remarkable power of human choice is in fact an image and reflection of God's own primal freedom and autonomy.

---

79 Westminster Confession of Faith, 3.8; in Schaff, 3:610. Here the "high mystery" refers to God's secret decree.

4. The Freedom of God

Although the importance of human freedom in *Paradise Lost* has been widely discussed by Milton scholars, the importance of the portrayal of the freedom of God in the poem has largely gone unnoticed. But as Virginia Mollenkott has noted, Milton's theology is concerned not only with human freedom, but with "freedom of the will both in God and in his creatures."[1] Indeed, from a systematic point of view, the freedom of God in *Paradise Lost* is primary; it is the ground and basis of all creaturely freedom. The poem's portrayal of God therefore properly centres on God's freedom. Even more vigorously than in Reformed orthodox theology, *Paradise Lost* depicts God as a being exalted in his utter freedom; he is free to create or not and free to redeem or not. Even his generation of the Son is a wholly free act, and thus the Son's very existence is, as in Arian theology, radically contingent.

The Free Creator

In the post-Reformation era, Reformed orthodox theology took up the medieval question of whether the work of creation is necessary or contingent. A small number of Reformed theologians argued for the necessity of God's outgoing works (*opera Dei ad extra*), claiming that the divine works flow from the divine nature in such a way that God does not possess genuine alternativity of choice. William Perkins, for example, asserts this position when he defines the divine decree as "that by which God in himselfe, hath necessarily, and yet freely, from all eternitie determined all things."[2] Yet the majority of Reformed orthodox divines, while maintaining the necessity of God's essence and existence, strongly affirmed the contingence of the works of God.[3] William

1   Virginia R. Mollenkott, "Free Will," in *A Milton Encyclopedia*, ed. William B. Hunter et al., 9 vols. (Lewisburg: Bucknell University Press, 1978–83), 3:114.
2   William Perkins, *A golden chaine: or, The description of theologie* (Cambridge, 1592), 18.
3   On the Reformed orthodox view of the necessity of the divine nature in relation to the contingence of the divine acts, see Andreas J. Beck, "Gisbertus Voetius (1589–1676): Basic Features of His Doctrine of God," in *Reformation and Scholasticism: An Ecu-*

Ames articulates the usual Reformed position when he writes that
"[w]hat God wills to do outwardly he wills not out of natural necessity,"[4] for "there is nothing in the world, that hath a necessary connex-
ion with the divine essence; and so nothing external comes from God
by any necessity of his nature, but from his wisdome and free-will."[5] In
the same vein, Zacharias Ursinus had written: "God created the world
not by an absolute necessity" but by his "immutable, yet utterly free
decree. Neither was God tied down to creating things, nor if he had
never created the world ... would he be on that account less good or
less blessed."[6] In this respect Reformed orthodoxy's emphasis on "the
utter freedom of God"[7] followed the lead of Duns Scotus, who had
written that the creative act "proceeds from God not from any necessity
... but from a pure freedom that is not moved, much less necessitated,
by anything outside itself."[8] The contingence of the work of creation
had in this way been maintained against pantheistic and emanationist
doctrines and, in the late seventeenth century, Reformed orthodoxy
sought in particular to defend divine contingence against the necessitarianism of Spinoza's theory of *Deus sive natura*, according to which
the will of God simply "cannot be other than it is."[9]

In contrast to Reformed orthodoxy, Arminian theology developed a
more circumscribed view of the divine freedom[10]—indeed, it restricted
God's freedom to such an extent that a Reformed divine like William
Twisse could accuse the Arminians of "making God himselfe a necessary Agent, devoyd of all liberty and freedome."[11] According to Arminian

---

   menical Enterprise, ed. Willem J. van Asselt and Eef Dekker (Grand Rapids: Baker,
   2001), 205–26.

4 William Ames, *The Marrow of Theology*, ed. and trans. John D. Eusden (Grand Rapids:
   Baker, 1968), 1.7.36.

5 William Ames, *The substance of Christian religion: or, A plain and easie draught of the
   Christian catechism* (London, 1659), 67.

6 Zacharias Ursinus, *Opera theologica*, 3 vols. (Heidelberg, 1612), 1:548; cited in Heppe,
   192.

7 The term is from Muller, *PRRD*, 3:447.

8 John Duns Scotus, *Quaestiones disputatae de rerum principio*, 4.1.3; in *Quaestiones disputatae de rerum principio, Tractatus de primo rerum omnium principio*, ed. R. Garcia (Florence, 1910).

9 See Baruch Spinoza, *Ethics*, ed. James Gutmann (New York: Hafner, 1949), 71.

10 See especially Richard A. Muller, "God, Predestination, and the Integrity of the
   Created Order: A Note on Patterns in Arminius' Theology," in *Later Calvinism: Inter-
   national Perspectives*, ed. W. Fred Graham (Kirksville: Sixteenth Century Journal
   Publishers, 1994), 431–46.

11 William Twisse, *The riches of Gods love unto the vessells of mercy, consistent with his
   absolute hatred or reprobation of the vessells of wrath*, 2 vols. (Oxford, 1653), 1:101.

theology, God "is not FREELY good,"[12] but he wills the good by a "natural necessity,"[13] that is, a necessity grounded in "his entire nature and essence."[14] The necessary goodness of the divine nature, Arminius writes, "constitutes an entire, total, and sufficient cause for the exclusion of liberty."[15] God is therefore neither "freely good," nor does he do "all things freely."[16] Rather, all the "acts of God," both his internal (*ad intra*) acts and his outgoing (*ad extra*) acts, find their "foundation"[17] and their "proximate and immediate principle" in the life and essence of God.[18] The will of God therefore "can only will that which is not opposed to the Divine Essence (which is the foundation both of his understanding and of his will)."[19] The divine will's liberty and range of possibilities are in this way limited and restricted by the nature of God. Although Arminius still insists on the freedom of God's creative act,[20] he understands freedom, as Richard Muller observes, not in the Reformed sense of "an utter freedom" by which God can do as he pleases "apart from consideration of external circumstances,"[21] but only in the sense of an intellectualist freedom by which "the [divine] intellect directs the [divine] will to act."[22] In this circumscribed account of the freedom of God, Arminian theology differs in a subtle but highly significant way from the Reformed orthodox vision of a God who is "the most free agent" and not in any sense "a natural and necessary agent."[23]

In its portrayal of creation, *Paradise Lost* exhibits close continuity with Reformed orthodoxy by affirming the freedom and contingence of

---

12 Jacobus Arminius, *The Works of James Arminius*, trans. James Nichols and William Nichols, 3 vols. (Grand Rapids: Baker, 1986), 2:34.

13 Simon Episcopius, *Opera theologica*, 2 vols. (London, 1678), 1:305.

14 Arminius, *Works*, 2:33. In contrast, representing the Reformed position, Richard Baxter, *The divine life in three treatises* (London, 1664), 131, writes: "God hath a natural *Freedome of Will*, being Determined to Will by nothing without him, nor liable to any Necessity."

15 Arminius, *Works*, 2:35.

16 Arminius, *Works*, 2:35.

17 Arminius, *Works*, 2:340.

18 Arminius, *Works*, 2:119.

19 Arminius, *Works*, 2:352.

20 See for example Arminius, *Works*, 2:356: "The creation was freely produced, not necessarily."

21 Muller, *PRRD*, 3:447.

22 Richard A. Muller, *God, Creation and Providence in the Thought of Jacob Arminius: Sources and Directions of Scholastic Protestantism in the Era of Early Orthodoxy* (Grand Rapids: Baker, 1991), 226. On Arminius's intellectualist view of freedom, see also idem, "The Priority of the Intellect in the Soteriology of Jacob Arminius," *Westminster Theological Journal* 55 (1993), 55–72.

23 Stephen Charnock, *The Existence and Attributes of God* (London, 1797), 371–72.

this creative act of God. As the Father commissions the Son to create the world, he explicitly asserts that his decision to create is a contingent one:[24]

> And thou my Word, begott'n Son, by thee
> This I perform, speak thou, and be it don:
> My overshadowing Spirit and might with thee
> I send along, ride forth, and bid the Deep
> Within appointed bounds be Heav'n and Earth,
> Boundless the Deep, because I am who fill
> Infinitude, nor vacuous the space.
> Though I uncircumscrib'd my self retire,
> And put not forth my goodness, which is free
> To act or not, Necessitie and Chance
> Approach not mee, and what I will is Fate. (7.163–73)

Creation is to be brought about by God's "goodness," and this goodness "is free / To act or not." That is, God himself is faced with alternative possible choices, and he is free to decide between these alternatives. His decision to create is thus contingent. Not only does the Father affirm his own volitional contingence in creation, but he also denies the contrary: "Necessitie" does not approach him. Nothing in God's own nature leads him inexorably to bring anything into being by a creative act. Further, while Arminian theology closely connected the divine acts to the necessary goodness of the divine nature, the God of *Paradise Lost* asserts that it is precisely his "goodness" that is contingently "free" and that remains untouched by necessity. God's goodness is therefore equally perfect and complete, regardless of whether or not he chooses to create. His goodness imposes no necessity on his actions.[25]

---

24 David Loewenstein, *Milton: Paradise Lost* (Cambridge: Cambridge University Press, 1993), 29, finds in this passage Milton's opposition to the predestinarian orthodoxy of Reformed theology. But the passage is concerned only with the question of the freedom or necessity of the divine creative act; the question of predestination is not in view.

25 For an analogy of this kind of compatibility between necessary goodness and contingent action, see Colin E. Gunton, *Becoming and Being: The Doctrine of God in Charles Hartshorne and Karl Barth* (Oxford: Oxford University Press, 1978), 147–48: "I may know from his consistent past behaviour that Smith loves his family, but that is not to say that I know which particular loving acts he will perform tomorrow or next week." The analogy breaks down, however, in the respect that the God of *Paradise Lost* can choose not only between alternative acts, but also (unlike human beings) between acting and not-acting.

In this decidedly "non-Arminian"[26] emphasis on the divine freedom in creation, *Paradise Lost* exhibits close continuity with the Reformed orthodox tradition. Indeed, A. S. P. Woodhouse has even suggested that "[t]here is no tenet of orthodox belief to which Milton
adheres more tenaciously than the voluntary character of the creative
act."[27] Engaging with the Reformed divines Ames and Wollebius, Stephen Fallon has shown the extent to which divine freedom in *Paradise
Lost* is continuous with Reformed orthodoxy. Fallon rightly notes that
"the God of *Paradise Lost* exhibits demonstrably more freedom of choice
than does the God of the theological compatibilists" like Hobbes or
Arminius: in the poem, God has "freedom to choose among equal alternative goods."[28] He is not constrained by nature to act in any particular
way; nor, more importantly, is he constrained by nature to act at all. He
is "free / To act or not."[29] With a similar emphasis on God's freedom to
refrain from acting, Milton's *De Doctrina Christiana* argues that "God
cannot rightly be called *actus purus* ... for thus he could do nothing except what he does do, and he would do that of necessity, although in
fact he is omnipotent and utterly free in his actions."[30] In such a conception, the possibilities of the freedom of God far exceed the possibilities of creaturely freedom. For, in Fallon's words, "[m]an is free to do
right or wrong, but he must act; God, on the other hand, can do only
right, but he is free to act or not."[31] The point, then, is not simply that
God might have chosen to create this world in a different way; rather,
Paradise Lost presents "the disorienting possibility that our world might
never have been created"[32]—that God, without compromising his

---

26 Stephen M. Fallon, "'To Act or Not': Milton's Conception of Divine Freedom," *Jour-
    nal of the History of Ideas* 49:3 (1988), 426 n. 4.

27 A. S. P. Woodhouse, "Notes on Milton's Views on the Creation: The Initial Phases,"
    Philological Quarterly 28 (1949), 215.

28 Fallon, "To Act or Not," 444, 448.

29 In parallel, see the summary of the Reformed orthodox position in Heppe, 192:
    "Above all it is fixed, that the creation of the world is a thoroughly free act of God, in
    fact an act of God free *libertate contradictionis* ... so that God could also refrain from
    creating."

30 *CPW* 6:145–46; *CM* 14:48. The concept of God as *actus purus* was especially develo-
    ped by Thomas Aquinas: for a recent discussion, see Fergus Kerr, *After Aquinas: Ver-
    sions of Thomism* (Oxford: Blackwell, 2002), 187–91, 199–203.

31 Fallon, "To Act or Not," 448.

32 Fallon, "To Act or Not," 449. Articulating the Thomist position, E. L. Mascall, *He
    Who Is: A Study in Traditional Theism* (London: Longmans, 1943), 95, observes: "The
    real miracle is not that God exists but that the world does." For a theological discus-
    sion of the possibility of nonexistence, and the "ontological shock" that this possibi-
    lity evokes, see Paul Tillich, *Systematic Theology*, 3 vols. (Chicago: University of Chi-
    cago Press, 1951–63), 1:126, 207–13.

goodness, might have chosen never to act at all.[33] Such a possibility strikingly highlights the contingence of God's creative act, and in turn the gracious character of all creaturely existence. Here the words of T. F. Torrance, one of the twentieth century's most vigorous advocates of theological contingence, may serve as a gloss on *Paradise Lost*'s account of the freedom of God in creation: "Since the Creator was free not to create," and since the creation was "a contingent act unconditioned by anything in God," the act of creation can be understood only as "an act of pure liberality and grace."[34] Reformed orthodox theology, with its emphasis on divine freedom, accentuated this theme of the graciousness of creation,[35] a theme that is summed up in the statement of Karl Barth: "Creation is grace."[36] In the same way, in *Paradise Lost* all creaturely existence is profoundly rooted in a contingent choice of God, so that the relationship between God and his creatures remains always and only a relationship grounded in the divine liberality. For this reason, when the newly created Adam awakes for the first time and knows himself to be a creature, his thoughts turn immediately to the liberality of the creator's goodness:

> Thou Sun, said I, faire Light,
> And thou enlight'nd Earth, so fresh and gay,
> Ye Hills and Dales, ye Rivers, Woods, and Plaines,
> And yee that live and move, fair Creatures, tell,
> Tell, if ye saw, how came I thus, how here?
> Not of my self; by some great Maker then,
> In goodness and in power præeminent;
> Tell me, how may I know him, how adore,

---

33   On the complex Reformed orthodox view of divine *volitio* and *nolitio*, see the account of Muller, *PRRD*, 3:456: "in the case of an event 'a,' God can will 'a' or will 'not-a'— but he can also 'not will a' without any necessity of willing 'not-a' and, indeed, he can 'not will a' and in the same moment 'not will not-a.'" Muller suggests that these distinctions between *volitio* and *nolitio* may be due to Scotist influences on Reformed orthodox theology.

34   T. F. Torrance, *Divine and Contingent Order* (Oxford: Oxford University Press, 1981), 34. See also the remark of Mascall, *He Who Is*, 109: "It is precisely because creation can give nothing whatever to God which in any way enhances his beatitude, that creation is an act of entire giving on the part of God.... In creating the world he gains nothing; that is why creation is an act of supreme love."

35   Muller, *PRRD*, 3:570, notes that in Reformed orthodoxy grace is "a characteristic of God's relations to the finite order," and is "fundamental to all of God's relationships with the world and especially with human beings" (3:570 n. 512).

36   Karl Barth, *Dogmatics in Outline*, trans. G. T. Thomson (London: SCM, 1949), 54. The idea that creation is grace had been stated already by Origen, and was developed by Augustine, Anselm, Luther and Calvin. See the historical discussion in Karl Barth, *Church Dogmatics*, ed. Geoffrey W. Bromiley and T. F. Torrance (Edinburgh: T&T Clark, 1956–77), III/1, 29–31.

> From whom I have that thus I move and live,
> And feel that I am happier then I know. (8.273–82)

As Fallon notes, Adam here "awakes at his creation to a sense of gratitude for life as a gift."[37] Creation is not a necessary expression of the
divine nature, but a free expression of God's pre-eminent "goodness."
And for this reason God can only be thanked and "adore[d]" for bestowing on Adam the gift of creaturely existence.

But while Reformed orthodox theology insisted that "no creature
was or could have been a cause ... in the act of creation,"[38] since any
cause external to the divine will itself would compromise the freedom
of God's creative act, *Paradise Lost* speaks of the angelic rebellion as a
"cause" of creation. Early in Book 7, Adam asks Raphael to explain:

> what cause
> Mov'd the Creator in his holy Rest
> Through all Eternitie so late to build
> In *Chaos*. (7.90–93)

In reply, Raphael does not even pause over the question of whether an
external "cause" is proper to the divine will; rather, he simply explains
that the cause of creation was the rebellion and expulsion from heaven
of Lucifer and "his flaming Legions" (7.134). When the Son returns
from his conquest over the rebellious spirits, the Father tells him of his
plan to make amends for the "many" who have forfeited their place in
heaven:

> I can repaire
> That detriment, if such it be to lose
> Self-lost, and in a moment will create
> Another World, out of one man a Race
> Of men innumerable, there to dwell,
> Not here, till by degrees of merit rais'd
> They op'n to themselves at length the way
> Up hither. (7.152–59)

And on hearing of this plan, the heavenly angels sing:

> to him
> Glorie and praise, whose wisdom had ordaind
> Good out of evil to create, in stead
> Of Spirits maligne a better Race to bring
> Into thir vacant room. (7.186–90)

---

37 Fallon, "To Act or Not," 445.
38 Ames, *Marrow of Theology*, 1.8.16.

God's creative act is, then, motivated by the vacancy in heaven left by the expelled angels. Satan had thought to lessen the number of God's worshippers (7.609–16), but God will re-people heaven with a better race. This concept of the re-peopling of heaven constitutes a significant theological risk in a poem that seeks to accentuate the freedom of God and to show that God is always "free / To act or not," untouched by any shadow of "Necessitie" (7.171–72). Indeed, the re-peopling theory, which can be traced back at least as far as Augustine,[39] had traditionally been accompanied by a necessitarian view of the will of God in creation. The most elaborate account of this theory is found in Anselm's *Cur deus homo*,[40] where Anselm posits the re-peopling of heaven as part of the "reason or necessity"[41] of creation and redemption alike. According to Anselm, it was necessary for God to exact payment for sin;[42] it was necessary that the number of elect human beings replace the number of fallen angels;[43] it was necessary that a satisfaction be made for sin, since sinful human beings cannot replace holy angels;[44] and it was necessary for God to become human, in order to make the necessary satisfaction for sin.[45] Anselm seeks also to maintain the freedom of God, by claiming that God "freely submits himself" to necessity,[46] but this note of divine freedom is itself subsumed under the overarching necessitarian framework.[47]

In describing the re-peopling of heaven as a "cause" of creation, *Paradise Lost* might seem similarly to risk sliding into such a necessitarian scheme. Yet the most theologically important aspect of *Paradise Lost*'s appropriation of the re-peopling theory is the way in which it modifies and corrects the Anselmic account. Before speaking of his desire to re-people heaven, the Father radically qualifies this "cause" of

---

39 See Augustine, *De civitate Dei contra paganos*, 22.1; in *PL* 41 and *NPNF* 2. For a historical survey of the idea of the re-peopling of heaven, see Grant McColley, *"Paradise Lost": An Account of Its Growth and Major Origins, with a Discussion of Milton's Use of Sources and Literary Patterns* (Chicago: Packard, 1940), 46–47.

40 Anselm, *Cur deus homo*; in *Opera omnia*, 6 vols. (Edinburgh: Thomas Nelson, 1938–61), 2:37–133.

41 Anselm, *Cur deus homo*, 1.1.

42 Anselm, *Cur deus homo*, 1.12.

43 Anselm, *Cur deus homo*, 1.16–17.

44 Anselm, *Cur deus homo*, 1.19.

45 Anselm, *Cur deus homo*, 1.20–23; 2.6–7.

46 Anselm, *Cur deus homo*, 2.5.

47 Perhaps the most striking example of Anselm's tendency to subsume freedom into a broader necessitarian framework is his paradoxical argument that Christ lays down his life freely, precisely because it is "necessary" that he should "die of his own free will" (*Cur deus homo*, 2.11; see also 2.17).

creation. Satan has, the Father says, drawn "many" away from "thir place" in heaven (7.144):

> Yet farr the greater part have kept, I see,
> Thir station, Heav'n yet populous retaines
> Number sufficient to possess her Realmes
> Though wide, and this high Temple to frequent
> With Ministeries due and solemn Rites. (7.145–49)

In spite of the fall of Satan and his hosts, the great majority of angels remains in heaven, and the number of these angels remains "sufficient." In this way God flatly counters Satan's boast that his rebellion has "emptied Heav'n" (1.633).[48] God has not suffered any loss; heaven remains "populous"; and there is accordingly no need for the number of fallen angels to be replaced. Only after making this crucial—and deeply non-Anselmic—point does God proceed to explain that he has, nevertheless, freely decided to re-people heaven. Of Satan, the Father says:

> But least his heart exalt him in the harme
> Already done, to have dispeopl'd Heav'n,
> My damage fondly deemd, I can repaire
> That detriment, if such it be to lose
> Self-lost, and in a moment will create
> Another World. (7.150–55)

Satan's claim "to have dispeopl'd Heav'n" is only "fondly deemd" by Satan to have damaged God. God has lost nothing, for the fallen angels are "Self-lost," that is, "lost to themselves rather than to God."[49] But still God claims that he "can" and "will" repair the situation, which he ironically calls a "detriment." By saying only that he "can" and "will," God emphasises the simple freedom of his decision to create. The rebellion of the angels is therefore, as Stephen Fallon notes, a "reason" for God's creative act, but not a "sufficient" reason;[50] or more precisely, it is simply the *occasion* for creation—an occasion that in no way impels the will of God to act. After all, it is precisely in this connection that God affirms his sheer freedom "To act or not" (7.172). Further, God claims that he will freely choose to re-people heaven with a "better Race" (7.189)—and what is more, he will re-people heaven not simply with a

---

48   As noted by Verity, 535.
49   Hughes, 349.
50   Fallon, "To Act or Not," 445. See also C. A. Patrides, *Milton and the Christian Tradition* (Oxford: Clarendon, 1966), 38.

fixed number of human beings, but with "men innumerable" (7.156). Thus, as Dennis Danielson observes, *Paradise Lost* does not envisage a mere "replacing of a certain number of angels with the same number of human beings," but instead the angels' fall is "more than compensated" by replacing a limited number of angels with an "innumerable" host of human beings.[51]

This over-compensation for the fallen angels especially highlights the freedom of God in creation. In contrast to any necessitarian view of the re-peopling of heaven, the God of *Paradise Lost* creates freely and contingently. He exercises his goodness by creating "Another World" (7.155) even when he has no need to do so.[52] He has lost nothing in the Satanic rebellion, so he stands to gain nothing for himself in the creation of a new world. As William Ames had said, there can ultimately be no reason for God's creative act, "beyond or above his free will."[53] This Reformed orthodox notion is deeply ingrained in *Paradise Lost*'s portrayal of the "cause" of creation. The poem thus appropriates the Anselmic theory of the re-peopling of heaven in order to achieve a fundamentally non-Anselmic effect: a more pronounced emphasis on the freedom and contingence of God's will, and therefore also on the gracious character of the creative act.[54] This feature of *Paradise Lost*'s theology illustrates the poem's distinctive tendency to appropriate existing theological concepts in such a way that these concepts are radically transformed.

Arian Freedom

Paradise Lost's emphasis on the freedom of God becomes even more pronounced, and this time in a highly heterodox way, in the poem's account of the Father's free generation of the Son. Trinitarian orthodoxy consistently regarded the internal works of God (*opera Dei ad intra*), in

---

51   Dennis R. Danielson, *Milton's Good God: A Study in Literary Theodicy* (Cambridge: Cambridge University Press, 1982), 233.

52   Michael Lieb, *The Dialectics of Creation: Patterns of Birth and Regeneration in Paradise Lost* (Boston: University of Massachusetts Press, 1970), 57 n. 3, also notes that the concept of the re-peopling of heaven reflects "the major pattern of the poem: creation springs from destruction as good springs from evil."

53   Ames, *The substance of Christian religion*, 68.

54   Out of a proper concern to insist that the concept of the re-peopling of heaven "does not make creation 'necessary,'" Fowler goes so far as to say that "Raphael nowhere advances any theory about the cause of man's creation" (Fowler, 365). Yet this uneasiness about the idea of a "cause" of creation seems ill-founded in view of the non-necessitarian function of the "cause" in *Paradise Lost*'s account.

which the Father generates the Son, and the Father and Son spirate the Spirit,[55] as "most necessary" acts of the divine essence;[56] by his necessary will (*voluntas necessaria*) "God the Father necessarily wills to beget God the Son."[57] This is a necessity in the strictest sense; it is, in the words of Francis Turretin, a necessity grounded in the divine "nature."[58] Responding to the Arian view that the Son is begotten not "by nature" but "by the freewill of the Father," William Perkins writes that the Son "is the Sonne of the Father by nature, *not by will*."[59] Since this generation of the Son by the Father is a necessity of the divine nature, it is viewed as an "eternall generation," which "hath neither beginning, middle, or ende."[60]

In sharp contrast to this orthodox trinitarian position, *Paradise Lost's* account of the generation of the Son is characterised not by necessity but by contingence. When the still solitary Adam expresses his desire for human companionship, God the Father replies:[61]

> What thinkst thou then of mee, and this my State,
> Seem I to thee sufficiently possest
> Of happiness, or not? who am alone

---

55 I am referring here to Western trinitarian orthodoxy, according to which both Father and Son spirate the Spirit. Eastern orthodoxy denied the validity of the Western *filioque* clause, and affirmed that the Father alone spirates the Spirit. Notwithstanding this division, however, the Eastern and Western churches were united in viewing the internal trinitarian works (*opera Trinitatis ad intra*) as taking place by a necessity of nature (*ex necessitate naturae*), and not by any indifferent freedom of the divine will.

56 John Duns Scotus, *God and Creatures: The Quodlibetal Questions*, trans. F. Alluntis and A. B. Wolter (Princeton: Princeton University Press, 1975), 16.1.5.

57 Muller, *PRRD*, 3:453.

58 Francis Turretin, *Institutes of Elenctic Theology*, ed. James T. Dennison, trans. George Musgrave Giger, 3 vols. (Phillipsburg: P&R, 1992–97), 3.29.22.

59 William Perkins, *An exposition of the symbole or creed of the apostles* (Cambridge, 1595), 143.

60 Perkins, *An exposition of the symbole or creed*, 137.

61 Some debate has focused on whether the divine speaker in this section of Book 8 is in fact the Father, or whether it might instead be the Son of God. According to James H. Sims, "*Paradise Lost*: 'Arian Document' or Christian Poem?" *Études Anglaises* 20 (1967), 343, Adam is speaking not with the Father but with the Son, and Sims thus argues that the theology of the dialogue should not be taken in an Arian sense. In contrast, Michael Bauman, *Milton's Arianism* (Frankfurt am Main: Peter Lang, 1987), 263–66, more convincingly argues that the divine speaker here can only be God the Father. Bauman rightly notes that, in the statement "Whom thou soughtst I am" (8.316), the divine speaker implicitly identifies himself as the "I AM" of Exodus 3:14, and thus as the monotheistic God of the Old Testament. It is worth noting, too, that when the "voice" of this divine speaker is compared with the respective voices of the Father and the Son elsewhere in the poem, it bears distinct resemblance to the voice of the Father.

> From all Eternitie, for none I know
> Second to mee or like, equal much less.
> How have I then with whom to hold converse
> Save with the Creatures which I made, and those
> To me inferiour, infinite descents
> Beneath what other Creatures are to thee? (8.403–11)

Adam responds with what is perhaps the poem's clearest statement of Arian theology:

> No need that thou
> Shouldst propagate, already infinite;
> And through all numbers absolute, though One;
> But Man by number is to manifest
> His single imperfection, and beget
> Like of his like, his Image multipli'd,
> In unitie defective, which requires
> Collateral love, and deerest amitie. (8.419–26)

According to Adam, God does not need to "propagate" or "beget." He is perfect and complete simply as "One"; his perfection is expressed by his numerical simplicity, in contrast to humanity's imperfection, which is witnessed by its need for numerical multiplication. This emphasis on numerical simplicity stands in continuity with Arian theology. Arius himself had described God as "monad" (μονάς) and therefore as "most solitary" (μονώτατος),[62] and the British Arian Samuel Clarke argued that the word "God" in scripture "never signifies a complex Notion of more Persons ... than One; but always means One Person only."[63] Similarly, the Socinians took it as axiomatic that "the divine essence is numerically one,"[64] so that their anti-trinitarian theology was motivated by "their radical assumption of the oneness of God."[65] In *Paradise Lost*, Adam's speech is allusively replete with theological terms like "propagate," "infinite," "absolute," "beget," "image" and "unitie"; but the most theologically significant term is "need"—"No need that thou / Shouldst propagate." Here "need" immediately calls up the entire Nicene tradition, which understood the Father's generation (γέννησις) of the Son to be a "necessary" act of the divine essence (οὐσία). Only by stressing this divine necessity could theologians maintain the eternal consubstantiality of the Son with the Father; in fact, in arguing for the

62   See Robert C. Gregg and Dennis E. Groh, *Early Arianism: A View of Salvation* (London: SCM, 1981), 87–91, 98–99.

63   Samuel Clarke, *The works of Samuel Clarke*, 4 vols. (London, 1738), 4:155.

64   *The Racovian Catechism*, ed. Thomas Rees (London, 1818), 4.1.

65   Muller, *PRRD*, 4:283.

restriction of the freedom of God, Arminius had insisted that too great
an emphasis on divine freedom would lead to Arianism: "For if [God]
be *freely* good, he ... does all things *freely*, even when he begets the Son
and breathes forth the Holy Spirit!"[66] Arian theology had indeed placed
the greatest possible emphasis on God's freedom, insisting that the Son
is generated not by necessity but "by a punctiliar act of God's free
will," and in this way it highlighted "[t]he freedom of God from all
limitations, his essential independence of all contingencies, and the
essential contingency of the Son's status as Son."[67] Thus Samuel Clarke
describes the generation of the Son as occurring "not by absolute *neces-*
sity of nature (which infers self-existence and independency) but by the
power of the *will* of the Father."[68] And according to Milton's *De Doctrina*
Christiana, the Father "begot his Son not from any natural necessity (*non*
necessitate naturae) but of his own free will," for God "always acts with
absolute freedom," and so "must have begotten his Son with absolute
freedom."[69] Indeed, according to the treatise God "stands in no need of
propagation (*propagatione*)."[70] This is exactly the point of Adam's affirmation that God does not "need" to propagate.[71] Even the propagation of the Son depends solely on the free decision of the divine will, so
that, as Michael Bauman observes, in *Paradise Lost* the Son's very existence is not necessary but contingent: "The Son need not ever have
existed."[72] Hence even *Paradise Lost*'s most notorious and controversial
"heresy" — its Arianism — is itself grounded in the poem's profound and
rigorously consistent commitment to the freedom of God.[73]

Further, the exaltation of the Son is not an eternal and necessary reality, but a contingent event that occurs at a particular temporal moment within the narrative action of *Paradise Lost*. Summoning the whole
"Empyreal Host" (5.583), the Father declares:

---

66   Arminius, *Works*, 2:35.
67   Peter Widdicombe, *The Fatherhood of God from Origen to Athanasius* (Oxford: Claren-
     don, 1994), 144. See also Gregg and Groh, *Early Arianism*, 161–76.
68   From a letter of Samuel Clarke, recorded in William Whiston, *Historical memoirs of the*
     life and writings of Dr. Samuel Clarke (London, 1730), 79.
69   *CPW* 6:209; *CM* 14:186.
70   *CPW* 6:209; *CM* 14:186.
71   The close parallel between the *De Doctrina* and *Paradise Lost* on this point has been
     rightly noted by Maurice Kelley, *This Great Argument: A Study of Milton's De Doctrina*
     Christiana as a Gloss Upon Paradise Lost (Princeton: Princeton University Press, 1941),
     120–21.
72   Bauman, *Milton's Arianism*, 267.
73   The same, I believe, may be said of the Arianism of the *De Doctrina Christiana*: see
     especially the argument in *CPW* 6:209; *CM* 14:184–86, which is succinct but no-
     netheless decisive for the whole structure of the treatise's theology of the Son of
     God.

> Hear all ye Angels, Progenie of Light,
> Thrones, Dominations, Princedoms, Vertues, Powers,
> Hear my Decree, which unrevok'd shall stand.
> This day I have begot whom I declare
> My onely Son, and on this holy Hill
> Him have anointed, whom ye now behold
> At my right hand; your Head I him appoint;
> And by my Self have sworn to him shall bow
> All knees in Heav'n, and shall confess him Lord. (5.600–8)[74]

Here the Father's public "begetting" of the Son is distinct from the moment of the Son's creation, since the Son had already existed before the angels were "By him created" (5.838);[75] as Bauman notes, the Son's begetting in this connection consists in the fact that he is exalted by the Father "to a position of high eminence which He did not previously possess."[76] The fact that the Son does not naturally or necessarily occupy this exalted position at the Father's "right hand" is crucial for the development of the narrative that follows. Satan, jealous of being suddenly "eclipst" by "Another" (5.775–76), feels himself "impaird" (5.665) by the exaltation of the Son, who has been "that day / Honourd by his great Father" (5.662–63). And so Satan rebels. The whole cosmic drama of *Paradise Lost* is therefore contingent on the event of the exaltation of the Son. And the contingence of the Son's exaltation is highlighted by the Father's insistence that this exaltation depends not on any intrinsic necessity—not, that is, on the fact that the Son is "consubstantial with the Father" (ὁμοούσιος τῷ πατρί), and is therefore already necessarily exalted[77]—but simply on the Father's "Decree." It is the free choice of

---

74 The Father's speech alludes to Psalm 2:7: "I will declare the decree: the LORD hath said unto me, Thou art my Son; this day have I begotten thee." This verse has a controversial history of trinitarian and anti-trinitarian interpretation in the post-Reformation era: see Muller, *PRRD*, 4:276, 285, 301–2. The theological appropriation of Psalm 2:7 at this point in the narrative of *Paradise Lost* deserves a detailed study against the background of the verse's interpretive history. For the *De Doctrina*'s interpretation of Psalm 2:7, see *CPW* 6:206–7; *CM* 14:184–86.

75 According to the *De Doctrina Christiana*, the "generation" or begetting of the Son can refer either to the Son's "production" or to his "exaltation" (*CPW* 6:205; *CM* 14:180). The same distinction seems to be implicit in this section of *Paradise Lost*, in which the already existent Son is publicly "begotten" by the Father with the result that he will henceforth sit at God's right hand.

76 Bauman, *Milton's Arianism*, 259. A similar view of the Son's exaltation is presented by the Socinian writer John Biddle in *A confession of faith touching the Holy Trinity* (London, 1648), 9–15.

77 Nicaeno–Constantinopolitan Creed; in Schaff, 2:57.

the Father to honour the Son in this way. This is a contingent choice, a decree that the Father need not and might not have made.

This distinctively Arian characterisation of divine freedom is accentuated further by the contingence of the work of redemption in *Paradise Lost*. An important theological function of the Father–Son colloquy in Book 3 is to portray dramatically the sheer contingence of God's decision to redeem the human race. When the Father declares that humankind "must die" (3.209) unless some other will pay the "rigid satisfaction, death for death" (3.212), there is stunned silence in heaven. In the midst of this silence, before the Son steps forward and offers himself as a sacrifice for humanity, the narrative voice points out the dramatic contingence of the entire plan of salvation:

> And now without redemption all mankind
> Must have bin lost, adjudg'd to Death and Hell
> By doom severe, *had not the Son of God,*
> In whom the fulness dwels of love divine,
> His dearest mediation thus renewd. (3.222–26; emphasis added)

The human race need not have been saved. There need not have been a mediator. The Son offers himself with true freedom, exhibiting what Desmond Hamlet calls the "creative use of His freedom and His responsibility."[78] Here the Son is not simply a natural and necessary expression of the Father's will; in the drama of the poem, his decision is not simply a given from the outset. On the contrary, as Barbara Lewalski observes, "Milton's Arianism allows him to portray the Son as a genuinely dramatic and heroic character, whose choices are made and whose actions are taken freely."[79] The Son exercises his freedom to bring about the will of the Father; in the words of John Rumrich, he is the "contingent" Son who "acts to fulfill the will of the one absolute being."[80] In this respect the theology of *Paradise Lost* is discontinuous with the Reformed orthodox insistence on the necessity of the work of salvation through Christ. The Puritan Stephen Charnock had argued

---

78 Desmond M. Hamlet, *One Greater Man: Justice and Damnation in Paradise Lost* (London: Associated University Presses, 1976), 18.

79 Barbara K. Lewalski, *The Life of John Milton: A Critical Biography* (Oxford: Blackwell, 2000), 473. This aspect of the narrative of *Paradise Lost* also stands in close continuity with early Arianism, which had placed great emphasis on the free and willing obedience of the Son: see Gregg and Groh, *Early Arianism*, 1–42, 77–129.

80 John P. Rumrich, *Milton Unbound: Controversy and Reinterpretation* (Cambridge: Cambridge University Press, 1996), 45.

elaborately for the necessity of Christ's death,[81] and Thomas Manton similarly writes: "Surely [Christ's] death was necessary, or God would never have appointed it; his bloody death suited with God's design."[82] Ames also speaks of the necessity by which God—being the kind of God he is—must necessarily provide a way of salvation.[83] The Amyraldian theologians insisted even more emphatically on the necessity of redemption. According to Amyraut, it would be "impossible" for the divine justice to leave human sin unpunished,[84] but it would be even more impossible for God not to be merciful,[85] since God's actions are strictly subordinated to his nature.[86] On account of his goodness, God "cannot but love" unfallen human beings; he is "unable not to love" those who are fallen but repentant.[87] Such concepts of divine necessity are entirely absent in *Paradise Lost*. Instead, the poem points to a vision of the totally uninhibited freedom of God. The Father need not have begotten the Son. The Son need not have redeemed humanity.

In this respect the Son occupies a crucial place in the theodicy of *Paradise Lost*. As Rumrich notes, "the Son's freely made decisions to obey the Father's will function as a striking counter-example to the decisions of Satan and Adam."[88] The Son is not simply a reflection of the Father's essence and will; his decision to offer himself is not a necessary emanation from the will of the Father. It is, rather, a free and utterly contingent decision, a decision that might never have been made. In typical Protestant fashion, the gracious character of the work of redemption is thus emphasised, albeit it in a distinctly heterodox way. Human salvation, like creation, is portrayed as a sheer gift, as something that need not and might not have taken place. The entire human race may well

---

81 Stephen Charnock, *The Works of Stephen Charnock*, 5 vols. (Edinburgh, 1864–66), 5:3–48. For an earlier argument for the necessity of redemption, see Peter Martyr Vermigli, *Loci communes* (London, 1576), 2.17.19.

82 Thomas Manton, *The Complete Works of Thomas Manton*, 20 vols. (London, 1870–74), 1:422.

83 Ames, *The substance of Christian religion*, 33.

84 Moïse Amyraut, *A treatise concerning religions, in refutation of the opinion which accounts all indifferent* (London, 1660), 459.

85 On this aspect of Amyraldian theology, see G. Michael Thomas, *The Extent of the Atonement: A Dilemma for Reformed Theology from Calvin to the Consensus, 1536–1675* (Carlisle: Paternoster, 1997), 170, 174, 179–80.

86 See Thomas, *The Extent of the Atonement*, 198.

87 Moïse Amyraut, *Mosis Amyraldi dissertationes theologicae quatuor* (Saumur, 1645), 30–31, 36–39; cited in Thomas, *The Extent of the Atonement*, 198.

88 John P. Rumrich, "Milton's Arianism: Why It Matters," in *Milton and Heresy*, ed. Stephen B. Dobranski and John P. Rumrich (Cambridge: Cambridge University Press, 1998), 86. See also John C. Ulreich, "'Substantially Express'd': Milton's Doctrine of the Incarnation," *Milton Studies* 39 (2000), 116–17.

have "bin lost," condemned to die "without redemption" (3.222–23) —
"had not the Son of God" freely decided to intervene (3.224–26).

Divine and Creaturely Freedom

In *Paradise Lost*, the radical freedom of God is, moreover, the ground of
all creaturely freedom. In the poem, creation is identified with liberation, so that God's creatures, being endowed with genuine autonomy,
are made to participate in and to reflect something of God's own freedom.

In *Paradise Lost*, God does not create from nothing (*ex nihilo*), as in
Reformed orthodox theology,[89] but from pre-existing matter (*ex materia*). As Raphael tells Adam:

> O *Adam*, one Almightie is, from whom
> All things proceed, and up to him return,
> If not deprav'd from good, created all
> Such to perfection, one first matter all,
> Indu'd with various forms, various degrees
> Of substance, and in things that live, of life;
> But more refin'd, more spiritous, and pure,
> As neerer to him plac't or neerer tending
> Each in thir several active Sphears assignd,
> Till body up to spirit work, in bounds
> Proportiond to each kind. (5.469–79)

All creatures, angels as much as human beings, have been formed from
the same "first matter." The "formless Mass" of primal matter constitutes "This Worlds material mould" (3.708–9); and this primal matter
(*materia prima*) itself "proceed[s]" from God's own being.[90] Further, God
initially brings forth this "first matter" through an act of self-
withdrawal and self-limitation:[91]

---

89 On the Reformed orthodox view of *creatio ex nihilo*, see Heppe, 196–99.

90 See the concise statement of Hughes: "Milton thought of creation as God's shaping
through the Word, his Son, of the unformed matter which originated in him" (Hughes, 193).

91 Recent interpretations of monist–materialist creation in *Paradise Lost* are still indebted to the account of creation by retraction in Denis Saurat, *Milton, Man and Thinker*
(London: J. M. Dent, 1944), 102–10, 236–38, an account which contains penetrating
insights in spite of its obvious deficiencies and imbalances: for criticisms, see especially R. J. Zwi Werblowsky, "Milton and the *Conjectura Cabbalistica*," *Journal of the
Warburg and Courtauld Institutes* 18 (1955), 90–113; and Kelley, *This Great Argument*,
205–13. Perhaps the most important problem in Saurat's reading is the exaggerated
interpretive weight that he places on lines 7.168–73. He claims that "these six lines

> I am who fill
> Infinitude, nor vacuous the space.
> Though I uncircumscrib'd my self retire,
> And put not forth my goodness, which is free
> To act or not. (7.168–72)

In this vision of the creative act, as Rumrich has argued, God retires from a certain "shadowy" part of his own material being, leaving behind a formless chaos of divine "material potency."[92] By freely "retir[ing]" from himself and limiting himself in this way, God creates the possibility of creaturely freedom.[93]

Although the monistic materialism of *Paradise Lost* was foreign to Arminian theology, the concept of divine self-limitation was often expressed by Arminian writers. Arminius himself, as Richard Muller notes, had viewed creation "as a self-limiting act of God,"[94] and had affirmed "the self-limitation of God in relation to the created order."[95] Victoria Silver has suggested that *Paradise Lost*'s account bears "distinct ... resemblances to the Arminian and Molinist doctrine of God's middle knowledge, in which deity by delimiting its active and determining goodness through covenant creates a domain of contingent order."[96] But whereas for Arminius the divine self-limitation derives from God's goodness, which seeks to create and to preserve creaturely freedom,[97] *Paradise Lost* more radically equates God's self-limitation with the very act of creation. In a single act and moment, God's withdrawal from himself creates a sphere that is other to God, and that possesses its own ontological autonomy: "since Milton's God is in some sense material, he need only withdraw his control from a portion of himself to leave freed matter in an area no longer controlled."[98] Denis Saurat is therefore

---

are the most important passage in *Paradise Lost*," and that from the retraction theory presented here "everything else derives" (238–39), since it constitutes "the very centre of [Milton's] metaphysics" (102).

92   Rumrich, *Milton Unbound*, 129, 144.

93   See Stephen M. Fallon, "*Paradise Lost* in Intellectual History," in *A Companion to Milton*, ed. Thomas N. Corns (Oxford: Blackwell, 2001), 339: "Chaos is that region from which God retires, refraining from putting forth his goodness. The distance won by this restraint accounts not only for the formlessness of Chaos, but also for the freedom of the universe created from the body of God, including the freedom of creatures."

94   Muller, *God, Creation and Providence in the Thought of Jacob Arminius*, 234, 268.

95   Muller, *God, Creation and Providence in the Thought of Jacob Arminius*, 239.

96   Victoria Silver, *Imperfect Sense: The Predicament of Milton's Irony* (Princeton: Princeton University Press, 2001), 358 n. 9.

97   See Muller, *God, Creation and Providence in the Thought of Jacob Arminius*, 239–40.

98   Harry F. Robins, *If This Be Heresy: A Study of Milton and Origen* (Illinois: University of Illinois Press, 1963), 93.

right when he remarks that "[t]he question of free will ... becomes with Milton ontological. Being is freedom."[99] By withdrawing ontologically from his own active essence, God freely relinquishes part of his own being, and in this way calls forth a created order, an ontological Other, the very being of which consists in its autonomy vis-à-vis God. Creation itself, as that from which God "retire[s]" (7.170), is therefore nothing other than a radical "liberation" of creaturely reality.[100] As Victoria Silver has noted, God occasions creaturely freedom by creating ontological "room" for his creatures.[101] God withdraws and circumscribes his own fullness in order to grant autonomous space to his creatures.[102]

To draw a perverse analogy, the autonomy of human creatures in *Paradise Lost* is rather like that of amorous Sin, who springs full-grown from Satan's head, no longer bounded by her maker, but wholly governed by her own will and affections (2.746–67). The point at which this analogy breaks down is also instructive. Whereas Satan's offspring is generated by an unconscious, unwilled emanation, God's creatures are granted their existence by a wholly free and therefore wholly gracious act of the divine will. They are free creatures whose autonomous existence is grounded in the freedom of God. In Stephen Fallon's succinct expression, "God freely grants freedom to his creatures,"[103] and in precisely this way God allows himself to become limited by his autonomous creatures. With their ontology deriving from the liberation of matter from the divine being, human creatures are thus free to decree and to actualise their own futures—they are literally "Authors to themselves in all" (3.122). In Hegelian terms, one might say that their being consists in their becoming, or at any rate in an intrinsic potency for becoming.

Creaturely freedom is, then, derived from divine freedom, just as creaturely being is derived from the divine being. God is, as Juliet Cummins observes, "the archetype of freedom."[104] The freedom of God's creatures is thus a reflection of God's own freedom; it is, in the words of Genesis 1:27, the "image of God." The narrative voice in *Paradise Lost* therefore describes the "filial freedom" of Adam and Eve

---

99   Saurat, *Milton, Man and Thinker*, 103.

100 Saurat, *Milton, Man and Thinker*, 104.

101 Silver, *Imperfect Sense*, 103.

102 The theme of God's self-withdrawal has become important in modern theology: see for instance Jürgen Moltmann, *God in Creation: A New Theology of Creation and the Spirit of God*, trans. Margaret Kohl (London: SCM, 1985), 86–89.

103 Stephen M. Fallon, *Milton among the Philosophers: Poetry and Materialism in Seventeenth-Century England* (Ithaca: Cornell University Press, 1991), 215.

104 Juliet L. Cummins, "The Metaphysics of Authorship in Milton's *Paradise Lost*" (Ph.D. diss., University of Sydney, 2000), 55.

(4.294);[105] and God tells Adam that "the spirit within thee free" is "My Image" (8.440–41). In spite of its monist–materialist underpinnings, this aspect of *Paradise Lost*'s theology stands in continuity with Reformed orthodox theology. Richard Baxter describes human freedom as "part of Gods Natural Image on Man";[106] and, articulating the Reformed conception of the relationship between divine and human freedoms, Baxter refers with approval to those medieval scholastics who had maintained "not only that there is *Contingency from God*, but that there could be no *Contingency* in the creature, if it had not its original in God: the Liberty of God being the fountain of Contingency."[107] In just the same way, all creaturely freedom in *Paradise Lost* reflects something of God's own being—for God himself is true freedom.

The portrayal of the freedom of God in *Paradise Lost* thus draws on a diverse range of theological traditions. In accentuating the sheer freedom of the creative act, the poem's theology is close to Reformed orthodoxy and discontinuous with Arminian theology's more circumscribed view of divine freedom. But in its depiction of the contingent freedom with which the Father generates the Son, the poem's theology departs radically from Reformed orthodoxy and Arminianism alike, and instead adopts an Arian position. *Paradise Lost*'s Arianism is itself grounded both in the poem's thoroughgoing commitment to the absolute freedom of God, and in its corresponding commitment to the contingence of all the divine acts. The fact that the entire plan of redemption is also radically contingent highlights not only this divine freedom, but also the *gracious* character of redemption. Throughout the poem, the freedom of God is thus consistently and rigorously affirmed.

Further, in the poem's theology all creaturely freedom is grounded in the deeper reality of contingent divine freedom. Like God's own freedom, this creaturely freedom is, as I will argue in the following chapter, characterised by the contingent ability to choose between alternative possibilities. But by its very nature the freedom of human beings is also mutable—it is a freedom that possesses the ability to choose unfreedom and thus to negate itself, by plunging into the spiritual enslavement of the fall.

---

105 See Danielson, *Milton's Good God*, 105, who notes that "filial" in this line "reminds us of the genetic relationship between the characteristics of parent and child, creator and creature, and hence of their corresponding value."

106 Richard Baxter, *Catholick theologie* (London, 1675), 115.

107 Baxter, *The divine life*, 131. According to Iain M. MacKenzie, *God's Order and Natural Law: The Works of the Laudian Divines* (Aldershot: Ashgate, 2002), 38, the Laudian divines conceived of the natural order in terms of a similar "double contingency," namely, a contingency *to* God as well as a contingency *from* God.

5. Human Freedom and the Fall

In *Paradise Lost* Adam and Eve are, like God, characterised by the ability to choose between alternative possibilities. God has placed them in an environment in which they are free to grow and to develop through a creative use of their freedom. Their freedom consists in an indifferent liberty to choose from among an abundance of possibilities, and their possession of right reason enables them to choose wisely and well. But by its very nature, human freedom also entails the possibility of turning away from God and falling. Adam and Eve are thus contingent agents, able freely to stand or to fall. The fall itself, I will argue in this chapter, is thus a contingent, self-determined act that is not necessitated by any causal influence. In the narrative of *Paradise Lost* the fall is depicted as an irrational possibility of human nature that stands in fundamental discontinuity with all the preceding choices of Adam and Eve. Further, the free act with which Adam and Eve fall is not only self-determined but also self-negating. Through its evil choice, human nature freely abdicates its own liberty of indifference, so that its range of possibilities is drastically narrowed. It becomes self-enslaved, lacking the freedom to rise beyond itself into genuine freedom. In this way *Paradise Lost* presents the fallen will as a will in need of liberation—a will in need of grace.

Freedom and Necessity

In post-Reformation theology, necessitarianism involved the assertion that every choice is the necessary effect of a prior cause, and the subsequent denial that alternative possible choices exist. A necessitated event is, then, the antithesis of a contingent event, which Duns Scotus had defined simply as anything "whose opposite could have occurred at the time that this actually did."[1] The necessity (*necessitas*) or contingence (*contingentia*) of human choice was discussed extensively in post-Reformation theology, and, as William Cunningham has noted, the

---

1   John Duns Scotus, *Philosophical Writings: A Selection*, trans. Allan Wolter (Edinburgh: Thomas Nelson, 1962), 59.

central question was whether a "liberty of spontaneity" is "sufficient for moral responsibility."[2] In other words, is *spontaneity* of choice a sufficient condition for human freedom, or must human freedom also involve *alternativity* of choice?[3] In the necessitarian view, the will is free merely by virtue of its ability to choose spontaneously or voluntarily, in accordance with its own inclination. This was the position generally adopted by Reformed orthodox divines. William Perkins, for instance, asserted both "necessitie and freedome of will," since "in the doing of a voluntarie action it is sufficient that it proceede of judgment."[4] And, according to Francis Turretin, the will's freedom consists only in its "willingness and spontaneity."[5]

In contrast to this Reformed view of freedom, Arminian theologians insisted not only that the will is able to choose spontaneously, but also that it possesses the genuine possibility of alternative choice. Articulating the Arminian position, Thomas Goad claimed that God has "poised some things in such an equal *possibility* of being or not being, and left it to his creatures *choice* to turn the *scale*, that in respect of him they fall out *contingently*; it being as possible for his creatures to have *omitted* them, as to have *done* them."[6] Similarly, Simon Episcopius argued that the human will is "indifferently disposed or enclined to the opposites or contraries," and that for this reason the will remains "free from all necessity whatever."[7] In short, for the Arminians the will's freedom is equated with its liberty of indifference (*libertas indifferentiae*) — its ability to choose either of two alternative possibilities at a given moment. In this view, the human will is therefore defined simply as "a Power either to do, or not to do."[8] Its freedom consists not merely in spontaneity of choice, but also in alternativity of choice. Arminian

---

2   William Cunningham, *The Reformers and the Theology of the Reformation* (Edinburgh, 1862), 498.

3   Here I have followed the useful summary of Eef Dekker, "An Ecumenical Debate Between Reformation and Counter-Reformation? Bellarmine and Ames on *liberum arbitrium*," in *Reformation and Scholasticism: An Ecumenical Enterprise*, ed. Willem J. van Asselt and Eef Dekker (Grand Rapids: Baker, 2001), 144.

4   William Perkins, *A treatise of Gods free grace, and mans free will* (Cambridge, 1601), 20.

5   Francis Turretin, *Institutes of Elenctic Theology*, ed. James T. Dennison, trans. George Musgrave Giger, 3 vols. (Phillipsburg: P&R, 1992–97), 6.5.11.

6   Thomas Goad, *Stimluus orthodoxus, sive Goadus redivivus: A disputation partly theological, partly metaphysical, concerning the necessity and contingency of events in the world, in respect of Gods eternal decree* (London, 1661), 2.

7   Simon Episcopius, *The confession or declaration of the ministers or pastors which in the United Provinces are called Remonstrants, concerning the chief points of Christian religion* (London, 1676), 109.

8   [Anon.], *An antidote against some principal errors of the predestinarians* (London, 1696), 8.

writers thus accused Reformed orthodoxy of affirming "inevitable necessity,"[9] "absolute necessity,"[10] and "fatal necessity";[11] and they attributed to Reformed orthodoxy the notion that "Sin be necessitated in some, as well as Vertue is in others."[12] According to Thomas Goad, the Reformed divines "go further" even than the Stoics, in as much as they "impose a *necessity* on all things whatsoever."[13] Milton's *De Doctrina Christiana* also takes up this characteristic Arminian criticism when it asserts: "From the concept of human freedom, all idea of necessity must be removed."[14]

Paradise Lost appropriates this Arminian polemic against Reformed orthodox necessitarianism. Throughout the poem, it is only fallen creatures who claim to be subject to necessity. When Satan claims to be "compell[ed]" to bring about the fall (4.391), the narrative voice remarks that "with necessitie, / The Tyrants plea," Satan has simply "excus'd his devilish deeds" (4.392–93). Similarly, confronted by God in the garden, the fallen Adam explains with a show of magnanimity that he himself would take the blame for the fall, except that "strict necessitie" and "calamitous constraint" compel him to place the blame squarely on Eve (10.131–32). While these fallen creatures claim to be necessitated, God himself states that if his creatures did not possess genuine freedom to obey or to disobey they would have "servd necessitie, / Not mee" (3.110–11); and God denies that any predestinarian decree has "necessitate[d]" the fall (10.44). Raphael explains to Adam that the human will is "not over-rul'd by Fate / Inextricable, or strict necessity" (5.527–28), and that God thus requires "Our voluntary service ... Not our necessitated" (5.529–30).

Such denials of any divine necessitation of human choice are coupled with a corresponding denial of Satan's power to coerce or necessitate the human will. If Satan were able to determine the human will, then Adam and Eve would lose their contingent freedom and, as a result, their moral responsibility for the fall. Thus the Father instructs Raphael to warn Adam that Satan:

> is plotting now
> The fall of others from like state of bliss;
> By violence, no, for that shall be withstood,

9   Goad, *Stimluus orthodoxus, sive Goadus redivivus,* 5.

10   John Goodwin, *Confidence dismounted* (London, 1651), 10.

11   Simon Episcopius, *Opera theologica,* 2 vols. (London, 1678), 2:209.

12   [Anon.], *An antidote against some principal errors,* 13.

13   Goad, *Stimluus orthodoxus, sive Goadus redivivus,* 3.

14   *CPW* 6:161; *CM* 14:76.

> But by deceit and lies; this let him know,
> Least wilfully transgressing he pretend
> Surprisal, unadmonisht, unforewarnd. (5.240–45)

For all his might, Satan is not capable of overpowering the human will, of effecting a fall "By violence."[15] Rather, his only strategy against pre-lapsarian humanity is "deceit and lies." Satan can only try to talk Adam and Eve into misusing their own freedom; he cannot interfere with their contingent ability to choose. Emphasising this point, the Puritan Thomas Boston insists that "the devil did only allure, he could not ravish [Adam's] consent," and that he "could only tempt, not force" the human will.[16] Thus in *Paradise Lost* if human beings are to fall at all, it can only be by "wilfully transgressing" (5.244). Addressing the heavenly angels, the Father says of Satan:

> I told ye then he should prevail and speed
> On his bad Errand, Man should be seduc't
> And flatterd out of all, believing lies
> Against his Maker; no Decree of mine
> Concurring to necessitate his Fall (10.40–44)

At a glance, the Father's language here may seem to approach a notion of Satanic causation: "Man" is said to be passively "seduc't" and "flatterd." But the active verb, "believing," places responsibility on the free human agent, who is not simply overwhelmed by Satanic seduction and flattery, but who in the last resort takes the active step of "believing" the "lies" of Satan. Still, the predominantly passive voice of these lines has the effect of grammatically distancing God from the fall, while in contrast Satan is described as having a specific and active role in bringing about the fall. But even Satan's role is reduced to a matter of mere rhetoric. He seduces, flatters and lies—in all this, there is clearly no coercion of the human will, and no "violence" against the autonomy of human freedom.

In the same lines, any divine coercion is also ruled out. In insisting that he has not "concur[red] to necessitate" the fall with any decree of predestination, God the Father invokes the Reformed orthodox concept

---

15   The language of "violence" against free will was common in post-Reformation theology. The Westminster Confession of Faith, 3.1, for example, denies that "violence [is] offered to the will of the creatures" by predestination (Schaff, 3:608); and Episcopius, *The confession or declaration*, 118, argues that Adam's will "was not forc't ... by any outward violent impulse."

16   Thomas Boston, *Commentary on the Shorter Catechism*, 2 vols. (Aberdeen, 1853), 1:248, 254.

of concurrence (*concursus*). According to Reformed orthodoxy, God's concurrence is the providential activity by which he moves created things to action through second causes, in such a way that "does not destroy second causes, but upholds them."[17] Johann Heinrich Heidegger defines concurrence as "the operation of God by which he co-operates directly with the second causes ... so as to urge or move them to action and to operate along with them."[18] In contrast to this theology of concurrence, the God of *Paradise Lost* is not causally related to human choice and action; in the poem, the divine will and the human will do not interact in any cause–effect relationship. According to God, any such notion of concurrence would mean ultimately that the fall of human beings had already been "necessitated" by the divine will.

In its sustained rejection of all kinds of necessitation, then, the theology of *Paradise Lost* stands in close continuity with one of the central concerns of seventeenth-century Arminian theology, and its recurring insistence on the contingence of human freedom sets the theological backdrop for the poem's portrayal of the fall.

Contingent Freedom

The account of the fall in *Paradise Lost* constitutes a powerful critique of necessitarianism, and it presents a narrative portrayal of the Arminian concept of a contingent liberty of indifference. In his defence of human freedom, God insists that the divine decree does not

> touch with lightest moment of impulse
> His free Will, to her own inclining left
> In even scale. (10.45–47)

Here the metaphor of the balance invokes the Arminian view of contingent freedom. The balance image was frequently used by post-Reformation writers to represent the theory of the will's liberty of indifference, according to which the self-determining will is essentially uninfluenced towards either good or evil. Being left in "even scale," the will directs its own course. Emphasising this indifference of the will,

---

17 Johannes Wollebius, *Compendium theologiae christianae*; in *Reformed Dogmatics*, ed. and trans. John W. Beardslee (Oxford: Oxford University Press, 1965), 1.6.1. For an extended account of the doctrine of concurrence in post-Reformation theology, see Karl Barth, *Church Dogmatics*, ed. G. W. Bromiley and T. F. Torrance (Edinburgh: T&T Clark, 1956–77), III/3, 90–154.

18 Johann Heinrich Heidegger, *Corpus theologiae* (Zurich, 1700), 7.28; cited in Heppe, 258.

God the Father says that divine action does not "touch" the will even "with lightest moment of impulse" — with "moment" denoting both the small particle of a balance,[19] and the "[c]ause or motive of action; determining influence."[20] The human will, poised on a balance, is not inclined or determined in even the smallest degree by any external influence. Further, the Father's assertion that the will is equally capable of being inclined in either of two contrary directions constitutes an implicit denial of any internal, natural necessity. According to internal necessitarianism, the will is irresistibly determined by its own inclinations; but in *Paradise Lost*, the will's choice between good and evil is entirely undetermined. It remains poised on the balance until it moves itself in one direction or the other. The power of human choice is therefore radically contingent.

This characteristically Arminian view of human freedom was vigorously condemned by Reformed orthodox theologians. Johann Heinrich Heidegger, for example, denies that Adam was created "indifferent to good and evil," arguing that "[s]uch indifference, lying as it were on the scales and fluctuating between right and wicked" would be "a flaw in the creature," since it implies that Adam does not possess a natural inclination towards righteousness.[21] In the same way, Francis Turretin argues that any "equilibrium" of the will must conflict with the will's created goodness, for the prelapsarian will "would not have been very good, if it had been disposed to vice equally with virtue."[22] Notwithstanding its emphasis on the indifference of the will, however, Arminian theology still maintained that the unfallen will possessed "an inclination to good."[23] For Arminian theologians, the concept of the will's "indifferency" did not imply an "[a]bsence of ... favour for one side rather than another,"[24] or a mere "apathy";[25] rather it meant simply that the will possesses "an equal power to take either of two courses."[26] The Arminian "balance model" of liberty thus means, in Dennis Danielson's words, that "in a given moral choice, necessary conditions exist that allow the agent to choose one way or the other."[27]

---

19   *OED* 3a.

20   *OED* 5.

21   Heidegger, *Corpus theologiae*, 6.100; cited in Heppe, 242–43.

22   Turretin, *Institutes*, 8.1.8.

23   Jacobus Arminius, *The Works of James Arminius*, trans. James Nichols and William Nichols, 3 vols. (Grand Rapids: Baker, 1986), 2:363.

24   *OED* I 1.

25   *OED* I 2.

26   *OED* I 3.

27   Dennis R. Danielson, *Milton's Good God: A Study in Literary Theodicy* (Cambridge: Cambridge University Press, 1982), 134.

For this reason, the liberty of indifference that characterises the will of Adam and Eve in *Paradise Lost* does not exclude the fact that their "right Reason" (12.84) will lead them to prefer certain moral choices over others. As Adam says, all the "Faculties" of the human soul "serve / Reason as chief" (5.101–2). Even love, the highest of human virtues, "hath his seat / In Reason" (8.590–91). The perfect freedom of the first human beings consists in the rectitude of their reason. It is by reason that they are able to choose freely between good and evil; and it is the "Sanctitie of Reason" (7.508) that enables them to recognise, approve and choose the good. The concept of right reason (*recta ratio*) was commonly invoked in post-Reformation theology, and was especially characteristic of the Arminian and Amyraldian theologies, both of which stressed the primacy of reason over will.[28] In the words of Moïse Amyraut: "Reason in innocence was that inward principle, that divine light set up in the soul of man ... by which we were both instructed in our duty and enabled to perform it."[29] The concept of right reason in *Paradise Lost* stands in continuity with this emphasis on the primacy of reason, and it contrasts with the Reformed orthodox emphasis on the primacy of the will.[30]

In the same way, in *Paradise Lost* "true Liberty" dwells "alwayes with right Reason," and, apart from right reason, liberty "hath no dividual being" (12.83–85). Freedom is, in other words, virtually synonymous with right reason: "Reason also is choice" (3.108).[31] In the words of Adam, "God left free the Will, for what obeyes / Reason, is free, and Reason he made right" (9.351–52). The rectitude of Eve's and Adam's reason does not, however, entail a necessitarian inclination towards the good, but only an ability to judge wisely between good and evil, and to make a purely self-determined decision on the basis of

---

28 See for example Episcopius, *Opera theologica*, 2:203. On the concept of right reason in the sixteenth and seventeenth centuries, see Robert Hoopes, *Right Reason in the English Renaissance* (Cambridge, Mass.: Harvard University Press, 1962).

29 Moïse Amyraut, *A discourse concerning the divine dreams mention'd in Scripture* (London, 1676), 15.

30 Here I differ from Georgia B. Christopher, *Milton and the Science of the Saints* (Princeton: Princeton University Press, 1982), 98–99, who interprets right reason in *Paradise Lost* in terms of Luther's equation of *recta ratio* with *fides*. In this reading, the concept of right reason in fact undermines any notion of autonomous reliance on rationality. But *Paradise Lost* places far more emphasis on reason qua reason than any such Lutheran interpretation allows. Accordingly, the poem's concept of right reason stands in continuity not with a Lutheran view of faith, or with a Reformed voluntarism, but with the intellectualist view of freedom articulated by Arminian and Amyraldian theologians.

31 The same sentiment is expressed in *Areopagitica*: "when God gave [Adam] reason, he gave him freedom to choose, for reason is but choosing" (*CPW* 2:527).

this judgment. Reason itself therefore guarantees both the *probability* of standing and the *possibility* of falling. As Adam says, "Firm we subsist, yet possible to swerve" (9.359). In their unfallen state, Adam and Eve are "firm" in the uprightness of their reason; but their freedom consists in their ability to incline their own wills, so that it is always possible for them to "swerve" from righteousness. The prelapsarian perfection of Adam and Eve consists precisely in this power of contingent choice — the ability to stand or to fall.

Prelapsarian perfection is thus not static but dynamic. Instructing Adam on the freedom of the will, Raphael says:

> That thou art happie, owe to God;
> That thou continu'st such, owe to thy self,
> That is, to thy obedience; therein stand.
> This was that caution giv'n thee; be advis'd.
> God made thee perfet, not immutable;
> And good he made thee, but to persevere
> He left it in thy power, ordaind thy will
> By nature free, not over-rul'd by Fate
> Inextricable, or strict necessity. (5.520–28)

In their original state Adam and Eve are "perfet," and as such they are able to persevere in obedient happiness. Yet according to Raphael they may continue in their happy state only by freely obeying the creator, for they are "perfet" but "not immutable." This distinction between perfection and mutability, so important for any theodicy based on the Genesis story, was strongly emphasised in Reformed orthodox theology. Thus in spite of his necessitarian view of freedom, William Perkins affirms that "[i]n *Adams* will there were two things, *Libertie* and *Mutabilitie*";[32] and according to the Westminster Confession: "Man, in his state of innocency, had freedom and power to will and to do that which is good and well-pleasing to God, but yet mutably, so that he might fall from it."[33] Such an ability to fall from perfection may itself seem to constitute an imperfection; but Reformed orthodox divines argued that "mutability" entails "no fault or imperfection" in human nature.[34]

In *Paradise Lost* this mutability entails not only the possibility of falling, but also the possibility of positive development. Through their free obedience to God, human beings may be "by degrees of merit rais'd" to a heavenly mode of existence (7.157); indeed, even the physi-

---

32   William Perkins, *The workes of that famous and worthie minister of Christ, in the Universitie of Cambridge, M. W. Perkins*, 3 vols. (Cambridge, 1608–9), 1:708.

33   Westminster Confession of Faith, 9.2; in Schaff, 3:623.

34   Turretin, *Institutes*, 8.1.7.

cal bodies of Adam and Eve may, through a process of gradual development, "turn all to spirit, / Improv'd by tract of time" (5.497–98). The perfection of human nature therefore cannot be a mere "static perfection."[35] Rather, as Barbara Lewalski notes, perfection in *Paradise Lost* is a matter of "challenge, choice, and growth";[36] it is "complex and constantly developing, not simple and stable."[37] Prelapsarian perfection is, in Danielson's words, "capable of enrichment and increase"; humanity's created state in Eden is only a "beginning," open to a future of diverse possibilities.[38] In the seventeenth century, this dynamic view of the perfection and freedom of the first human beings was affirmed by Walter Raleigh: "God gave man to himselfe, to be his owne guide, his owne workeman, and his owne painter, that he might frame or describe unto himselfe what hee pleased, and make election of his own forme."[39]

In *Paradise Lost*, Eve affirms the richness of her alternative choices and possibilities, even as she talks with the serpent about the forbidden tree:

> For many are the Trees of God that grow
> In Paradise, and various, yet unknown
> To us, in such abundance lies our choice,
> As leaves a greater store of Fruit untoucht. (9.618–21)

Human choice in the garden is characterised by "such abundance" that the great majority of possibilities and choices are never realised. Indeed, while post-Reformation writers usually suggested that the fall of Adam and Eve had taken place on the same day as their creation,[40] the

---

35   As noted by Danielson, *Milton's Good God*, 178.

36   Barbara K. Lewalski, *The Life of John Milton: A Critical Biography* (Oxford: Blackwell, 2000), 466.

37   Barbara K. Lewalski, "Innocence and Experience in Milton's Eden," in *New Essays on Paradise Lost*, ed. Thomas Kranidas (Berkeley: University of California Press, 1969), 99. Tillyard's famous criticism of prelapsarian life thus rests on a misunderstanding of the dynamic nature of prelapsarian perfection: see E. M. W. Tillyard, *Milton* (London: Chatto & Windus, 1930), 282–83: "Adam and Eve are in the hopeless position of Old Age pensioners enjoying perpetual youth.... Any genuine activity would be better than utter stagnation." With similar misunderstanding, A. J. A. Waldock, "*Paradise Lost*" *and Its Critics* (Cambridge: Cambridge University Press, 1947), 125, speaks of Edenic life as "an eternity of boredom."

38   Dennis R. Danielson, "The Fall and Milton's Theodicy," in *The Cambridge Companion to Milton*, ed. Dennis R. Danielson (Cambridge: Cambridge University Press, 1999), 154.

39   Walter Raleigh, *The History of the World*, ed. C. A. Patrides (Philadelphia: Temple University Press, 1971), 142.

40   See for example Thomas Watson, *A body of practical divinity* (London, 1692), 79: "the most probable and received Opinion is, That *Adam* fell the very same day in which

narrative of *Paradise Lost* withholds the fall for several days, in order to portray dramatically Eve's and Adam's dynamic and evolving process of growth through the exercise of their freedom. Before falling, they use their freedom to engage creatively in prayer and education, gardening and lovemaking, conversation and cooking. This rich variety of activities indicates something of the variety of their prelapsarian possibilities. Further, the divine prohibition itself is not a narrow restriction placed upon human freedom, but in its simplicity even this prohibition serves to illustrate the richness and openness of freedom. As Eve tells the serpent, the prohibition of the tree of knowledge is the "Sole Daughter of [God's] voice"; in all other respects, "we live / Law to our selves, our Reason is our Law" (9.653–54). The divine prohibition is therefore light and easy—"One easie prohibition" (4.433)—in view of the abundance of prelapsarian choice. As John Downham says of Adam and Eve: "having but one onely Commandement, and that so easie to keepe, as to abstaine from one onely fruit, in so great plentie and varietie of other, yet they brake it."[41] And similarly, Arminius had written that the first sin was "easily avoidable by man in the midst of such abundant plenty of good and various fruits."[42] But if the fall is inexcusable in light of the "abundance" of Adam's and Eve's possible choices, in *Paradise Lost* the fall is also possible only because of the human will's ability to choose and to actualise its own future, and to do so vis-à-vis a multitude of alternative possibilities. By making Adam and Eve free for a future of development and growth, God has also endowed their freedom with the contingent possibility of falling. The possibility of falling in itself is therefore not a sinister flaw in human nature, but an aspect of the rich freedom of that nature.

---

he was created"; and thus Adam did not take up even "one night's lodging in Paradise." According to the more detailed chronology of John Lightfoot, *The works of the reverend and learned John Lightfoot, D.D.*, 2 vols. (London, 1684), 1:1–3, heaven and earth were created "in a moment," with the angels being created "in the very same instant"; but when human beings were created, certain angels became devils "through spite at man," and thus set out at once to ruin humanity, with the result that the human race fell on the same day. In this scheme angels and humans alike become fallen on the same day—they begin to exist and then begin to sin almost instantaneously.

41 John Downham, *The summe of sacred divinitie first briefly and methodically propounded, and then more largely and cleerly handled and explained* (London, 1620), 234.

42 Arminius, *Works*, 2:155.

Contingence and Theodicy

The emphasis on the contingent freedom of human choice is of special significance in *Paradise Lost*'s theodicy. A justification of the ways of God based on the Genesis story must seek to explain not only why God allowed the first human beings to fall, but also why he allowed them to be subject to temptation—subject, that is, to the mere possibility of falling—in the first place. In *Paradise Lost*, this question of the possibility of falling is answered with the concept of contingent freedom. Speaking of God, Raphael tells Adam:

> Our voluntary service he requires,
> Not our necessitated, such with him
> Findes no acceptance, nor can find, for how
> Can hearts, not free, be tri'd whether they serve
> Willing or no, who will but what they must
> By Destinie, and can no other choose? (5.529–34)

According to Raphael, a necessitated will is a will that does not choose contingently; it possesses no alternative possibility, and thus "can no other choose." No choice is truly free, and no obedience truly acceptable to God, unless possible alternative choices also exist: in Stanley Fish's words, "the possibility (or capability) of falling is what gives the act of standing meaning."[43] God thus places Adam and Eve in the garden in order that they should serve him freely; and in order to guarantee authentic freedom, and consequently the possibility of authentic obedience, God also establishes the possibility of the alternative choice of disobedience.

The power to choose contingently between the alternative possibilities of obedience and disobedience, then, is not accidental but essential to freedom in *Paradise Lost*, just as it is essential to freedom in Arminian theology. Thus in the poem the possibility of falling is present from the beginning as part of human nature, as a vital component of the freedom of the human will. As Milton had asserted in *Areopagitica*, without the possibility of choosing between good and evil, Adam would have been "a meer artificiall *Adam*," more puppet than human.[44] The choice of God to grant contingent freedom to Adam and Eve is in this way justified. Even the possibility of falling is in fact a possibility

---

43 Stanley E. Fish, *How Milton Works* (Cambridge, Mass.: Harvard University Press, 2001), 527.

44 *CPW* 2:527.

granted by the gracious God who provides for his creatures not "artificiall" but genuine freedom.

The angels enjoy a similar freedom through contingence. Comparing human beings to angels, the Father affirms that both are created "just and right, / Sufficient to have stood, though free to fall" (3.98–99):

> Such I created all th' Ethereal Powers
> And Spirits, both them who stood and them who faild;
> Freely they stood who stood, and fell who fell. (3.100–2)

Likewise Raphael contrasts the contingent obedience of the unfallen angels with the disobedience of the fallen:

> My self and all th' Angelic Host that stand
> In sight of God enthron'd, our happie state
> Hold, as you yours, while our obedience holds;
> On other surety none; freely we serve,
> Because we freely love, as in our will
> To love or not; in this we stand or fall:
> And som are fall'n, to disobedience fall'n,
> And so from Heav'n to deepest Hell; O fall
> From what high state of bliss into what woe! (5.535–43)

The angels stand only by free obedience. They do not obey God as a result of any volitional necessity, for their wills retain the power "To love or not." Following Augustine and Thomas Aquinas, Reformed orthodoxy emphasised the volitional immutability of the righteous angels; once these angels had persevered in obedience, they were "confirmed in good and endowed with full happiness so that they immutably cleave to God with perfect obedience."[45] According to Reformed orthodoxy, such angels can never again possess even the hypothetical possibility of falling away. Arminian theology agreed with Reformed orthodoxy on this point: Arminius writes that the "good Angels" have an "infused habit" of goodness, and have received from God a "confirmation in habitual goodness."[46] But the portrayal of angelic freedom in *Paradise Lost* departs explicitly from this theological position. According to Raphael, the angels maintain their "happie state" only while they continue obediently to exercise their free choice. They have received no divine confirmation in righteousness; their wills remain indifferent, able at any moment either "To love or not." The angels thus

---

45   William Ames, *The Marrow of Theology*, ed. and trans. John D. Eusden (Grand Rapids: Baker, 1968), 1.10.18.
46   Arminius, *Works*, 2:361.

have "other surety none," apart from their own free obedience. Their obedience is always a contingent obedience, characterised by the possibility of the alternative choice of disobedience.[47] The fallen angels, too, possessed the same alternativity of choice before they rebelled; they too were able to direct their own wills according to "Right reason" (6.42). Gazing at the sun through tears, Satan declaims:

> Hadst thou the same free Will and Power to stand?
> Thou hadst: whom hast thou then or what to accuse,
> But Heav'ns free Love dealt equally to all? (4.66–68)

In this fleeting confession, Satan acknowledges that "Heav'ns free love" has secured for all the angels the power of freedom and the alternativity of choice. The authentic freedom of all the angels was assured by their liberty of indifference, their self-determining ability to love or not: "firm they might have stood, / Yet fell" (6.911–12).

A Free Fall

The fact that in *Paradise Lost* there is no essential difference between human freedom and angelic freedom highlights the absence of any necessity from "Mans First Disobedience" (1.1). Some angels, possessing the same ability to fall, chose instead to stand firm; and just so, the poem's human protagonists might have chosen to stand and not to fall. The whole episode of the fall is thus characterised by radical contingence. All Eve's and Adam's choices might have been otherwise; all that happens might not have happened. Readers of the episode of the fall in *Paradise Lost* enjoy the privileged perspective of knowing from the outset how the story will end, and this foresight can too easily give rise to a necessitarian reading of the fall. Joseph Summers rightly cautions: "As we read the poem with our hindsight and the occasional reminders of God's foreknowledge, we can, if we are not careful, construct an image of inexorable necessity in the development of the

---

47 John P. Rumrich, *Milton Unbound: Controversy and Reinterpretation* (Cambridge: Cambridge University Press, 1996), 16, therefore seems mistaken when he suggests that "the continued obedience of the good angels seems, if not automatic, almost inevitable after the war in heaven. Having seen what they have seen, who could disobey?" One might equally ask how Adam could disobey, having heard what he has heard about the angelic rebellion. But such questions simply highlight the irrationality of disobedience, rather than any immutability of creaturely choice.

events to their final outcome."[48] In *Paradise Lost*, even God's foreknowledge of the fall had "no influence on thir fault" (3.118)—and nor does the reader's privileged knowledge render the fall certain or necessary. In particular, the fall is not theologically necessitated by the fact that certain events in the developing narrative seem to be leading towards this crucial event.[49]

The separation of Eve from Adam, initiated by the industrious suggestion of Eve, is of particular importance in this connection:

> Let us divide our labours, thou where choice
> Leads thee, or where most needs, whether to wind
> The Woodbine round this Arbour, or direct
> The clasping Ivie where to climb, while I
> In yonder Spring of Roses intermixt
> With Myrtle, find what to redress till Noon. (9.214–19)

The fact that the fall could not have taken place in the way that it does without this division of labour has led many readers to posit a necessary connection between the separation and the ensuing fall. Barbara Lewalski, for instance, asserts that "Eve's proposal that they undertake separate gardening tasks as a means to greater efficiency is shown to lead directly to the Fall";[50] and A. G. George speaks of a "transgressive separation," claiming that the eating of the forbidden fruit is "only the completion of the fall."[51] But in contrast to such readings, other critics have rightly seen that Eve's decision to work alone is not invalidated by the fact that the fall takes place soon afterwards.[52] Indeed, as

---

48 Joseph H. Summers, *The Muse's Method: An Introduction to Paradise Lost* (London: Chatto & Windus, 1962), 148.

49 In this respect, a traditional Aristotelian theory of "plot" does not offer an appropriate interpretive approach to *Paradise Lost*. According to Aristotle, *Poetics*, 1452a, the most effective narrative is one in which incidents "occur unexpectedly and at the same time in consequence of one another"; in particular, the change of the hero's fortunes should take place not merely *post hoc* but *propter hoc*, arising "out of the structure of the Plot itself, so as to be the consequence, necessary or probable, of the antecedents." To approach the episode of the fall in *Paradise Lost* through this kind of necessitarian narrative framework is to miss the fact that *Paradise Lost* attempts a very different and more challenging kind of narrative, in which the decisive action is not necessary (*propter hoc*), but radically contingent (*post hoc*).

50 Barbara K. Lewalski, "Milton on Women—Yet Once More," *Milton Studies* 6 (1974), 6.

51 A. G. George, *Milton and the Nature of Man: A Descriptive Study of Paradise Lost in Terms of the Concept of Man as the Image of God* (London: Asia Publishing House, 1974), 142–43.

52 See especially Susannah B. Mintz, *Threshold Poetics: Milton and Intersubjectivity* (Newark: University of Delaware Press, 2003), 142–51; Diane Kelsey McColley, *Milton's Eve* (Urbana: University of Illinois Press, 1983), 140–86; and Joan Malory Webber, "The Politics of Poetry: Feminism and *Paradise Lost*," *Milton Studies* 14 (1980), 3–24.

Marilyn Farwell notes, Eve's desire for temporary solitude may be viewed as "a logical step in her growth."[53] Although Eve does in fact fall, it is a mistake to read the fall back into the separation scene, such that the fall becomes a foregone conclusion. Eve's capacity to resist temptation alone is, as David Gay observes, "necessary to the integrity of the poem." If the separation entails the fall, then the epic's argument lapses into "notions of fate rather than providence," necessity rather than freedom.[54] There can of course be no hermeneutically naïve approach to this scene; the reader knows that the fall is imminent, just as the narrative voice does when it laments that "hapless Eve" will be "deceav'd" and will fail (9.404). But mere chronology and occasion do not amount to causation. Eve will fall; and had she remained with Adam she might not have fallen. But even as she leaves him to work alone in the garden, she possesses fully the capacity to stand. She may still resist temptation and decide not to fall. Whatever psychological, existential and relational implications her separation from Adam may have, the separation itself has not compromised her innocence or her liberty of indifference.

In a perceptive argument, Stanley Fish has thus correctly pointed to the causal "irrelevance" of the separation scene:

> The decision of an absolutely free will cannot be determined by forces outside it, and, in a causal sense, such a decision has no antecedents. I would suggest that the point of the scenes in Paradise from Book 4 to Book 9 is their irrelevance, as determining factors, to the moment of crisis experienced by the characters.[55]

But while the division of labour may be irrelevant as a cause of the fall, the whole scene is important as a depiction of the rich freedoms of prelapsarian life. Indeed, the possibility of Eve's solitude is itself an expression of her perfect freedom.[56] Eve is right when, responding to Adam's argument that together they are safer against temptation, she says:

> Let us not then suspect our happie State
> Left so imperfet by the Maker wise,
> As not secure to single or combin'd:

---

53   Marilyn R. Farwell, "Eve, the Separation Scene, and the Renaissance Idea of Androgyny," *Milton Studies* 16 (1982), 15.

54   David Gay, *The Endless Kingdom: Milton's Scriptural Society* (Newark: University of Delaware Press, 2002), 86.

55   Stanley E. Fish, "Discovery as Form in *Paradise Lost*," in *New Essays on Paradise Lost*, ed. Thomas Kranidas (Berkeley: University of California Press, 1969), 6.

56   See Arthur E. Barker, "*Paradise Lost*: The Relevance of Regeneration," in *Paradise Lost: A Tercentenary Tribute*, ed. Balachandra Rajan (Toronto: University of Toronto Press, 1969), 63–64.

> Fraile is our happiness, if this be so,
> And *Eden* were no *Eden* thus expos'd. (9.337–41)

Eve has rightly understood the perfection of human nature and the ability of the human will to withstand temptation and to choose good instead of evil. The fact that she will so soon fall does not negate the validity of her insight at this point. Adam, moreover, is right to allow Eve at last to go. His decision is based on a recognition of her freedom: "Go; for thy stay, not free, absents thee more" (9.372).[57] Adam could have compelled Eve to stay with him only by compromising her freedom, and he realises that such a restriction of her choice would render her "not free." It would entail a resort to "force" —and "force upon free Will hath here no place" (9.1173–74). If Eve were to lose her freedom in this way, it would be a worse fate than any temptation she might encounter alone in the garden. William Riley Parker's suggestion that the fall began with Adam's "fall from responsibility and good judgment when he yielded to Eve's whim to work apart" therefore seems mistaken[58]—on the contrary, a different kind of fall would have begun had Adam chosen to make his wife "not free," by compelling her to stay with him against her own will and judgment. The fall, then, cannot be causally traced back to the separation scene. Throughout this scene, Eve and Adam remain innocent beings, both of them making creative use of their contingent freedom in face of a dynamic range of alternative choices and possibilities. When Eve departs from Adam, she "actively chooses ..., takes the risk of being alone, and reaches toward the possibility of alternatives."[59]

But although she is free to stand—and although she might have stood—Eve freely falls:

> her rash hand in evil hour
> Forth reaching to the Fruit, she pluckd, she eat:
> Earth felt the wound, and Nature from her seat
> Sighing through all her Works gave signs of woe,
> That all was lost. (9.780–84)

---

57 Joan S. Bennett, "'Go': Milton's Antinomianism and the Separation Scene in *Paradise Lost*, Book 9," *PMLA* 98 (1983), 401, argues that, instead of either compelling Eve to stay or commanding her to go, Adam should have simply "withheld his permission for her to go." According to Bennett, when Adam tells Eve to "Go" he is in fact giving her "a positive command," and is thus acting "legalistically." Adam's statement should not, however, be categorised as a "command"; on the contrary, it is a conditional statement: "if thou think, trial unsought may finde / Us both securer ... / Go" (9.370–72). And Eve herself understands this statement not as a command, but simply as "thy permission" (9.378).

58 William Riley Parker, *Milton: A Biography*, 2 vols. (Oxford: Clarendon, 1968), 1:512.

59 Mintz, *Threshold Poetics*, 150.

While the poem offers a detailed exploration of the process of Eve's deception, it presents no specific psychological analysis of the movement of her will. Similarly, the movement of Adam's will is not directly portrayed. As Boyd Berry observes, "we do not ... see Adam and Eve change their minds," but we see them only "with *changed* minds."[60] When Eve tells Adam that she has "tasted" (9.874), and urges him also to "taste, that equal Lot / May joine us" (9.881–82), an "Astonied" Adam, chilled with "horror" (9.890), declares that he has made his choice. Speaking first to himself, Adam says:

> Certain my resolution is to Die;
> How can I live without thee, how forgoe
> Thy sweet Converse and Love so dearly joind,
> To live again in these wilde Woods forlorn?
> Should God create another *Eve*, and I
> Another Rib afford, yet loss of thee
> Would never from my heart; no no, I feel
> The Link of Nature draw me: Flesh of Flesh,
> Bone of my Bone thou art, and from thy State
> Mine never shall be parted, bliss or woe. (9.907–16)

This soliloquy reveals the suddenness with which Adam decides to fall. Even before he speaks of his reasons for falling, his "resolution" is already "Certain." But when he comes to articulate the reason for his choice, he claims that it is not his own freedom, but the "Link of Nature" that "draw[s]" him. His choice, he says, is necessitated by a power greater than that of his own will. Turning to Eve, Adam repeats this statement of necessitation even more strongly:

> I with thee have fixt my Lot,
> Certain to undergoe like doom; if Death
> Consort with thee, Death is to mee as Life;
> So forcible within my heart I feel
> The Bond of Nature draw me to my owne,
> My own in thee, for what thou art is mine;
> Our State cannot be severd, we are one,
> One Flesh; to loose thee were to loose my self. (9.952–59)

Adam claims that he is drawn so "forcibl[y]" by the "Bond of Nature" that he simply "cannot" be parted from Eve.

Some readers have been so impressed by Adam's profession of necessitation at this point that they have interpreted the whole episode of

---

60 Boyd M. Berry, *Process of Speech: Puritan Religious Writing and Paradise Lost* (Baltimore: Johns Hopkins University Press, 1976), 253.

the fall in necessitarian terms. J. B. Savage, for instance, suggests that Adam's choice "is compelled as a necessary consequence," and that under the circumstances the fall is "irresistible and inevitable."[61] According to A. J. A. Waldock, Adam's two declarations of necessity are "the two most important passages in *Paradise Lost*,"[62] and Waldock employs the necessitarianism of these declarations as an interpretive key to Adam's fall. Similarly, Robert Crosman argues that *Paradise Lost* depicts "a tragic Adam unable to resist temptation."[63] Such necessitarian readings simplify Adam's transgression to such an extent that the essential theological mystery of the fall is explained away—namely, the mystery of an uncaused act of will in which reason contradicts itself by choosing the irrational possibility of sin and death.[64] This is, however, a mystery that defies reductive necessitarian explanations.[65] In the words of Thomas Watson, sin is "absurd and irrational"; it "makes a Man act not only *wickedly*, but *foolishly*."[66] In a word, sin is "madnesse."[67] In *Paradise Lost* the fall is a real possibility of human nature, but it is an irrational possibility that can be actualised only by a flagrant denial and contradiction of the judgment of "right reason." The poem's portrayal of the fall can therefore be understood only when all notions of necessity are set aside, and when "Mans First Disobedience" (1.1) is seen in its sheer singularity, in its utter discontinuity with everything that has transpired in prelapsarian life. Søren Kierkegaard's description of the fall is thus apposite here: "By the qualitative leap sin came into the

---

61 J. B. Savage, "Freedom and Necessity in *Paradise Lost*," *ELH* 44 (1977), 305–7.

62 Waldock, *"Paradise Lost" and Its Critics*, 46.

63 Robert Crosman, *Reading Paradise Lost* (Bloomington: Indiana University Press, 1980), 178–79.

64 Necessitarian readings also tend to assume that some element of fallenness is a necessary precondition for the fall. Such an assumption rests on a misapprehension of the basic idea of the fall—in the words of Rudolf Bultmann, *Theology of the New Testament*, trans. Kendrick Grobel, 2 vols. (London: SCM, 1951–55), 1:251: "Sin came into the world by sinning."

65 On the other hand, this mystery also defies reductive attempts to demonstrate its logical contradictoriness. Such attempts, which rest on necessitarian assumptions about the nature of freedom, have been offered by Savage, "Freedom and Necessity in *Paradise Lost*," 286–311; Mili N. Clark, "The Mechanics of Creation: Non-Contradiction and Natural Necessity in *Paradise Lost*," *English Literary Renaissance* 7:2 (1977), 207–42; and R. D. Bedford, "Time, Freedom, and Foreknowledge in *Paradise Lost*," *Milton Studies* 16 (1982), 61–76. Given *Paradise Lost*'s view of contingent, indifferent freedom, there is nothing intrinsically impossible about a free fall—even though such a fall is intrinsically irrational.

66 Watson, *A body of practical divinity*, 77.

67 William Ames, *The substance of Christian religion: or, A plain and easie draught of the Christian catechism* (London, 1659), 29.

world."[68] Indeed, John Tanner has argued that just as in Kierkegaard's thought sin is always "a qualitative leap, inexplicable as the sum of quantitative determinants,"[69] so also in *Paradise Lost* the emergence of sin is "radically incommensurable" and "irrational."[70] The fall of Adam and Eve ultimately resembles an existential leap more than a conditioned (i.e. caused) and rational choice. It is a leap from reason to unreason, from innocence to fallenness, not a gradual transition in which one step predictably and necessarily follows another. Ultimately then, on a theological level little more can be said about Adam's fall than that "he knew better, and he ate anyway."[71] As William Riley Parker observes, Adam's choice is not fixed by any circumstances. Adam is not persuaded or seduced by Eve; his decision is simply a "foolish" gesture, "a suicidal, useless, thoroughly human choice."[72] From the moment of his creation Adam does, of course, possess the *ability* to fall, because of his contingent liberty of indifference; but he never possesses a sound *reason* to fall, and in this sense one cannot accurately speak of any cause of his fall. At the moment of decision, he simply uses his freedom to plunge—without reason and against reason—into ruin.

More particularly, the narrative account of Adam's fall shows that his choice is not necessitated by the prior fall of Eve. As G. K. Hunter observes: "Milton could easily have shown an Adam who was betrayed by fleshly weakness, unable to resist the seductive and carnally irresistible Eve"; but, on the contrary: "Adam's speech of resolution and tragic knowledge that he is to die is spoken ... *to himself*, without persuasion and interruption from Eve. When he speaks to her his mind is already made up."[73] Adam has a "Certain ... resolution" to fall (9.907), even before he speaks of the bond of nature, or of the unity of marriage, or of the sweetness of Eve's companionship. With his gestures of tragic necessitation, he is, as Dennis Burden points out, seeking simply to justify a course of action on which he has already settled.[74]

A necessitarian reading of Adam's fall can be maintained only at the expense of the view of contingent freedom that has been developed consistently throughout the entire poem. Everything that the reader has

68 Søren Kierkegaard, *The Concept of Dread*, trans. Walter Lowrie (London: Oxford University Press, 1944), 99.
69 John S. Tanner, *Anxiety in Eden: A Kierkegaardian Reading of Paradise Lost* (New York: Oxford University Press, 1992), 33.
70 Tanner, *Anxiety in Eden*, 45.
71 David M. Miller, *John Milton: Poetry* (Boston: Twayne, 1978), 137.
72 Parker, *Milton*, 1:515.
73 G. K. Hunter, *Paradise Lost* (London: George Allen & Unwin, 1980), 197.
74 Dennis H. Burden, *The Logical Epic: A Study of the Argument of Paradise Lost* (London: Routledge & Kegan Paul, 1967), 164.

learned about the contingence of human freedom is a preparation for this decisive moment, when Adam claims to be "draw[n]" by "Nature" into disobedience (9.914; 9.956), and when he laments that he "cannot" resist falling along with Eve (9.958). Raphael had already corrected Adam on this point, when the latter claimed to be enslaved by his wife's "loveliness": "Accuse not Nature," warns Raphael, "shee hath don her part; / Do thou but thine" (8.561–62). In attempting to shrug off his moral responsibility and to impute the cause of his disobedience to "Nature," Adam is in reality denying the truth about his own nature: that he is the free image of God, possessing the power to choose between good and evil, and that he is volitionally autonomous in face of all external circumstances and internal inclinations alike, so that nothing can determine the movement of his will. Indeed, in his speech to Eve, Adam himself admits that his decision is purely self-determined— "I with thee have fixt my Lot" (9.952)—even though he immediately contradicts this admission, adopting instead, like the Satanic theologians, a notion of "Fixt Fate" (2.560).

In *Paradise Lost*, there can be no authentic freedom and therefore no moral responsibility without the contingence of the will. If this is recognised, then Adam's denial of his contingent liberty of indifference must itself be taken as a reflection and expression of his turn from God towards disobedience. This feature of *Paradise Lost* is best understood in the context of the opinion, widespread in post-Reformation theology, that Adam fell as soon as he decided to eat the fruit,[75] so that he was already fallen before he had physically broken the divine prohibition. In the words of William Ames: "The first motion or step of ... disobedience necessarily came before the act of eating, so that it may truly be said that man was a sinner before he did the eating."[76] Similarly, the Adam who soliloquises about his necessitation by the "Link of Nature" (9.914) is an already fallen Adam.[77] In denying his own freedom, Adam seeks to rid his actions of their moral implications—to act without consequences. But in the theology of *Paradise Lost* there can be no moral choice without consequences, for built into the very structure of the poem's universe is the volitional autonomy of created beings, and the alternativity of choice with which free creatures actualise their own

---

75 Thus Fish, *How Milton Works*, 555, observes that "Adam falls ... somewhere in the middle of line 894."

76 Ames, *Marrow of Theology*, 1.11.6.

77 See in this connection Beverley Sherry, "Speech in *Paradise Lost*," *Milton Studies* 8 (1975), 259, who notes that in *Paradise Lost* the "monologue" is "a characteristically fallen mode of utterance." Sherry thus speaks of Adam's and Eve's "Satanic tendency to soliloquise."

futures. The one who chooses to fall must therefore be responsible for his or her own choice and its ruinous consequences. The God of *Paradise Lost* is thus justified when he says of humanity:

> whose fault?
> Whose but his own? ingrate, he had of mee
> All he could have; I made him just and right,
> Sufficient to have stood, though free to fall. (3.96–99)

The fact that both Adam and Eve are "Sufficient to have stood, though free to fall" should be basic to any reading of the episode of the fall in *Paradise Lost*. If Adam and Eve themselves seem to contradict this fact, it is only because fallen creatures, having already exercised their freedom "to fall," are subsequently quick to deny their sufficiency "to have stood." Such denials reflect not their original freedom, but their present state of corruption. Ultimately, in spite of all external circumstances and internal motivations, Eve and Adam might have stood. In the words of Arminius, it was "the duty of man" to resist all internal and external "causes" of sin, and this resistance was entirely "in his power": "This resistance might have been effected by his repelling and rejecting the causes which operated outwardly, and by reducing into order and subjecting ... those which impelled inwardly."[78] Viewed in this light, the "causes" of the fall are not really causes in the proper sense at all. There is finally no cause, except for the free, contingent and self-determined choice of a human being.[79] It is this Arminian view of contingent freedom that the whole episode of the fall in *Paradise Lost* so dramatically enacts.

Freedom Enthralled

The fall thus takes place by an act of human freedom. But this act is not only an expression of freedom. It is at the same moment also a negation of freedom, in which the human will becomes enslaved.[80] In its pro-

---

78 Arminius, *Works*, 2:153.
79 In a different connection, Jeffrey Burton Russell, *The Prince of Darkness: Radical Evil and the Power of Good in History* (London: Thames & Hudson, 1988), 190, has said of Milton's Satan: "If Satan fell freely, there is no cause of his fall, for there can be no cause of a truly free-will act."
80 For a twentieth-century statement of this theological concept, see Reinhold Niebuhr, *The Nature and Destiny of Man: A Christian Interpretation*, 2 vols. (London: Nisbet, 1941–43), 1:17: "Man contradicts himself within the terms of his true essence. His essence is free self-determination. His sin is the wrong use of his freedom and its con-

nounced emphasis on the enslavement of the fallen will, *Parai se Lost* is closely continuous with Reformed orthodox theology; this is, indeed, one of the most strikingly orthodox features of the poem's theology, although it is a feature that has received little attention in Milton scholarship. Many readers of the poem continue to follow Sir Herbert Grierson's simplistic characterisation of its theology as "Pelagian."[81] In contrast, William Riley Parker is one of the few scholars to have recognised the important role of the concept of lost freedom in *Parai se Lost*. According to Parker, one of the poem's "dominant ideas" is that "'tyranny must be,' 'true liberty' having been lost to the human race since Adam's 'original lapse' from 'right reason.'"[82] This important insight, recently restated by Marshall Grossman[83] and developed by William Walker,[84] is crucial not only for an understanding of *Parai se Lost*'s view of the fall, but also for an understanding of its theology of grace. In the poem, the unfallen will is poised in a liberty of indifference between good and evil; but the fall decisively tips the balance towards evil, so that the freedom to choose the good is lost. Human nature is thus left with an inclination towards evil, which cannot be overcome except by the liberating grace of God.

The portrayal of original sin in *Parai se Lost* brings the poem's theology remarkably close to the Reformed orthodox concept of "total depravity." *Parai se Lost* consistently affirms the Augustinian notion of original sin (*peccatum or g nale*),[85] according to which all human beings were present "in" Adam when he fell,[86] and have in this way become partakers of Adam's guilt (*reatus*) and corruption (*corrupt o*).[87] As God

---

sequent destruction." Like Milton, Niebuhr emphasises that this act of self-enslavement is itself an expression of freedom: "Man is most free in the discovery that he is not free" (1:276).

81   Herbert J. C. Grierson, *Cross Currents in English Literature of the Seventeenth Century* (London: Chatto & Windus, 1958), 267.

82   Parker, *Milton*, 1:591.

83   Marshall Grossman, *"Authors to Themselves": Milton and the Revelation of History* (Cambridge: Cambridge University Press, 1987), 148–49.

84   William Walker, "Human Nature in Republican Tradition and *Paradise Lost*," *Early Modern Literary Studies* 10:1 (2004), 32–41 <http://purl.oclc.org/emls/10-1/walkmilt.htm>.

85   On the parallels between *Paradise Lost* and Augustine regarding original sin, see Peter A. Fiore, *Milton and Augustine: Patterns of Augustinian Thought in Paradise Lost* (University Park: Pennsylvania State University Press, 1981), 42–60. Fiore suggests that original sin is one of the doctrines "most central to the theological framework of *Paradise Lost*" (42).

86   Augustine, *De civitate Dei*, 13.14.

87   This Augustinian distinction between guilt and corruption was taken up in Reformed orthodox theology. See for instance Amandus Polanus, *Syntagma theologiae christianae* (Geneva, 1617), 6.3.

the Father says, if Adam falls, he will perish "with his whole posteritie" (3.209). Adam's and Eve's understanding of this concept of original sin motivates much of their despair after the fall. Adam laments that everything he "shall beget, / Is propagated curse" (10.728–29), so that the creator's command to *"Encrease and multiplie"* has, by a bitter irony, become "death to heare" (10.730–31). In all this, *Paradise Lost's* theology is discontinuous with both Pelagian[88] and Socinian[89] denials of original sin. Further, the poem's view of original sin is continuous with the Reformation and post-Reformation emphasis on the positive corruption of original sin,[90] as opposed to Roman Catholic theology's claim that original sin is simply a privation of the supernatural gift of original righteousness.[91] Pondering his unborn offspring, which now "stands curst" in him (10.818), Adam asks:

> But from mee what can proceed,
> But all corrupt, both Mind and Will deprav'd,
> Not to do onely, but to will the same
> With mee? (10.824–27)

As a result of the fall, Adam's offspring must be "all corrupt"—that is, "all" of Adam's offspring will be corrupt, and each member of Adam's offspring will be "all" corrupt.[92] This totality of human corruption is such that human nature is "deprav'd" in "both Mind and Will." Reformed orthodox theology similarly emphasised the corruption of both intellect and will. Theodore Beza writes that "man's understanding and

---

88 For the Pelagian view of original sin, see Augustine, *De gratia Christi et de peccato originali contra Pelagium, ad Albinam, Pinianum, et Melaniam,* 2.1–48; in *PL* 44 and *NPNF* 5.

89 Formulating the Socinian position, *The Racovian Catechism,* ed. Thomas Rees (London, 1818), 10, presents an uncompromising denial of original sin: "the fall of Adam, as it was but one act, could not have power to deprave his own nature, much less that of his posterity." As William Poole, *Milton and the Idea of the Fall* (Cambridge: Cambridge University Press, 2005), 159, notes, *Paradise Lost* "could not be less Socinian" in its depiction of original sin.

90 For an elaborate Reformed orthodox discussion of original sin, see Anthony Burgess, *The doctrine of original sin, asserted and vindicated against the old and new adversaries thereof* (London, 1659).

91 For an example of this Roman Catholic position, see Anselm, *Opera omnia,* 6 vols. (Edinburgh: Thomas Nelson, 1938–61), 2:169–70. Closer to the Protestant position was Thomas Aquinas's affirmation of both a privative and a positive aspect of original sin: see Thomas, *Summa theologiae,* 1a2ae.82.1. The argument of Fiore, *Milton and Augustine,* 52–55, that Milton, with Roman Catholic theology, regards original sin only as the loss of the gift of original righteousness is unconvincing.

92 See the annotation of Bentley, 334.

will" are "blind and froward" respectively;[93] and Stephen Charnock
speaks of human nature's "darkened wisdom" and "enslaved will."[94]
Similarly Johannes Wollebius writes that "the intellect ... is beclouded,"
while "the will ... has lost its rectitude."[95] Arminianism followed Reformed orthodoxy in this respect, also denying that fallen human beings can either "think" (*cogitare*) or "will" (*velle*) anything good,[96] since
sin both "darken[s] our Minds" and "pervert[s] our Wills."[97] This emphasis on the corruption of both reason and will was an expression of
the totality of corruption: "Sin hath made its sickly impressions in
every faculty."[98] The Reformed orthodox concept of total depravity
(*corruptio totalis*) was a statement not of the absoluteness of human corruption—as though human beings were as sinful as they could be—but
of its pervasiveness throughout "the whole man."[99] Calvin had asserted
that "the whole person" is "so deluged, as it were, that no part remains
exempt from sin";[100] and William Perkins speaks similarly of "the
whole body and soule" as corrupted by original sin.[101] In the same way,
in *Paradise Lost* Adam claims that original sin will cause both the "Mind
and Will" of his descendents to be "deprav'd." Because of the fall, human reason is darkened, and the will is condemned to follow the evil
will of Adam, and "to will the same." Human nature has, as Michael
later says, been subjected to a "natural pravitie" (12.288).[102]

---

93 Theodore Beza, *A booke of Christian questions and answers, wherein are set foorth the cheef
    points of the Christian religion* (London, 1572), 27.
94 Stephen Charnock, *The Works of Stephen Charnock*, 5 vols. (Edinburgh, 1864–66),
    3:169.
95 Wollebius, *Compendium theologiae christianae*, 1.10.1.
96 *Articuli Arminiani sive remonstrantia*, 3; in Schaff, 3:546–47.
97 Episcopius, *The confession or declaration*, 121.
98 Charnock, *The Works of Stephen Charnock*, 3:171.
99 Ames, *The substance of Christian religion*, 15.
100 John Calvin, *Institutes of the Christian Religion*, trans. Henry Beveridge, 2 vols. (Grand
    Rapids: Eerdmans, 1989), 2.1.9.
101 William Perkins, *An exposition of the symbole or creed of the apostles* (Cambridge, 1595),
    112.
102 Commenting on this line, William J. Grace, *Ideas in Milton* (Notre Dame: University
    of Notre Dame Press, 1968), 5, suggests that "Michael here speaks as a straightfor-
    ward Calvinist." Although this expression is incautious, it is clearly not without
    some justification. In contrast, it is less justified when Edward Wagenknecht, *The
    Personality of Milton* (Normon: University of Oklahoma Press, 1970), 141, speaks
    simply of Milton's "rejection of total depravity." Basil Willey, *The Seventeenth Centu-
    ry Background: Studies in the Thought of the Age in Relation to Poetry and Religion* (Lon-
    don: Chatto & Windus, 1957), 241, rightly suggests that "Milton stands half-way
    between those who ... hold the utter depravity of the natural man, and those who ...
    believe unreservedly in his goodness."

But human nature is not only thoroughly corrupt in the theology of *Paradise Lost*; it is also, and more importantly, radically enslaved. After insisting that the unfallen Adam and Eve are "free to fall" (3.99), God the Father says: "I formd them free, and free they must remain, / Till they enthrall themselves" (3.124–25). This concise statement indicates the profound effect of the fall on human freedom. The freedom in which prelapsarian Adam and Eve were created is qualified by the preposition—"Till." Freedom, according to God, is not necessarily a permanent feature of human nature. It can be compromised by human beings themselves. Adam and Eve are to remain free only "Till" they "enthrall themselves." As elsewhere in *Paradise Lost*, "enthrall" does not denote a pleasing, merely figurative captivity; rather the word is used with full literal force: "To reduce to the condition of a thrall; ... to enslave, bring into bondage."[103] In the sixteenth century, Edwin Sandys had described the fallen will as being "in such thraldom and slavery unto sin, that it cannot like of any thing spiritual and heavenly";[104] and Reformed divines like William Prynne and John Owen speak in the same way of the will's "cursed thraldome,"[105] asserting that the fallen will "is corrupted, enthralled, and under a miserable bondage," to such an extent that human beings "can doe nothing but sinne."[106] So too, *Paradise Lost* refers to this kind of enslavement of the will (*servo arbitrio*) when it describes human nature as "forfeit and enthralld / By sin" (3.176–77).

According to Michael, human freedom—defined as right reason—is negated and lost through sin:

> Since thy original lapse, true Libertie
> Is lost, which alwayes with right Reason dwells
> Twinnd, and from her hath no dividual being:
> Reason in man obscur'd, or not obeyd,
> Immediatly inordinate desires
> And upstart Passions catch the Government

---

103 *OED* 1.

104 Edwin Sandys, *The Sermons of Edwin Sandys*, ed. John Ayre (Cambridge, 1841), 21.

105 William Prynne, *God, no impostor, nor deluder: or, An answer to a Popish and Arminian cavill, in the defence of free-will, and universall grace* (London, 1630), 24.

106 John Owen, *Theomachia autexousiastike: or, A display of Arminianisme, being a discovery of the old Pelagian idol free-will, with the new goddesse contingency* (London, 1643), 139. This view of the will's depravity did not, however, entail the negation of the will's volitional character, but only its inability to perform spiritually good choices. See James Ussher, *An answer to a challenge made by a Iesuite in Ireland* (London, 1631), 515–16: "And now since the Fall of *Adam* wee say ... that freedome of Will remayneth still among men; but the abilitie which once it had, to performe spirituall duties and things pertayning to salvation, is quite lost and extinguished."

> From Reason, and to servitude reduce
> Man till then free. (12.83–90)

The "true Libertie" of the created human nature is now "lost." The will
is no longer governed by "right Reason," but by the desires and passions of sin. After the fall, "Understanding rul'd not, and the Will /
Heard not her lore" (9.1127–28). The primacy of right reason is thus
lost. Human nature is reduced to an internal "servitude" — it is enslaved not to any outward necessitating force, but to itself. In the words
of Luther, human nature is "curved in upon itself" (*incurvatus in se*),[107]
enslaved by its own inclination to sin, and lacking the power to transcend and so to escape the enslaving self.[108] Here Abdiel's words to
Satan also offer a fitting description of human enslavement: "Thy self
not free, but to thy self enthralld" (6.181). Enthralled to itself, human
nature has "lost" its power of contingent choice; the will is no longer
poised indifferently between good and evil, but it is radically and ines-
capably inclined to evil. Michael adds that this theological form of unfreedom is the source of all forms of political tyranny:

> Therefore since hee permits
> Within himself unworthie Powers to reign
> Over free Reason, God in Judgement just
> Subjects him from without to violent Lords;
> Who oft as undeservedly enthrall
> His outward freedom: Tyrannie must be,
> Though to the Tyrant thereby no excuse. (12.90–96)

Significantly, the enslavement of the human will is depicted here as
purely self-caused: "hee permits" sin to reign "Within himself" (12.90–
91). The loss of "outward freedom" through political tyranny is simply
a consequence of this self-caused loss of inward liberty.

The most important feature of human beings' enslavement to sin is
their lack of power to seek or even to desire the grace of God. According to the Son of God, grace can come to human beings only "unimplor'd" and "unsought" (3.231):

> Happie for Man, so coming; hee her aide
> Can never seek, once dead in sins and lost;

---

107 Luther often uses the expression: it is, for example, repeated throughout his lectures
on Romans. See *Luther's Works*, ed. J. Pelikan and H. T. Lehmann, 55 vols. (St Louis
and Philadelphia: Concordia and Fortress, 1958–86), 25:245, 291, 345, 351.

108 Thus Sherry, "Speech in *Paradise Lost*," 259, notes the connection between the solilo-
quies of Adam and Eve and the way in which these fallen characters "turn away
from each other and from God into themselves."

> Attonement for himself or offering meet,
> Indebted and undon, hath none to bring. (3.232–35)

Fallen human beings "Can never seek" the grace of salvation, for they are utterly "undon" in their fallenness, even to the extent of being "dead in sins." The metaphor of spiritual death was widely employed in post-Reformation theology as a profound expression of both the pervasive corruption and the sheer helplessness of the human condition. This "deadness" metaphor was especially asserted in polemic against Roman Catholic theology, which took offence at the Reformation idea of humanity's total helplessness. Against Luther, Erasmus of Rotterdam had written that "although the freedom of the will has been wounded by sin, it is not dead; and although it has been lamed, so that we are more inclined to evil than to good before we receive grace, it has not been destroyed."[109]

In contrast, post-Reformation Reformed theologians speak unequivocally—as does *Paradise Lost*—of human nature as "dead in sins." William Perkins, for example, describes the fallen will as "not onely sicke and weake, but even starke dead";[110] and John Downham claims that human nature "is not only decayed, and in part hurt and wounded by the fall of *Adam*, but utterly dead in sinne."[111] Likewise William Ames depicts human nature as "altogether drowned in sin and death."[112] This metaphor of death illustrates the extent of the human will's unfreedom: it no more possesses the power to turn to God than a corpse possesses the power to lift itself from the tomb.[113] The human will, enslaved to sin, is thus utterly helpless. This point was affirmed with equal emphasis by Arminian writers.[114] Episcopius, for instance,

---

109 Desiderius Erasmus, *Collected Works of Erasmus*, 86 vols. (Toronto: University of Toronto Press, 1974–93), 76:26–27.

110 William Perkins, *The workes of that famous and worthie minister of Christ, in the Universitie of Cambridge, M. W. Perkins*, 3 vols. (Cambridge, 1608–9), 1:552.

111 Downham, *The summe of sacred divinitie*, 240.

112 Ames, *The substance of Christian religion*, 14.

113 This was a common analogy in Reformed orthodox theology. See for instance Pierre du Moulin, *The anatomy of Arminianisme* (London, 1620), 302: "as the Carkasse cannot dispose nor prepare it selfe to the resurrection... So man in the state of sinne, and before his regeneration, hath nothing whereby he may dispose himselfe, or further his regeneration and spirituall new birth."

114 This aspect of post-Reformation Arminianism has frequently been misunderstood. Even a leading historian like Christopher Hill has perpetuated a caricatured view of Arminianism's theology of the fallen will. See Christopher Hill, "From Lollards to Levellers," in *Rebels and Their Causes: Essays in Honour of A. L. Morton*, ed. Maurice Cornforth (London: Lawrence & Wishart, 1978), 58, where Arminianism is defined as "the doctrine that men may save themselves by their own efforts." In contrast, the statement of the eighteenth-century Arminian John Wesley, *The question, what is an*

speaks of the "servitude of sin,"[115] and argues that "we can neither shake off the miserable Yoak of Sin, nor do any thing truly good."[116] Similarly Arminius writes that the human will "is not free from the first fall,"[117] for it is "not only wounded, maimed, infirm, bent, and weakened; but ... also imprisoned, destroyed, and lost."[118] The fallen will is thus an impotent "slave."[119] In affirming that the human will is "enthralled" and "dead in sin," *Paradise Lost*'s theology thus stands in continuity with the Reformation theology of sin that was affirmed by Reformed orthodoxy and Arminianism alike; and it has little in common with the radical theology of an Anabaptist like Balthasar Hubmaier, who had condemned Luther's view of the fallen will as "rubbish,"[120] claiming instead that human nature "has remained utterly upright and intact before, during and after the Fall";[121] or with Socinian theology, which insisted that "the nature of man is by no means so depraved as that he is deprived of the liberty and power of obeying or not obeying God."[122]

The distinctive emphasis in *Paradise Lost* is, however, not so much on the enslavement of human nature as such, but on the self-enslaving power of human choice. Far from being mere victims of sin, Adam and Eve actively "enthrall themselves" (3.125). The enslavement of their wills is therefore not simply a negation of their freedom, but a striking expression of it: Adam and Eve are so free that they can even relinquish and negate their own freedom. This paradox had already been stated by Augustine: "it was by the bad use of free will that man destroyed both it and himself."[123] Freedom is lost through freedom. The twentieth-century theologian Emil Brunner expresses this paradox with a striking analogy: "Like someone who has shrieked too loudly and has lost his voice, so we have been boastful in our freedom, and now free-

---

Arminian? answered (Bristol, 1770), 5, is hyperbolic but closer to the truth: "No man that ever lived, not *John Calvin* himself, ever asserted ... Original Sin ... in more strong, more clear and express terms, than *Arminius* has done."

115 Episcopius, *The confession or declaration*, 123.

116 Episcopius, *The confession or declaration*, 127.

117 Arminius, *Works*, 2:194.

118 Arminius, *Works*, 2:192.

119 Arminius, *Works*, 2:192–94.

120 Balthasar Hubmaier, *On Free Will*, in *Spiritual and Anabaptist Writers: Documents Illustrative of the Radical Reformation*, ed. G. H. Williams (London: SCM, 1957), 131.

121 Hubmaier, *On Free Will*, 120.

122 *Racovian Catechism*, 10.

123 Augustine, *Enchiridion de fide, spe et charitate*, 30; in *PL* 40 and *NPNF* 3.

dom ... has been lost."[124] And with a different analogy, William Ames describes sin as "a bargain, in which the sinner for the enjoyment or use of some short pleasure, out of a madnesse sells himself into slavery."[125] In the same way, Adam and Eve freely abdicate their freedom in *Paradise Lost*. They have shrieked too loudly and lost their voice. They have "chosen to have no choice."[126]

Further, this choice to have no choice is not simply a once-for-all act that takes place at the moment of the fall; it is a continuing act, in which the human will consistently and "freely" chooses its own enslavement. In the words of Thomas Watson, human beings are slaves who "willingly obey" the "Tyrant" that rules over them. They are "willing to be Slaves, they will not take their Freedom; they kiss their Fetters."[127] In the same way, William Ames writes that, although fallen human beings "serve a most miserable servitude ... to sin," they do not desire to "shake off this slavish yoke," since "their very will it selfe, and the spirit of their minde is possessed by this slavery."[128] Augustine had made this point when he insisted that in spite of its enslavement to sin, the fallen will is "freely enslaved."[129] So too, in *Paradise Lost*, the will that enslaves itself is freely enslaved; it continues to choose as if it were free, even though it has in fact lost the liberty of indifference and the governance of right reason. Such a will is, in the words of Calvin, "a voluntary slave."[130]

In this chapter I have argued that, in continuity with the anti-Calvinist polemics of Arminian theology, *Paradise Lost* consistently repudiates necessitarian views of human freedom. In the poem, as in Arminianism, authentic freedom and moral responsibility are considered to be impossible without alternativity of choice. So in *Paradise Lost* human freedom is portrayed in Arminian terms as a liberty of indifference, in which the will is poised between alternative possibilities, possessing the power to determine its own course, and guided by "right reason," which enables it to judge well and to prefer what is good. All the

---

124 Emil Brunner, *Man in Revolt: A Christian Anthropology*, trans. Olive Wyon (London: Lutterworth, 1939), 135.
125 Ames, *The substance of Christian religion*, 29.
126 C. S. Lewis, *A Preface to Paradise Lost* (London: Oxford University Press, 1942), 102. Lewis is referring here to Satan, but his comment is also apt as a description of the fallen human condition.
127 Watson, *A body of practical divinity*, 86.
128 Ames, *The substance of Christian religion*, 25–26.
129 Augustine, *Enchiridion*, 30.
130 Calvin, *Institutes*, 2.2.7.

choices of Adam and Eve in the events leading up to the fall are therefore contingent choices, and the fall is possible only because of Adam's and Eve's freedom of alternative choice. Not being necessitated by anything, the fall is itself brought about purely by the freely willed and self-determined decisions of human beings. Having an abundant range of freedoms, the first human beings freely choose to fall.

But in the poem the act of falling is viewed as both an expression and a negation of freedom. In this respect, the theology of *Paradise Lost* stands in close continuity with the Reformed orthodox conception of original sin as total depravity. While the unfallen will is characterised by a rich abundance of alternative possibilities and by the power to choose and to actualise such possibilities, the fallen will, in contrast, is characterised by a restricted narrowness: a radical loss of alternative possibilities. Human nature has become slavishly turned in upon itself, and its horizons have in this way been drastically narrowed and restricted. Such a corrupted human nature cannot raise itself from itself; it cannot transcend itself in order to grasp again the genuine freedom that consists in abundant alternative possibilities. Such an enslaved will must, in other words, be liberated — it must be set free from itself in order to receive anew the power of freedom.[131]

As I will argue in the following chapter, *Paradise Lost*'s account of universal, liberating grace constitutes a dramatic theological qualification of its depiction of the corrupting power of original sin. Left to itself, fallen human nature can only be corrupt and enslaved. But it has not been left to itself: the same humanity that has been ruined by Adam has also been "Restore[d]" by "one greater Man" (1.4–5). It has been liberated by grace, and granted the fresh possibility of receiving the gift of salvation through the Son of God.

---

131 See the parallel statement of Arminius, *Works*, 2:157: "With these evils [all people] would remain oppressed for ever, unless they were liberated by Christ Jesus; to whom be glory for ever."

6. Grace, Conversion and Freedom

According to Sir Walter Raleigh, *Paradise Lost*'s entire plot "radiates" from a single point: the moment when Eve plucks and eats the forbidden fruit. Referring to this moment, Raleigh remarks that "there is not an incident, hardly a line of the poem, but leads backwards or forwards to those central lines in the Ninth Book."[1] In this influential reading, subsequently adopted by James Holly Hanford and, initially, by E. M. W. Tillyard,[2] the moment of the fall tended to eclipse other significant themes in the epic, such as obedience, restoration and grace. Accepting Raleigh's claim that the epic action centres on the single episode of the fall, A. J. A. Waldock was able to offer a devastating critique of the entire poem by arguing that this episode ultimately fails.[3] The force of Waldock's argument led to a substantial defection from Raleigh's theory. In "The Crisis of *Paradise Lost*," still one of the most important studies of the poem's portrayal of conversion, Tillyard repudiated his earlier position and argued instead for an "adjustment of balance,"[4] in which "the centre of importance should be shifted to [Adam's and Eve's] regenerate action after the Fall."[5] By thus raising the conversion scene to a place of eminence within the epic narrative, Tillyard also attempted to compensate for the comparative neglect of this part of the poem, and several scholars have followed him in recognising the crucial significance of this scene in *Paradise Lost*. G. A. Wilkes, for example, identifies its importance within the context of the poem's theodicy, arguing that the conversion of Adam and Eve exhibits "the operation of Providence in bringing forth good from evil."[6] C. A. Patrides suggests

---

1 Walter Raleigh, *Milton* (London, 1900), 81–82.
2 See James Holly Hanford, *A Milton Handbook* (New York: Appleton, 1961), 213; and E. M. W. Tillyard, *Milton* (London: Chatto & Windus, 1930), 245–49.
3 A. J. A. Waldock, *"Paradise Lost" and Its Critics* (Cambridge: Cambridge University Press, 1947), 25–64.
4 E. M. W. Tillyard, *Studies in Milton* (London: Chatto & Windus, 1951), 51.
5 Tillyard, *Studies in Milton*, 45.
6 G. A. Wilkes, *The Thesis of Paradise Lost* (Melbourne: Melbourne University Press, 1961), 35–36. In a similar way, John T. Shawcross, *With Mortal Voice: The Creation of Paradise Lost* (Lexington: University Press of Kentucky, 1982), 24–25, argues that the heavenly colloquy in Book 3 is the poem's climax, and that this climax highlights the providence of God in providing salvation even before the need for it exists.

that the conversion of Adam and Eve is "one of the most important though least understood incidents in *Paradise Lost*,"[7] and Robert Crosman speaks of the closing lines of Book 10, where Eve and Adam water the ground with penitent tears, as "perhaps the greatest moment of Milton's poem."[8]

The theological significance of the conversion scene, however, remains often overlooked, especially by readers who view this scene as no more than a depiction of reconciliation between two estranged human beings. John Broadbent, for instance, argues that Eve and Adam simply "become plain wife and husband" in their penitence;[9] and according to Michael Wilding, "[w]hat finally emerges at the end of Book 10" is simply "human dignity."[10] Similarly, Tillyard misses the theological meaning of conversion entirely when he describes the scene as an account of "two ordinary human beings ... coming together in ordinary human decency."[11]

The stated aim of *Paradise Lost* is not, of course, to portray "ordinary human decency," but to demonstrate the triumph of the goodness of God over evil. This demonstration of God's good providence rests in part on the fact that Adam and Eve are not left in their misery, but are restored by divine grace. The conversion scene can be fully understood only against the backdrop of the fall, and, correspondingly, the fall is seen in its proper light only when it is viewed in relation to the ensuing intervention of the grace of God. "Mans First Disobedience, and the Fruit / Of that Forbidd'n Tree" (1.1–2) have subjected human nature to a radical corruption. Human freedom has become enslaved to the tyrannical power of the sinful self. But the fall and the power of sin occupy centre stage in the poem only "*till* one greater Man / Restore us" (1.4–5; emphasis added). The gracious providence of God does not leave human nature in its fallen state, but brings forth good from evil by triumphing over the power of original sin and liberating the human will from its dark enthrallment. Roland Frye has rightly remarked that the whole of *Paradise Lost*, "as an assertion of eternal providence," is "far less concerned with the commission of sin than with the triumph

7   C. A. Patrides, *Milton and the Christian Tradition* (Oxford: Clarendon, 1966), 210.

8   Robert Crosman, *Reading Paradise Lost* (Bloomington: Indiana University Press, 1980), 204.

9   John B. Broadbent, *Some Graver Subject: An Essay on Paradise Lost* (London: Chatto & Windus, 1960), 266.

10   Michael Wilding, *Milton's Paradise Lost* (Sydney: Sydney University Press, 1969), 107.

11   Tillyard, *Studies in Milton*, 43.

of grace."[12] Indeed, within the narrative of *Paradise Lost*, the destructive power of the fall is subsumed under the overarching framework of the providence of God, which works to bring good from evil by showing grace and mercy to the fallen human race. The fall of Adam and Eve is not the final word, for "over wrauth Grace shall abound" (12.478), so that God's "Mercy first and last shall brightest shine" (3.134).

Universal Prevenient Grace

The close of Book 10 in *Paradise Lost* finds Adam and Eve confessing their sins, begging for divine pardon, and "with tears / Watering the ground" (10.1101–2). Patrides has drawn attention to the "unexpectedness and uncharacteristic nature of this incident,"[13] and Joseph Summers similarly notes that we know of "no reason, no set of natural circumstances whereby we could predict or expect that love could be rekindled after such abusive lust and such hatred, that life could again be welcomed after such despair."[14] The fact that Eve and Adam become penitent at all, after all that has taken place, bears witness to the intervention of the grace of God. And as Book 11 opens, the narrative voice explains that their repentance is due to the influence of that grace:

> Thus they in lowliest plight repentant stood
> Praying, for from the Mercie-seat above
> Prevenient Grace descending had remov'd
> The stonie from thir hearts, and made new flesh
> Regenerat grow instead, that sighs now breath'd
> Unutterable, which the Spirit of prayer
> Inspir'd. (11.1–7)

Here the narrative voice describes the conversion of Adam and Eve with richly allusive biblical and theological language. Reference to the theological concept of "Prevenient Grace" (*gratia praeveniens*) is especially important, since this concept is central to the theology of conversion in *Paradise Lost*, and was also a central feature of the major post-Reformation controversies regarding grace and conversion.

---

12 Roland M. Frye, *God, Man, and Satan: Patterns of Christian Thought and Life in Paradise Lost, Pilgrim's Progress, and the Great Theologians* (Princeton: Princeton University Press, 1960), 70.

13 Patrides, *Milton and the Christian Tradition*, 210.

14 Joseph H. Summers, *The Muse's Method: An Introduction to Paradise Lost* (London: Chatto & Windus, 1962), 108.

Following Augustine,[15] medieval theology distinguished between exciting, operating and prevenient grace on the one hand, and assisting, cooperating and subsequent grace on the other. For writers like Anselm, Bernard of Clairvaux and Thomas Aquinas, prevenient grace was understood to be a divine work that prepares human beings for the subsequent grace of justification, without including any element of human cooperation.[16] According to Duns Scotus, William of Ockham and Gabriel Biel, on the other hand, fallen human beings retain the ability to prepare themselves for the subsequent bestowal of grace.[17] The former position was taken up by the Protestant reformers, who affirmed that the will remains entirely passive in its initial conversion by prevenient grace. Thus Calvin writes that the fallen will is "converted solely by the power of God" through "prevenient grace,"[18] and that the will itself possesses not even "the minutest ability" to cooperate with grace, until it has already been "wholly transformed and renovated."[19] Reacting against this Protestant position, counter-Reformation Catholic theology anathematised the idea "that man's free will, when moved and excited by God, gives no cooperation by assenting to God's exciting and calling," and that the will cannot in any way "dispose and prepare itself" for salvation.[20] In this counter-Reformation view, then, prevenient grace alone does not prepare human beings for salvation, but it aids and enables them to prepare themselves.[21]

In the seventeenth century, the concept of prevenient grace was at the heart of the divergence of Arminian theology from Reformed orthodoxy. A focal point of the controversy between the two theological traditions was the question whether the mode of conversion is resistible or irresistible. This question was, according to Francis Turretin, "the principle hinge of the controversy" between Reformed orthodoxy and Arminianism,[22] and Arminius himself claimed that "the whole contro-

---

15   See Augustine, *De gratia et libero arbitrio*, 33; in *PL* 44 and *NPNF* 5.

16   See for example Bernard of Clairvaux, *De gratia et libero arbitrio*, 14.46–47; in *PL* 182.

17   On the different medieval views of prevenient grace, see Heiko A. Oberman, *Forerunners of the Reformation: The Shape of Late Medieval Thought* (Philadelphia: Fortress, 1981), 123–41.

18   John Calvin *Institutes of the Christian Religion*, trans. Henry Beveridge, 2 vols. (Grand Rapids: Eerdmans, 1989), 2.3.7.

19   Calvin, *Institutes*, 2.3.6.

20   *Canones et decreta Concilii Tridentini*, 6.4; in Tanner, 2:679.

21   For an important early Protestant critique of the counter-Reformation view of prevenient grace, see Martin Chemnitz, *Examination of the Council of Trent*, trans. Fred Kramer, 4 vols. (St Louis: Concordia, 1986), 1:553–64.

22   Francis Turretin, *Institutes of Elenctic Theology*, ed. James T. Dennison, trans. George Musgrave Giger, 3 vols. (Phillipsburg: P&R, 1992–97), 15.6.1.

versy" concerning grace "reduces itself to the solution of this question, 'Is the grace of God a certain, irresistible force?'"[23] The Reformed orthodox concept of irresistible grace (*gratia irresistiblis*) affirmed both the infallible efficacy of grace and the passivity of the human will in the first moment of conversion. The human will is rendered passive by its total depravity (*corruptio totalis*); therefore "those who attribute to unredeemed man either a free will or powers by which he might do good or prepare himself for conversion and God's grace, are seeking a house in ashes."[24] Since human beings cannot prepare themselves for conversion, they are simply "overpower[ed]"[25] by the grace of God, and "invincibly" and irresistibly converted;[26] and "at the first moment" of such conversion the human will remains "in a purely passive state."[27] Indeed, "man is as passive in his Regeneration, as in his first generation."[28] For Reformed orthodoxy, then, prevenient grace is the grace that irresistibly converts the elect without any human cooperation. In contrast to this Reformed view, the Arminian concept of resistible grace (*gratia resistibilis*) affirmed both the universality of grace and the role of the human will in cooperating with it. In Arminian theology, the beginning of conversion is effected by a cooperation between divine grace and the human will. The influence of prevenient grace enables the fallen will to cooperate with grace, and so to be converted.[29] This prevenient grace is thus universally bestowed, but it "does not [always] obtain its effect"; fallen human beings retain "freedom of will, and a capability of resisting the Holy Spirit, of rejecting the proffered grace of God."[30] In short, for Arminianism the initial influence of prevenient grace is only a

---

23 Jacobus Arminius, *The Works of James Arminius*, trans. James Nichols and William Nichols, 3 vols. (Grand Rapids: Baker, 1986), 1:664. Historians of theology like James Orr and B. B. Warfield emphasise the centrality of the idea of irresistible grace to the whole theological system of Reformed orthodoxy. See James Orr, *The Progress of Dogma* (London, 1901), 299; and B. B. Warfield, *Calvin and Calvinism* (New York: Oxford University Press, 1931), 359: "What lies at the heart of [Reformed] soteriology is the absolute exclusion of the creaturely element in the initiation of the saving process."

24 Johannes Wollebius, *Compendium theologiae christianae*; in *Reformed Dogmatics*, ed. and trans. John W. Beardslee (Oxford: Oxford University Press, 1965), 1.10.1.

25 John Lightfoot, *The works of the reverend and learned John Lightfoot, D.D.*, 2 vols. (London, 1684), 1:1291.

26 Stephen Charnock, *The Existence and Attributes of God* (London, 1797), 419–20.

27 Bartholomaeus Keckermann, *Systema sacrosanctae theologiae* (Heidelberg, 1602), 263–64; cited in Heppe, 520.

28 John Cotton, *The new covenant* (London, 1654), 55.

29 For a useful discussion of the Arminian view of prevenient grace, see H. O. Wiley, *Christian Theology*, 3 vols. (Kansas City: Beacon Hill, 1940–43), 2:352–57.

30 Arminius, *Works*, 2:721–22.

necessary condition for conversion, while for Reformed orthodoxy the initial influence of grace is a *sufficient* condition for conversion.

When the narrative voice in *Paradise Lost* speaks of "Prevenient Grace," it thus evokes this complex history of theological controversy. The term "Prevenient Grace" can denote such a range of theological and polemical positions that *Paradise Lost*'s view of this concept needs to be explored in some detail.

The poem's concept of prevenient grace is, in the first place, sharply discontinuous with the Roman Catholic view that the human heart is able to prepare (or "prevent") itself for salvation. Addressing the Father in Book 3, the Son of God says:

> Man shall find Grace;
> And shall Grace not find means, that finds her way,
> The speediest of thy winged messengers,
> To visit all thy creatures, and to all
> Comes unprevented, unimplor'd, unsought,
> Happie for Man, so coming; hee her aide
> Can never seek, once dead in sins and lost. (3.227–33)

The Son's theological emphasis here is both on the inability of the human will to turn to God, and, correspondingly, on the sheer initiative of God's turning to humanity in grace. The fallen human beings who, through the enslavement of their wills, could not even "seek" the aid of grace, will now become the recipients of it. Grace is thus described as "unprevented"—literally, "not prepared for,"[31] signifying that fallen human beings who are "dead in sins" cannot in any way prepare themselves for salvation. In this respect *Paradise Lost* sides with the common Reformed orthodox polemic[32] against the Roman Catholic doctrine of prevenient grace, as expressed by the Council of Trent.[33] Further, the poem's denial of a human preparation for conversion (*preparatio ad conversionem*) also contrasts with the form of preparationism that be-

---

31   In his annotation, Bentley fails to realise that "prevented" is a theological term, and he thus writes: "How *Unprevented* can stand here, does not appear; unless in this Meaning, *comes unimplor'd, if not prevented*. But that would diminish the gracious favour, set forth here" (Bentley, 86). On the contrary, the meaning of "unprevented" highlights the gratuitousness of grace.

32   For an example of Reformed orthodox polemic against the Roman Catholic position, see Jeremias Bastingius, *An exposition or commentarie upon the Catechisme of Christian Religion* (Cambridge, 1589), 8: "Therefore this errour of the schoolemen is to be corrected, who thinke that men are able ... to doe good works of preparation, that is such as goe before the grace of God in us, and yet that they deserve grace of congruitie, as they barbarouslie speake."

33   *Canones et decreta Concilii Tridentini*, 6.5–6; in Tanner, 2:672–73.

came prominent among many Puritans in England and New England.[34] According to Thomas Hooker, for example, "when the heart is fitted and prepared, the Lord Jesus comes immediately into it";[35] and John Cotton writes that "if we smooth the way for Him, then He will come into our hearts."[36] In affirming that preparation is solely a work of God, the theology of *Paradise Lost* is closer to the Reformed orthodox theology of Richard Sibbes, who insists that all "preparations themselves are of God,"[37] and of the Westminster Confession, which asserts that "natural man, being ... dead in sin, is not able, by his own strength, to convert himself, or to prepare himself thereunto."[38] In *Paradise Lost*, the beginning of conversion thus arises solely from the initiative of God's grace, and not from any self-preparation of the human heart. Grace, in other words, "Comes unprevented" precisely because it is itself prevenient.

The Son of God therefore points out that it is "Happie for Man" that grace comes unprevented, since "hee her aide / Can never seek, once dead in sins and lost" (3.232–33). Grace cannot be prepared for or even sought by human beings in their fallen state, so that even the seeking of grace must already be a response to grace. As Luther had said, "this very wishing and asking, seeking or knocking, is the gift of prevenient grace, not of our eliciting will."[39] In contrast to any notion of self-preparation, the Son's affirmation that "Man shall find Grace" is thus a statement of the initiative of grace, in continuity with Reformation theology.

On the other hand, *Paradise Lost*'s theology of prevenient grace departs from the Reformation and Reformed view of particular and irresistible grace. According to Reformed orthodoxy, divine grace comes only to the particular number of elect individuals who have been chosen out of the corrupt mass (*corrupta massa*). But in *Paradise Lost*, the triumph of grace over sin is given expression in the universality of

---

34 On the development of Puritan preparationism, see R. T. Kendall, *Calvin and English Calvinism to 1649* (Oxford: Oxford University Press, 1979); Bernhard Citron, *New Birth: A Study of the Evangelical Doctrine of Conversion in the Protestant Fathers* (Edinburgh: Edinburgh University Press, 1951), 53–59; and Norman Pettit, *The Heart Prepared: Grace and Conversion in Puritan Spiritual Life* (New Haven: Yale University Press, 1966).

35 Thomas Hooker, *The soules humiliation* (London, 1638), 170.

36 John Cotton, *Christ the fountaine of life* (London, 1651), 40–41.

37 Richard Sibbes, *The Complete Works of Richard Sibbes*, 7 vols. (Edinburgh, 1862–64), 6:522.

38 Westminster Confession of Faith, 9.3; in Schaff, 3:623.

39 Martin Luther, *Luther's Works*, ed. J. Pelikan and H. T. Lehmann, 55 vols. (St Louis and Philadelphia: Concordia and Fortress, 1958–86), 29:125.

grace: grace comes "to all" (3.230), and God is "Merciful over all his works, with good / Still overcoming evil" (12.565–66).

The universality of grace was a particularly pronounced theme among Arminian and Amyraldian theologians in the seventeenth century. According to Amyraldian theology, the grace of salvation is "universal and common to all men," but this grace becomes effective only if human beings fulfil the condition of responding to Christ in faith—and only the elect members of the human race can in fact fulfil this condition.[40] In Amyraldian theology, then, the universalism of grace is no more than a "hypothetical universalism." In principle, God is gracious to all, but in reality his grace is received only by those for whom it has been specially predestined. Arminianism, in contrast, affirmed God's "serious intention to save all":[41] the gift of "Sufficient Grace" is "given to all Men" and "denied to none."[42] According to *Paradise Lost*'s theology, too, the grace of God is in the fullest sense *universal* grace (*gratia universalis*)—it is, as in Arminianism, not merely for all "diverse sorts" of people in general,[43] but "for each and every person" (*pro omnibus et singulis hominibus*).[44] It is the gift of God to all those human beings who have been corrupted and enslaved through the fall.

In the passage already quoted (3.227–33), the Son highlights God's readiness to be gracious to his creatures, describing grace as the "speediest" of God's angels. To recall Sonnet XIX, of the "Thousands" who "speed" at God's bidding, grace is quickest. And this divine eagerness to save has as its object not merely the elect, but "all [God's] creatures." Grace is thus universal: it "visit[s]" and "Comes" to all those who through the fall are "dead in sins and lost." This universal grace is the direct antithesis of the universal corruption of original sin, and of Satan's plan to "Draw after him the whole Race of mankind" (3.161). Through the work of redemption, God will "save ... the whole

---

40 Moïse Amyraut, *Brief traitté de la predestination et de ses principales dependances* (Saumur, 1634), 89–90, 163.

41 Simon Episcopius, *The confession or declaration of the ministers or pastors which in the United Provinces are called Remonstrants, concerning the chief points of Christian religion* (London, 1676), 201.

42 Francis Gordon, *An essay upon predestination and grace* (Edinburgh, 1712), 33, 35.

43 According to Reformed orthodox interpretation, God is gracious to all kinds of people, but not to each individual member of the human race. See for example Pierre du Moulin, *The anatomy of Arminianisme* (London, 1620), 248, who denies that "all" means "all ... particular men"; Sebastian Benfield, *Eight sermons publikely preached in the University of Oxford* (Oxford, 1614), 4, who argues that "all" refers to "all sorts of particulars, not each particular of all sorts"; and George Abbot, *The reasons which Doctour Hill hath brought* (Oxford, 1604), 19, who writes: "all intendeth many, or diverse of diverse sorts, not universally every one."

44 *Articuli Arminiani sive remonstrantia*, 2; in Schaff, 3:546.

Race lost" (3.279–80). The prevenient grace of God is for all. It is, as Arminius says, a grace that arises "from [God's] general love towards all mankind."[45]

Further, according to *Paradise Lost* the effect of this prevenient grace is a universal liberation of humanity from the enslaving power of original sin. The liberty of indifference (*libertas indifferentiae*) that was lost in the fall is restored to all people through prevenient grace. As God the Father says of fallen humanity:

> once more I will renew
> His lapsed powers, though forfeit and enthralld
> By sin to foul exorbitant desires;
> Upheld by mee, yet once more he shall stand
> On even ground against his mortal foe,
> By mee upheld, that he may know how frail
> His fall'n condition is, and to mee ow
> All his deliv'rance, and to none but mee. (3.175–82)

Through sin, the "powers" of human nature have been lost and enslaved. But by his grace God "renew[s]" these "lapsed powers."[46] He restores the freedom that human beings have forfeited, and liberates the will that has become "enthralld." The act of God's grace is, then, one of radical renewal, in which the destructive effects of the fall are reversed and the lost freedom of human nature is restored.[47] Substantially the same position had been stated by Arminius, according to whom prevenient grace "raises up again those who are conquered and have fallen" and "establishes and supplies them with new strength."[48] The *De Doctrina Christiana*, too, places great emphasis on the universal liberation of fallen human beings through grace. According to the treatise, regenerating grace "restores a person's natural faculties of right judgment and free will,"[49] so that the "lost freedom of will"[50] is restored

---

45   Arminius, *Works*, 2:722.

46   For a similar use of terminology, see the Westminster Confession of Faith, 10.1; in Schaff, 3:624: the grace of regeneration involves a "renewing" of the "wills" of the elect.

47   Dennis R. Danielson, "The Fall and Milton's Theodicy," in *The Cambridge Companion to Milton*, ed. Dennis R. Danielson (Cambridge: Cambridge University Press, 1999), 156–57, rightly observes that "[a]lthough free will is impaired by the Fall," prevenient grace "enables the fallen will to turn to God."

48   Arminius, *Works*, 2:700.

49   *CPW* 6:461; *CM* 15:366.

50   *CPW* 6:187; *CM* 14:134.

"to its former liberty."[51] This is precisely the meaning of prevenient grace in *Paradise Lost*.

In the poem, the liberating act of God's grace grants to all human beings the ability "once more" to "stand / On even ground." The will's liberty of indifference, in which it stands "In even scale" (10.47), has been lost in the fall. Instead of standing poised between good and evil with an equal possibility of either choice, the will is now inclined to evil, governed not by right reason but by "foul exorbitant desires," and as such it is incapable of choosing the good. But this sinful and enslaving inclination of the will is countered and conquered by the grace of God. "[O]nce more" the human will is set free for the possibility of the good and the right, and is placed on the scales of indifferent choice. The Arminian theologian John Goodwin similarly writes that the grace of God enables human beings to decide "whether they will or no," giving them a possibility of willing salvation, but also "a possibility ... of nilling."[52] And in the same way Arminius regards prevenient grace as bringing about a restoration of the liberty of indifference, in which the individual becomes capable both of "freely assent[ing]" to grace and of freely "withholding his assent."[53] So too in *Paradise Lost*, prevenient grace places the human will's power of choice back on the balanced scales, so that the alternative decision between good and evil becomes an authentic possibility.

This liberating work of grace is not described in *Paradise Lost* as a purification of human nature or a transformation of the sinful will, but as an upholding of human freedom: the powers of human nature are "Upheld by mee ... By mee upheld" (3.178–80). Human beings retain their "fall'n condition," remaining sinfully "frail" (3.180–81). But in the midst of this frailty and fallenness they are "upheld" by the grace of God. The spatial metaphor here evokes the image of human creatures being suspended over the abyss by the hand of God. They are, in one sense, "fall'n," and at each moment their natural tendency is to continue falling; but they are simultaneously upheld and preserved from falling. Reformed orthodox theologians commonly used this image to describe God's providential conservation (*conservatio*) of created things. According to this Reformed view, the creation that came from nothing (*ex nihilo*) also possesses a natural tendency to return to nothingness; at each moment it must therefore be upheld by divine providence, and

---

51   *CPW* 6:462; *CM* 15:370.
52   John Goodwin, *The remedie of unreasonableness* (London, 1650), 8.
53   Arminius, *Works*, 2:722.

prevented from sinking back into the abyss of non-being.[54] As Thomas Boston writes, creaturely being "must be upheld by God as a ball in the air," or it would return to non-being as naturally as the ball falls to the ground.[55] And in the words of William Ames, "God *holds as it were in his hand* the creature, that it fall not back to ... nothing";[56] for "[e]very creature would return to that state of nothing whence it came if God did not uphold it."[57] Arminian theology also highlighted this aspect of God's providence, which seemed a simple corollary of the idea of creation *ex nihilo*. Thus Robert Leighton, for example, writes: "If we believe that all things were produced out of nothing, the consequence is, that, by the same powerful hand that created them, they must be preserved and supported to keep them from falling back into their primitive nothing."[58] In *Paradise Lost* the providence of God does not serve this ontological function, for in the poem's theology creaturely being is derived not from nothingness but from the primal matter of God's own being, so that it is the divine being itself, not nothingness, from which "All things proceed" and to which they tend to "return" (5.469–70). The image of the upholding of creaturely being is thus appropriated in *Paradise Lost* in the context of human freedom, instead of the context of human ontology. It is the *freedom* of human nature that is "upheld" by the grace of God. Human freedom since the fall has a natural tendency to evil, and it would necessarily fall towards evil except for the upholding grace of God. This grace returns the will to its primitive state of indifference; it preserves the will from its tendency to collapse into self-enslavement, and enables it "once more" to "stand / On even ground" with the self-determining power to choose between good and evil. In the words of the *De Doctrina Christiana*, God thus graciously "gives us the power to act freely, of which we have been incapable since the fall."[59]

Universal prevenient grace, then, is not a grace that secures salvation, but only a grace that secures the *possibility* of salvation through the restoration of human freedom. As Dennis Danielson observes, "God's

---

54 On the Reformed orthodox concept of *conservatio*, see Karl Barth, *Church Dogmatics*, ed. Geoffrey W. Bromiley and T. F. Torrance (Edinburgh: T&T Clark, 1956–77), III/3, 58–90; and G. C. Berkouwer, *The Providence of God*, trans. Lewis B. Smedes (Grand Rapids: Eerdmans, 1952), 50–82.

55 Thomas Boston, *Commentary on the Shorter Catechism*, 2 vols. (Aberdeen, 1853), 1:188.

56 William Ames, *The substance of Christian religion: or, A plain and easie draught of the Christian catechism* (London, 1659), 69.

57 William Ames, *The Marrow of Theology*, ed. and trans. John D. Eusden (Grand Rapids: Baker, 1968), 1.9.17.

58 Robert Leighton, *Theological Lectures* (London, 1821), 98–99.

59 *CPW* 6:457; *CM* 15:356.

grace explains how man's repentance is possible ... but does not finally account for the fact that it actually takes place."[60] Preserved from the enslaving power of original sin, the human will is upheld "on even ground," able to choose or to reject the offer of salvation. Continuing his account of his gracious plan for fallen humanity, God thus says:

> Some I have chosen of peculiar grace
> Elect above the rest; so is my will:
> The rest shall hear me call, and oft be warnd
> Thir sinful state, and to appease betimes
> Th' incensed Deitie, while offerd Grace
> Invites; for I will cleer thir senses dark,
> What may suffice, and soft'n stonie hearts
> To pray, repent, and bring obedience due.
> To prayer, repentance, and obedience due,
> Though but endevord with sincere intent,
> Mine eare shall not be slow, mine eye not shut. (3.183–93)

Because of prevenient grace, salvation is a universal possibility. God's "peculiar grace" specially singles out some individuals, but the divine "call" to salvation comes to all the "rest" of humanity. All are invited to respond to "offerd Grace." Even the conversion of Adam and Eve in *Paradise Lost* is a picture not of any work of "peculiar grace," but of a universal human possibility, a possibility that is created for all by the liberating power of the prevenient grace of God.

While some Reformed orthodox writers denied that grace is universally offered,[61] most affirmed that all people are, in some sense, invited to partake of salvation. Johannes Wollebius, for instance, writes that even "the reprobate" are "called in earnest, and salvation is offered to them on condition of faith."[62] But the Reformed understanding of total depravity meant that the "condition" of such a universal offer of salvation could not be met by any except the elect, who are regenerated by the "absolutely irresistible" grace of God.[63] In this Reformed view, then, the universal offer of salvation is reduced to a nominal offer which God himself knows cannot possibly be accepted except by the elect. In contrast, Arminian theology spoke of the same universal offer of salvation,

---

60 Dennis R. Danielson, *Milton's Good God: A Study in Literary Theodicy* (Cambridge: Cambridge University Press, 1982), 88.

61 See for example William Prynne, *God, no impostor, nor deluder: or, An answer to a Popish and Arminian cavill, in the defence of free-will, and universall grace* (London, 1630), 2–3, who argues that the proclamation of grace is only for the sake of the elect, and is "intended unto them alone."

62 Wollebius, *Compendium theologiae christianae*, 1.20.2.

63 Wollebius, *Compendium theologiae christianae*, 1.28.1.

but affirmed also that the operation of sufficient grace (*gratia sufficiens*) removes the effects of human sinfulness enough to enable all fallen individuals to accept this offer. As Simon Episcopius writes, God gives sinners grace "sufficient for their yielding Faith and Obedience, when he calleth them by the Gospel";[64] and, in the words of Arminius, all fallen human beings are "excited, impelled, drawn and assisted by grace," but their liberty of indifference means that "in the very moment in which they actually assent [to grace], they possess the capability of not assenting."[65] This Arminian view of sufficient grace stands in continuity with God's reference in *Paradise Lost* to the invitation of "offerd Grace." Indeed, the theologically crucial term in God's speech is "suffice": God graciously reverses the effects of original sin to an extent that is sufficient for the salvation of all people.

Thus while the human mind had been darkened and blinded by original sin, God now graciously "cleer[s]" the minds of all fallen human beings. And while the will had been enthralled by sin, the hearts of all fallen human beings are now "soft'n[ed]" by grace. These metaphors of the enlightening of the mind and the softening of the heart were frequently used by post-Reformation writers. Richard Baxter, for example, speaks of God's "taking the hard heart out of us, and giving hearts of flesh,"[66] while Arminius writes that "the hardness of [man's] stony heart" is "changed into the softness of flesh" in conversion;[67] and Johann Heinrich Heidegger writes that God "illumines the reason to conviction of the truth."[68] In Reformed orthodox theology, such descriptions of the enlightening of the mind and softening of the heart could refer only to regeneration itself.[69] But in *Paradise Lost*, as in Arminianism, it is precisely the unregenerate heart that is softened by grace, so that it can respond to the offer of salvation. And the response to the offer of salvation is "To pray, repent, and bring obedience due." When fallen human beings, liberated and enabled by grace, freely turn to God with such prayer, penitence and obedience, they become not merely recipients of universal grace, but partakers of salvation.

---

64 Episcopius, *The confession or declaration*, 201.

65 Arminius, *Works*, 2:722. For an example of Reformed orthodox polemic against the Arminian concept of sufficient grace, see du Moulin, *The anatomy of Arminianisme*, 358–422.

66 Richard Baxter, *Aphorismes of justification* (London, 1649), 8.

67 Arminius, *Works*, 2:194–95.

68 Johann Heinrich Heidegger, *Corpus theologiae* (Zurich, 1700), 21.27; cited in Heppe, 520.

69 See for example the Westminster Confession of Faith, 10.1; in Schaff, 3:624; and Wollebius, *Compendium theologiae christianae*, 1.28.1.

The Conversion of Adam and Eve

This concept of universal prevenient grace, which is explicated theologically in Book 3, is portrayed dramatically in the conversion of Adam and Eve in Books 10 and 11. When Adam and Eve stand praying at the opening of Book 11, the Son of God presents their prayers to the Father and intercedes on their behalf:

> See Father, what first fruits on Earth are sprung
> From thy implanted Grace in Man, these Sighs
> And Prayers, which in this Gold'n Censer, mixt
> With Incense, I thy Priest before thee bring,
> Fruits of more pleasing savour from thy seed
> Sown with contrition in his heart, then those
> Which his own hand manuring all the Trees
> Of Paradise could have produc't, ere fall'n
> From innocence. Now therefore bend thine eare
> To supplication, heare his sighs though mute;
> Unskilful with what words to pray, let mee
> Interpret for him, mee his Advocate
> And propitiation, all his works on mee
> Good or not good ingraft, my Merit those
> Shall perfet, and for these my Death shall pay.
> Accept me, and in mee from these receave
> The smell of peace toward Mankinde, let him live
> Before thee reconcil'd. (11.22–39)

This is a depiction of the Reformed orthodox understanding of the intercessory work of Christ, according to which the Son of God performs the "oblation of the persons of the redeemed, sanctifying their prayers, and all their services, rendering them acceptable to God, through the savour of his own merits."[70] In the words of Stephen Charnock, Christ is "our priest in the court of heaven," who "plead[s]" for human redemption, "both before the tribunal of justice and the throne of mercy."[71] Responding to this intercession, the Father grants the Son's request, and as a result Eve and Adam immediately become aware that their prayer for grace has been answered. They find "Strength added from above," and "new hope" that has sprung "Out of despaire" (11.138–39).

---

70   Charles Hodge, *Systematic Theology*, 3 vols. (Grand Rapids: Eerdmans, 1946), 2:593–94.

71   Stephen Charnock, *The Works of Stephen Charnock*, 5 vols. (Edinburgh, 1864–66), 5:101.

Beginning his speech, significantly, with a reference to faith, the newly regenerate Adam marvels at the efficacy of prayer:

> *Eve*, easily may Faith admit, that all
> The good which we enjoy, from Heav'n descends;
> But that from us aught should ascend to Heav'n
> So prevalent as to concerne the mind
> Of God high-blest, or to incline his will,
> Hard to belief may seem; yet this will Prayer,
> Or one short sigh of human breath, up-borne
> Ev'n to the Seat of God. For since I saught
> By Prayer th' offended Deitie to appease,
> Kneeld and before him humbl'd all my heart,
> Methought I saw him placable and mild,
> Bending his eare; perswasion in me grew
> That I was heard with favour; peace returnd
> Home to my brest, and to my memorie
> His promise, that thy Seed shall bruise our Foe;
> Which then not minded in dismay, yet now
> Assures me that the bitterness of death
> Is past, and we shall live. (11.141–58)

This devotional meditation on prayer, repentance and grace forms a striking contrast and complement to the preceding speech of the Son. Both speeches, as well as the opening comments of the narrative voice, contain a subtle interplay of echoed words and phrases, which serves to highlight the paradoxical unity of divine grace and human freedom in salvation.[72] Adam marvels that God responds to just "one short sigh of human breath" (11.147);[73] but it is in fact the Son who pleads for the Father to "heare his sighs though mute" (11.31). Adam speaks of his prayer ascending, being "up-borne" (11.147); but the narrative voice has said already that "Prevenient Grace descending" has enabled Adam's repentance (11.3), and that "the Spirit of prayer" has "Inspir'd" this repentance (11.6–7). Adam says that his prayer ascends "to the Seat of God" in order to obtain mercy (11.148); but the narrative voice has

---

72 Referring to the sequence of biblical episodes related by Michael in Books 11 and 12, Marshall Grossman, *"Authors to Themselves": Milton and the Revelation of History* (Cambridge: Cambridge University Press, 1987), 167, notes that "[i]n the last two books of the poem, subtle juxtapositions, cross-references, and internal allusions replace local poetic effects." As I note here, this effect operates from the beginning of Book 11, and is important in the theological portrayal of Eve's and Adam's conversion.

73 The "sigh" was a common way of describing prayer in the seventeenth century. See for example Ames, *Marrow of Theology*, 2.9.12: "The prayers of the godly are called in the Scriptures ... *Sighs too deep for words.*"

told us that the grace that anteceded Adam's prayer came "from the Mercie-seat above" (11.2–3). Adam remarks that, in response to prayer, he perceived God "Bending his eare" (11.152); but it is the Son who pleads with the Father: "Now therefore bend thine eare" (11.30). In response to his prayer, Adam feels "peace" returning "to my brest" (11.153–54); but it is the Son who offers himself to the Father as a propitiation, saying, "Accept me, and in mee from these receave / The smell of peace toward Mankinde" (11.37–38). Adam says that his prayer has "incline[d]" God's will (11.145); but the Father–Son colloquy makes it clear that God's will is inclined by the intercession of the Son. Most importantly, Adam recognises that God has revoked the threatened sentence of death. The divine promise of the protevangelium, Adam says, "Assures me that the bitterness of death / Is past, and we shall live" (11.157–58). Yet the death sentence has in fact been redirected, not revoked; only by being placed on the Son is it removed from humankind. It is the Son who now stands in place of Adam and Eve: "my Death shall pay," he says, for their sinful deeds (11.36).[74]

Thus a richly ironic interplay of verbal echoes and allusions illustrates the two sides of regeneration: the divine initiative, and the free human response. Adam is aware only of the human role in initiating conversion through freely willed prayer and repentance; but the reader is privy to the initiative of grace that has liberated Adam and Eve and enabled them freely to turn towards the God who has already turned towards them. All that Adam says, then, is true, but all that he says is qualified and deepened by the reality of the primacy of prevenient grace. As Summers perceptively remarks: "The ironies are touching. Everything that Adam says is true, but none of it is true in the sense which he imagines."[75] At this point in the narrative, there is more to the grace of God than is dreamt of in Adam's theology. Still, the fact that Adam is unaware of the primacy of grace in enabling and inspiring his conversion dramatically highlights the sheer human freedom with which he experiences and chooses his conversion. For this reason, it is a mistake to read the dramatic conversion scene (in which everything depends on human freedom) as an experiential contradiction of the theol-

---

74 According to Broadbent, *Some Braver Subject*, 267, the portrayal of contrition in *Paradise Lost* is dramatically and theologically flawed because, while Adam and Eve "as yet know nothing of the crucifixion," true Christian contrition must be motivated by the sufferings of Christ. But such a criticism fails to appreciate both the theological centrality of the Son of God in the conversion scene, and the fact that the graciousness of God is dramatically heightened by the reader's awareness, and Adam's ignorance, of the Son's role.

75 Summers, *The Muse's Method*, 192.

ogy of conversion in Book 3 (in which everything depends on grace).[76] Rather, the dogma and drama of conversion should be taken together as the two sides of a single divine–human event. In short, as Neil Forsyth observes, the "paradox of Grace and free will" in the poem consists in the fact that "the freedom of Adam and Eve to repent is itself the experience of Grace";[77] and, one might add, the work of grace itself consists in the restored freedom of Adam and Eve. Enabled by prevenient grace, they are lifted to a position of genuine freedom, in which their conversion is possible but not assured, and in which (just as in the first instance everything depends upon grace) the decisive movement towards God and "away from the abyss"[78] depends on the freedom of their own wills. This relationship between divine grace and human freedom is expressed in paradoxical rhetoric by God:

> Man shall not quite be lost, but sav'd who will,
> Yet not of will in him, but Grace in mee
> Freely vouchsaf't. (3.173–75)

As Danielson notes, in these lines God affirms both that the human will "is decisive but not by itself efficacious," and that "grace is absolutely necessary for salvation but does not overrule the human will."[79] The freedom by which human beings may decisively "will" to be "sav'd" is itself grounded in grace.

Continuing Conversion

In *Paradise Lost* the conversion of Adam and Eve is, moreover, not simply a once-for-all event that confirms them in a regenerate state. On the contrary, their initial experience of conversion is only the first step in a dynamic and lifelong process. As Georgia Christopher notes, "faith" in the poem is "not a steady state, but one of fluctuating growth in which

---

76   Such a reading is offered by Rachel Falconer, *Orpheus Dis(re)membered: Milton and the Myth of the Poet–Hero* (Sheffield: Sheffield Academic Press, 1996), 163. According to Falconer, "the narrative action of Book 10 militates against ... [Book 3's] interpretation of grace, both dramatically and theologically."

77   Neil Forsyth, *The Satanic Epic* (Princeton: Princeton University Press, 2003), 293–94.

78   Balachandra Rajan, *The Lofty Rhyme: A Study of Milton's Major Poetry* (Coral Gables: University of Miami Press, 1970), 77.

79   Danielson, *Milton's Good God*, 86. See also Stephen M. Fallon, "*Paradise Lost* in Intellectual History," in *A Companion to Milton*, ed. Thomas N. Corns (Oxford: Blackwell, 2001), 333.

'subsequent grace' repeats with variations the paradigm of 'prevenient grace.'"[80] Michael tells Adam:

> thy Prayers are heard, and Death,
> Then due by sentence when thou didst transgress,
> Defeated of his seisure many dayes
> Giv'n thee of Grace, wherein thou mayst repent,
> And one bad act with many deeds well done
> Mayst cover. (11.252–57)

Adam's repentance is not a completed work. The "many dayes" of life that are granted him are days in which he must continue to "repent" of his sin, and to live out this repentance with "many deeds well done." Reformed orthodox theologians, with their emphases on God's eternal decree, the decisive event of justification, and the inability of believers to fall away from grace, tended to view conversion as a single event that fixed forever the spiritual state and destiny of the individual.[81] In contrast, however, the Reformation theologians had viewed conversion as a process that continues throughout the Christian life. In the first of his *Ninety-five Theses* (1517), Luther had declared that "[w]hen our Lord and Master Jesus Christ said, 'Repent,' he willed the entire life of believers to be one of repentance";[82] and Calvin similarly believed that repentance is not a single event but "the goal towards which [believers] must keep running during the whole course of their lives," so that regeneration is accomplished not "in a moment, a day, or a year," but only by a long process.[83] In this respect, Arminian theology remained close to Reformation thought by conceiving of conversion as a dynamic process; Episcopius, for instance, regards grace as "carry[ing] on ... saving conversion gradually unto the end."[84] In Arminianism the unstable nature of this dynamic process is highlighted most strikingly in

---

80 Georgia B. Christopher, *Milton and the Science of the Saints* (Princeton: Princeton University Press, 1982), 182.

81 On the Reformed orthodox doctrine of the perseverance of the saints (*perseverantia sanctorum*), according to which it is impossible for the regenerate elect to fall from grace, see G. C. Berkouwer, *Faith and Perseverance*, trans. Robert D. Knudsen (Grand Rapids: Eerdmans, 1958), especially 39–80. Milton's *De Doctrina Christiana* presents a theology of perseverance that relies formally on the Reformed orthodox position, while introducing an Arminian emphasis on conditionality. Thus according to the treatise all those who are elect and regenerate will "PERSEVERE TO THE END," but only "SO LONG AS THEY DO NOT PROVE WANTING IN THEMSELVES, AND SO LONG AS THEY CONTINUE IN FAITH AND CHARITY" (*CPW* 6:505; *CM* 16:70).

82 Luther, *Works*, 31:25.

83 Calvin, *Institutes*, 3.3.9.

84 Episcopius, *The confession or declaration*, 207.

the teaching that believers can fall away from grace: "so long as we are
in this world, he that now standeth should feare least he fall."[85] So too,
in *Paradise Lost* the human beings who have experienced conversion
remain always subject to the possibility of falling again. Affirming the
vital importance of the influence of grace, God the Father says of regenerate humanity:

> He sorrows now, repents, and prayes contrite,
> My motions in him: longer then they move,
> His heart I know, how variable and vain
> Self-left. (11.90–93)[86]

Reformed orthodoxy and Arminianism alike attributed human conversion to such divine "motions." According to Arminius, by the "motion
of the regenerating Spirit" fallen human beings are brought "to confess
their sins, to mourn on account of them, to desire deliverance, and to
seek out the Deliverer";[87] and the Reformed writer Joseph Alleine
speaks of the Holy Spirit implanting in the human soul "good motions," which are "the offers, and essays, and calls, and strivings of the
spirit."[88] But according to *Paradise Lost*, the "motions" of grace are involved not merely in the initial conversion of human beings, but in a
sustained process of conversion. The frail will of the regenerate believer
relies constantly on these "motions" — if the liberating influence of
grace were to withdraw, the will would lapse back into enslavement.
Even the converted will thus continues to be upheld by the grace of
God; grace continues to grant the freedom that enables it to turn to God
anew at each instant. Thus not only the beginning but also the con-
tinuation of the regenerate life depends on the human will's coopera-

---

85 Thomas Browne, *The copie of the sermon preached before the Universitie at St. Maries in
    Oxford* (Oxford, 1634), 51.

86 The syntax of line 91, "longer then they move," poses considerable interpretive
    difficulties. Fowler unravels the passage thus: "I know his heart will outlast these
    [motions] to good, and I know how variable and vain it will become if left to itself"
    (Fowler, 569); and, more simply, Verity: "I know man's variableness after my influ-
    ences cease to work in him" (Verity, 617). But the problem with these glosses, I sug-
    gest, is their implication that the motions to good will in fact eventually expire. That
    the motions will cease to "move" the human heart seems purely hypothetical, so that
    the lines might be glossed: "I know how variable and vain his heart would be if my
    motions ceased to move it, and left it to itself." In his proposed amendment of this
    passage, Bentley thus gets the sense right: "My Motions in him: SHOULD THEY CEASE
    TO move, / His Heart I know how variable and vain" (Bentley, 351).

87 Arminius, *Works*, 2:17.

88 Joseph Alleine, *A sure guide to heaven: or, An earnest invitation to sinners to turn to God*
    (London, 1668), 92. See also Joseph Hussey, *The glory of Christ unveil'd* (London,
    1706), 705.

tion with, and response to, the liberating work of grace. Such a view of grace as the agent of dynamic, continuing conversion had been affirmed by Arminius when he described grace as "THE COMMENCEMENT, THE CONTINUANCE AND THE CONSUMMATION OF ALL GOOD."[89]

In *Paradise Lost*'s third book, God the Father highlights the progressive nature of conversion while laying primary emphasis on the decisive role of the human will:

> I will place within them as a guide
> My Umpire *Conscience*, whom if they will hear,
> Light after light well us'd they shall attain,
> And to the end persisting, safe arrive. (3.194–97)

Even for those who have been converted by grace, the goal of salvation is by no means assured. Human beings do not yet possess the security of salvation; they are on the way (*in via*) to eternal life, but are not yet "safe," and have not yet "arrive[d]." Persistence is therefore necessary—a persistent choice to follow the internal light of conscience, a persistent exercise of freedom in which the human agent turns away from sin and towards God. In short, a moment-by-moment conversion is necessary if the individual is finally to "arrive" safely at the bliss of eternal salvation.

Hence the whole life of Adam and Eve, from the initial event of their conversion onwards, is to be—as was their Edenic life—an expression of the possibilities of contingent freedom. It is to be a journey of freedom, growth and development. For this reason, *Paradise Lost* ends with a vision of a future radically open to the possibilities of human freedom, a freedom that is upheld and "guide[d]" by the gracious providence of God, and at the same time "solitarie" in its ability to choose and to actualise the future:

> Som natural tears they dropd, but wip'd them soon;
> The World was all before them, where to choose
> Thir place of rest, and Providence thir guide:
> They hand in hand with wandring steps and slow,
> Through *Eden* took thir solitarie way. (12.645–49)

The self-enslaving narrowness of sin is left behind, as the first human beings turn freely to face a world of choice and possibility.

---

89   Arminius, *Works*, 1:664.

Conclusion

This study arose from a conviction that characterisations of *Paradise Lost*'s theology as either "orthodox" or "heretical" were simplistic, and that the poem's theology of freedom in particular was more complex and more individual in its appropriation of diverse theological concepts and traditions than has been widely recognised. I therefore set out to resituate the poem in its post-Reformation theological context, in order to identify the points of continuity and discontinuity between its theology and the theologies of the various post-Reformation schools and traditions. Beginning with an overview of the historical development of the theology of freedom, my study has followed the idea of freedom as it unfolds throughout the narrative of *Paradise Lost*, attempting progressively to tease out the complexities of the poem's theology and to explore the ways in which it both draws on and reformulates diverse theological concepts and traditions.

I found that, in continuity with the anti-Calvinist polemics of Arminianism, the poem critiques Reformed orthodox views of God and freedom. The grotesque parody of Calvinist predestinarianism expressed by Satan and the fallen angels in Books 1 and 2 is depicted in *Paradise Lost* as a heresy that misrepresents God by claiming that he compromises his own goodness and negates creaturely freedom. The theology of freedom progressively articulated throughout the rest of the poem constitutes a vigorous and sustained correction of this Satanic theology. God is portrayed in the poem as a free being whose principal concern is the authentic freedom of his creatures. To this end he predestines the freedom of human nature, and allows this nature, as his own image in humanity, to predestine and to actualise its own future. Far from negating the freedom of his creatures, the God of *Paradise Lost* creates room for creaturely self-determination by withdrawing his own being from that of his creatures in the act of creation. Through this divine self-withdrawal the creature comes to be characterised by a God-like autonomy, so that even the self-limited creator himself cannot trespass into the realm of free human decision. This radical depiction of creaturely freedom, while creatively drawing on Arminian concepts of divine self-limitation, is sharply discontinuous with the more circumscribed understandings of creaturely freedom in post-Reformation theology.

In *Paradise Lost* the freedom of creatures is characterised above all by indifferent contingence: the ability to choose in a purely self-determined way between alternative possibilities. This view of an indifferent and contingent will is, I have attempted to show, the most significant and far-reaching point of continuity between the poem's theology and the theology of Arminianism. Like Arminianism, and in contrast to Reformed orthodoxy, the poem views human freedom as consisting essentially in the power to choose between alternatives. This contingent alternativity of choice is not voluntaristically governed by the will, but is intellectually governed by right reason, as in Arminianism and Amyraldism. Such an account of human freedom becomes the crucial theological underpinning of the poem's portrayal of the fall of Adam and Eve as an event that might not and need not have taken place. The narrative of the fall in *Paradise Lost* involves, then, an elaborate enactment of the Arminian theology of contingent freedom.

But while the poem's portrayal of the fall is broadly continuous with an Arminian view of freedom, its depiction of the fallen will stands, perhaps surprisingly, in forthright continuity with the Reformed orthodox notion of total depravity. The human will that was created free has become enslaved through the fall. True freedom, which consists in a contingent liberty of indifference, has been lost—not because God has negated it, but because the free human agents have themselves freely renounced this freedom, and in so doing have become enslaved to themselves. It is in this connection that the poem adopts the theological concept of original sin, thus affirming that all human beings have become self-enslaved through the first decisive act of human disobedience.

Balancing this view of the universal enslavement of sin is the poem's emphasis on the universal liberating operation of divine grace. By the grace of God, the poem asserts, all human beings are liberated from the tyranny of sin. Their wills are returned to a state of contingent indifference so that they are again able to choose freely between good and evil. While this theology of universal grace is in some respects continuous with Arminian and Amyraldian views of grace, it offers a more profoundly universal vision, in which salvation is not merely a hypothetical but a genuine possibility for every human being. Indeed, the poem's account of predestination in Book 3 emphasises this point by denying the existence of any divine decree of reprobation, and by reducing reprobation to a provisional and temporal event in which human agents freely reject the electing grace of God. This account of reprobation presents a radical departure from the formal structure of post-Reformation predestinarian theology, in which divine predestination was consistently viewed as a double decree comprising both election and reprobation. The poem's theology thus exhibits genuine originality by universalising the grace of election and relativising the notion of reprobation in a way that strikingly emphasises the freedom of human agents. Because all human beings have been elected by God to salvation, and because all are recipients of liberating prevenient grace, no one is ever beyond the possibility of redemption. Indeed, although in continuity with the major post-Reformation traditions *Paradise Lost* affirms that some human beings will ultimately perish, the general tendency of its theology is in the direction of a thoroughgoing universalism. In the poem the fact that some people will finally perish is not, as in Reformed orthodoxy, a reflection of the nature of grace itself, but rather a reflection of the remarkable power of human freedom—a freedom that can even negate the electing grace of God.

I have also argued in this study that a consistent feature of *Paradise Lost*'s theology of freedom is its emphasis on process and development. The first created human beings, endowed with autonomous freedom, are placed by God in an environment that calls for the creative exercise of choice, so that the being of Adam and Eve consists in a state of becoming, in a continuing process of decision and development. Eve's and Adam's Edenic life is characterised by an abundance of alternative possibilities and by the contingent liberty of indifference that enables them freely to actualise such possibilities. This openness of choice and possibility is tragically lost through the fall, and is displaced by a self-focused narrowness and a self-chosen poverty of genuine possibilities.

But the same freedom is, in *Paradise Lost*, restored by the grace of conversion. Through grace, the human self is turned back towards God and the abundance of choice that characterised prelapsarian existence is restored. In the poem this conversion is not, as in Reformed orthodoxy, a once-for-all event, but, as in Reformation theology and Arminianism, a continuing process in which human beings progressively exercise their freedoms and actualise their futures in the face of alternative possibilities.

One of the most interesting features of the theology of *Paradise Lost* that has emerged in this study is the distinctive way in which the poem appropriates orthodox theological concepts, but presses them in a direction that is fundamentally opposed to post-Reformation orthodoxy. The poem's depiction of the fallen will, for instance, employs a Reformed orthodox view of the gracious liberation of the enslaved will, but it so universalises this concept of grace that the Reformed idea of enslavement is drastically undermined, and instead all human beings are viewed as free either to accept or to reject salvation. Similarly, *Paradise Lost*'s portrayal of the freedom of God's creative act is continuous with Reformed orthodoxy's high view of divine freedom; but in the poem this markedly orthodox insistence on the freedom of God is developed so consistently and so rigorously that the result is an Arian conception of the Son of God in which the Father generates and exalts the Son through sheer freedom alone, so that the very existence of the Son—and thus also the existence of redemption—is rendered radically contingent. These features of *Paradise Lost*'s theology illustrate the ways in which the poem draws on existing theological concepts but transforms and transcends them so that the idea of freedom receives the greatest possible emphasis.

The theology of *Paradise Lost* is then not simply orthodox or heretical, nor is it merely an eclectic amalgam of existing theologies. In moving beyond such readings, the present study seeks to foster an enhanced appreciation of the complex and nuanced ways in which Milton draws on the wide range of theological traditions available to him, while ultimately charting his own individual course. The theology he articulates in the poem is, in other words, itself a creative exercise and a forthright demonstration of human freedom. It is a highly individual, sharply focused and rigorously developed theology that is grounded in a profound commitment to the idea of freedom, and that seeks at every significant point to give expression to this freedom. The depth of this commitment to freedom is itself the most striking and most original dimension of the poem's theology. More than anything else, this underlying commitment gives distinctive shape to the poem's theological structure, and drives the creative reformulation of diverse theological concepts into Milton's hard-won and uniquely personal justification of the ways of God to men.

Bibliography

For texts printed in collected editions, the following abbreviations are used:

ANF   *The Ante-Nicene Fathers*, 10 vols.
NPNF   Schaff, *Nicene and Post-Nicene Fathers*, 14 vols.
PL   Migne, *Patrologia Latina*, 221 vols.

Milton Editions

Bentley, Richard, ed. *Milton's Paradise Lost: A New Edition*. London, 1732.

Bush, Douglas, ed. *The Complete Poetical Works of John Milton*. Boston: Houghton Mifflin, 1965.

Darbishire, Helen, ed. *The Poetical Works of John Milton*. 2 vols. Oxford: Clarendon, 1952–55.

Flannagan, Roy, ed. *The Riverside Milton*. Boston: Houghton Mifflin, 1998.

Fowler, Alastair, ed. *John Milton: Paradise Lost*. London: Longman, 1968.

Hughes, Merritt Y., ed. *John Milton: Complete Poems and Major Prose*. New York: Odyssey, 1957.

Newton, Thomas, ed. *Paradise Lost: A Poem, in Twelve Books*. 2 vols. London, 1749.

Patterson, Frank A., et al. *The Works of John Milton*. 18 vols. in 21. New York: Columbia University Press, 1931–38.

Todd, Henry J., ed. *The Poetical Works of John Milton: With Notes by Various Authors*. 4 vols. London, 1809.

Verity, A. W., ed. *Milton: Paradise Lost*. Cambridge, 1910.

Wolfe, Don M., et al. *Complete Prose Works of John Milton*. 8 vols. New Haven: Yale University Press, 1953–82.

Primary Sources

[Anon.]. *An antidote against some principal errors of the predestinarians*. London, 1696.

Abbot, George. *The reasons which Doctour Hill hath brought*. Oxford, 1604.

Addison, Joseph. *The Tatler*. Glasgow, 1754.

Alleine, Joseph. *A sure guide to heaven: or, An earnest invitation to sinners to turn to God*. London, 1668.

Ambrose, Isaac. *The compleat works of that eminent minister of God's word, Mr. Isaac Ambrose*. London, 1701.

Ames, William. *The Marrow of Theology*. Ed. and trans. John D. Eusden. Grand Rapids: Baker, 1968.

——. *The substance of Christian religion: or, A plain and easie draught of the Christian catechism*. London, 1659.

Amyraut, Moïse. *A discourse concerning the divine dreams mention'd in Scripture*. London, 1676.

——. *A treatise concerning religions, in refutation of the opinion which accounts all indifferent*. London, 1660.

——. *Brief traitté de la predestination et de ses principales dependances*. Saumur, 1634.

——. *Mosis Amyraldi dissertationes theologicae quatuor*. Saumur, 1645.

——. *Paraphrases sur les epistres de l'apostre s. Paul au Galates, Ephesiens, Philippiens, Colossiens, I Thessaloniciens, II Thessaloniciens*. Saumur, 1645.

——. *Sermons sur divers textes de la sainte ecriture*. Saumur, 1653.

Anselm. *Truth, Freedom, and Evil: Three Philosophical Dialogues*. Ed. and trans. J. Hopkins and H. Richardson. New York: Harper & Row, 1967.

——. *Opera omnia*. 6 vols. Edinburgh: Thomas Nelson, 1938–61.

——. *Trinity, Incarnation, and Redemption: Theological Treatises*. Ed. and trans. J. Hopkins and H. Richardson. New York: Harper & Row, 1970.

The Ante-Nicene Fathers: Translations of the Writings of the Fathers Down to A.D. 325. 10 vols. Grand Rapids: Eerdmans, 1956–62.

Aristotle. *The Complete Works of Aristotle*. Ed. Jonathan Barnes. 2 vols. Princeton: Princeton University Press, 1984.

Arminius, Jacobus. *The Works of James Arminius*. Trans. James Nichols and William Nichols. 3 vols. London, Grand Rapids: Baker, 1986.

Augustine. *De civitate Dei contra paganos*. In *PL* 41 and *NPNF* 2.

——. *De correptione et gratia*. In *PL* 44 and *NPNF* 5.

——. *De gratia Christi et de peccato originali contra Pelagium, ad Albinam, Pinianum, et Melaniam*. In *PL* 44 and *NPNF* 5.

——. *De gratia et libero arbitrio*. In *PL* 44 and *NPNF* 5.

——. *De praedestinatione sanctorum ad Prosperum et Hilarium*. In *PL* 44 and *NPNF* 5.

——. *De spiritu et littera*. In *PL* 44 and *NPNF* 5.

——. *Enchiridion de fide, spe et charitate*. In *PL* 40 and *NPNF* 3.

——. *In evangelium Ioannis tractatus*. In *PL* 35 and *NPNF* 7.

Bastingius, Jeremias. *An exposition or commentarie upon the Catechisme of Christian Religion*. Cambridge, 1589.

Baxter, Richard. *Aphorismes of justification*. London, 1649.

——. *Catholick theologie*. London, 1675.

——. *The divine life in three treatises*. London, 1664.

Bellarmine, Robert. *Disputationes de controversiis christianae fidei, adversus hujus temporis haereticos*. 4 vols. Rome, 1586–93.

Benfield, Sebastian. *Eight sermons publikely preached in the University of Oxford*. Oxford, 1614.

Bernard of Clairvaux. *De gratia et libero arbitrio*. In *PL* 182.

Bertius, Petrus. *The life and death of James Arminius and Simon Episcopius, professors of divinity in the University of Leyden in Holland*. London, 1672.

Beza, Theodore. *A booke of Christian questions and answers, wherein are set foorth the cheef points of the Christian religion*. London, 1572.

―――. *Tabula praedestinationis*. Geneva, 1555.

Biddle, John. *A confession of faith touching the Holy Trinity*. London, 1648.

Boston, Thomas. *Commentary on the Shorter Catechism*. 2 vols. Aberdeen, 1853.

―――. *Human nature in its four-fold state*. Edinburgh, 1720.

Browne, Thomas. *The copie of the sermon preached before the Universitie at St. Maries in Oxford*. Oxford, 1634.

Bunyan, John. *A holy life, the beauty of Christianity: or, An exhortation to Christians to be holy*. London, 1684.

Burgess, Anthony. *The doctrine of original sin, asserted and vindicated against the old and new adversaries thereof*. London, 1659.

Burthogge, Richard. *Christianity a revealed mystery*. London, 1702.

Calvin, John. *Commentaries on the Epistle of Paul the Apostle to the Romans*. Trans. John Owen. Edinburgh, 1849.

―――. *Commentaries on the First Book of Moses, Called Genesis*. Trans. John King. 2 vols. Edinburgh, 1847.

―――. *Commentary on the Book of the Prophet Isaiah*. Trans. William Pringle. 4 vols. Edinburgh, 1850.

―――. *Institutes of the Christian Religion*. Trans. Henry Beveridge. 2 vols. Grand Rapids: Eerdmans, 1989.

―――. *Institutio christianae religionis*. Geneva, 1563.

Cameron, John. *An examination of those plausible appearances which seeme most to commend the Romish Church, and to prejudice the Reformed*. Oxford, 1626.

Charnock, Stephen. *The Existence and Attributes of God*. London, 1797.

―――. *The Works of Stephen Charnock*. 5 vols. Edinburgh, 1864–66.

Chemnitz, Martin. *Examination of the Council of Trent*. Trans. Fred Kramer. 4 vols. St Louis: Concordia, 1986.

―――. *Loci Theologici*. Trans. J. A. O. Preus. 2 vols. St Louis: Concordia, 1989.

Cicero, Marcus Tullius. *De Oratore; De Fato; Paradoxa Stoicorum; De Partitione Oratoria*. Cambridge, Mass.: Harvard University Press, 1942.

Clarke, Samuel. *A generall martyrologie ... whereunto are added, the lives of sundry modern divines*. London, 1651.

————. *The works of Samuel Clarke.* 4 vols. London, 1738.

Cotton, John. *Christ the fountaine of life.* London, 1651.

————. *The new covenant.* London, 1654.

Dante Alighieri. *The Divine Comedy.* Ed. and trans. Charles S. Singleton. 6 vols. Princeton: Princeton University Press, 1970–75.

Day, William. *Man's destruction, prov'd to be of himself: in which, the Antinomian and Arminian errors are confuted.* London, 1713.

Dickson, David. *Truths victory over error.* Edinburgh, 1684.

Downham, John. *The summe of sacred divinitie first briefly and methodically propounded, and then more largly and cleerly handled and explained.* London, 1620.

Du Moulin, Pierre. *The anatomy of Arminianisme.* London, 1620.

Duns Scotus, John. *Duns Scotus on the Will and Morality.* Ed. and trans. Allan B. Wolter. Washington: Catholic University Press of America, 1986.

————. *God and Creatures: The Quodlibetal Questions.* Trans. F. Alluntis and A. B. Wolter. Princeton: Princeton University Press, 1975.

————. *Opera omnia.* Ed. Luke Wadding. 26 vols. Paris, 1891–95.

————. *Philosophical Writings: A Selection.* Trans. Allan Wolter. Edinburgh: Thomas Nelson, 1962.

————. *Quaestiones disputatae de rerum principio, Tractatus de primo rerum omnium principio.* Ed. R. Garcia. Florence, 1910.

Edwards, John. *Theologia reformata, or the body and substance of the Christian religion.* London, 1713.

————. *Veritas redux: Evangelical truths restored.* 2 vols. London, 1707.

Edwards, Jonathan. *A careful and strict enquiry into the modern prevailing notions of … freedom of will.* London, 1762.

Episcopius, Simon. *Opera theologica.* 2 vols. London, 1678.

————. *The confession or declaration of the ministers or pastors which in the United Provinces are called Remonstrants, concerning the chief points of Christian religion.* London, 1676.

Erasmus, Desiderius. *Collected Works of Erasmus.* 86 vols. Toronto: University of Toronto Press, 1974–93.

Flavel, John. *The whole works of the Reverend Mr. John Flavel.* 2 vols. London, 1701.

Goad, Thomas. *Stimluus orthodoxus, sive Goadus redivivus: A disputation partly theological, partly metaphysical, concerning the necessity and contingency of events in the world, in respect of Gods eternal decree.* London, 1661.

Goodwin, John. *An exposition of the nineth chapter of the Epistle to the Romans.* London, 1653.

———. *Confidence dismounted.* London, 1651.

———. *Redemption redeemed.* London, 1651.

———. *The agreement and distance of brethren.* London, 1652.

———. *The banner of justification displayed.* London, 1659.

———. *The remedie of unreasonableness.* London, 1650.

Gordon, Francis. *An essay upon predestination and grace.* Edinburgh, 1712.

Hooker, Thomas. *The soules humiliation.* London, 1638.

Hopkins, Ezekiel. *The works of the Right Reverend and learned Ezekiel Hopkins.* London, 1701

Hubmaier, Balthasar. *On Free Will.* In *Spiritual and Anabaptist Writers: Documents Illustrative of the Radical Reformation.* Ed. G. H. Williams. London: SCM, 1957. 112–35.

Hussey, Joseph. *The glory of Christ unveil'd.* London, 1706.

Irenaeus. *Against Heresies.* In *ANF* 1.

Jackson, Thomas. *Works.* 12 vols. Oxford, 1844.

Justin Martyr. *First Apology.* In *ANF* 1.

Keckermann, Bartholomaeus. *Systema sacrosanctae theologiae.* Heidelberg, 1602.

Kyd, Thomas. *The Spanish Tragedy.* Ed. Philip Edwards. London: Methuen, 1959.

Leigh, Edward. *A system or body of divinity.* London, 1662.

Leighton, Robert. *Theological Lectures.* London, 1821.

Lightfoot, John. *The works of the reverend and learned John Lightfoot, D.D.* 2 vols. London, 1684.

Luther, Martin. *D. Martin Luthers Werke: Kritische Gesamtausgabe.* 66 vols. Weimar: Hermann Böhlaus Nachfolger, 1883–1987.

———. *Luther's Works*. Ed. J. Pelikan and H. T. Lehmann. 55 vols. St Louis and Philadelphia: Concordia and Fortress, 1958–86.

Manton, Thomas. *The Complete Works of Thomas Manton*. 20 vols. London, 1870–74.

Migne, J. P., ed. *Patrologia Latina Cursus Completus*. 221 vols. Paris, 1844–55.

Molina, Luis de. *Concordia liberi arbitrii cum gratiae donis, divina praescientia, providentia, praedestinatione et reprobatione*. Ed. Johann Rabeneck. Onia: Collegium Maximum Societatis Jesu, 1953.

More, Henry. *Divine dialogues: containing sundry disquisitions and instructions concerning the attributes and providence of God*. London, 1668.

Origen. *De principiis*. In *ANF* 4.

Owen, John. *Theomachia autexousiastike: or, A display of Arminianisme, being a discovery of the old Pelagian idol free-will, with the new goddesse contingency*. London, 1643.

———. *Pneumatologia: or, A discourse concerning the Holy Spirit*. London, 1674.

Pascal, Blaise. *Pensées*. Trans. W. F. Trotter. London, 1908.

Perkins, William. *A golden chaine: or, The description of theologie*. Cambridge, 1592.

———. *A treatise on Gods free grace, and mans free will*. Cambridge, 1601.

———. *An exposition of the symbole or creed of the apostles*. Cambridge, 1595.

———. *The workes of that famous and worthie minister of Christ, in the Universitie of Cambridge, M. W. Perkins*. 3 vols. Cambridge, 1608–9.

Peter Lombard. *Sententiae in IV libris distinctae*. Rome: Editiones Collegii S. Bonaventurae ad Claras Aquas, 1971–81.

Phillips, Edward. "The Life of Mr. John Milton." In *Letters of state, written by Mr. John Milton: ... to which is added, an account of his life*. London, 1694.

Polanus, Amandus. *Syntagma theologiae christianae*. Geneva, 1617.

Pope, Alexander. *The first epistle of the second book of Horace, imitated*. London, 1737.

Prynne, William. *God, no impostor, nor deluder: or, An answer to a Popish and Arminian cavill, in the defence of the free-will, and universall grace*. London, 1630.

The Racovian Catechism. Ed. Thomas Rees. London, 1818.

Raleigh, Walter. *The History of the World*. Ed. C. A. Patrides. Philadelphia: Temple University Press, 1971.

Rijssen, Leonhardus. *Francisci Turretini compendium theologiae didactico–elencticae ex theologorum nostrorum institutionibus auctum et illustratum*. Amsterdam, 1695.

Schaff, Philip, ed. *A Select Library of the Nicene and Post-Nicene Fathers of the Christian Church*. First Series. 14 vols. Grand Rapids: Eerdmans, 1979.

———, ed. *The Creeds of Christendom: With a History and Critical Notes*. 3 vols. New York, 1919.

Sandys, Edwin. *The Sermons of Edwin Sandys*. Ed. John Ayre. Cambridge, 1841.

Sharp, John. *Fifteen sermons preached on several occasions*. London, 1701.

Sibbes, Richard. *The Complete Works of Richard Sibbes*. 7 vols. Edinburgh, 1862–64.

Spinoza, Baruch. *Ethics*. Ed. James Gutmann. New York: Hafner, 1949.

Tanner, Norman P., ed. *Decrees of the Ecumenical Councils*. 2 vols. London: Sheed & Ward, 1990.

Taylor, John. *A narrative of Mr. Joseph Rawson's case*. London, 1742.

Tertullian. *Adversus Praxeam*. In *PL* 2 and *ANF* 3.

———. *De praescriptionibus adversus haereticos*. In *PL* 2 and *ANF* 3.

Thomas Aquinas. *Summa Theologiae*. 60 vols. London: Blackfriars, 1964–76.

———. *Summa Theologica*. Trans. Fathers of the English Dominican Province. 3 vols. New York: Benziger Brothers, 1947–48.

Toland, John. *The life of John Milton*. London, 1699.

Toplady, Augustus. *The Church of England vindicated from the charge of Arminianism*. London, 1769.

Trelcatius, Lucas. *A briefe institution of the common places of sacred divinitie*. London, 1610.

Turretin, Francis. *Institutes of Elenctic Theology*. Ed. James T. Dennison. Trans. George Musgrave Giger. 3 vols. Phillipsburg: P&R, 1992–97.

Twisse, William. *Riches of Gods love unto the vessells of mercy, consistent with his absolute hatred or reprobation of the vessells of wrath*. 2 vols. Oxford, 1653.

Ursinus, Zacharias. *Opera theologica*. 3 vols. Heidelberg, 1612.

Ussher, James. *A body of divinitie, or the summe and substance of Christian religion*. London, 1653.

———. *An answer to a challenge made by a Iesuite in Ireland*. London, 1631.

Vermigli, Peter Martyr. *Loci communes*. London, 1576.

Watson, Thomas. *A body of practical divinity*. London, 1692.

Wesley, John. *The question, what is an Arminian? answered*. Bristol, 1770.

Whiston, Henry. *A short treatise of the great worth and best kind of nobility*. London, 1661.

Whiston, William. *Historical memoirs of the life and writings of Dr. Samuel Clarke*. London, 1730.

William of Ockham. *Predestination, God's Foreknowledge, and Future Contingents*. Ed. and trans. Marilyn McCord Adams and Norman Kretzmann. New York: Appleton, 1969.

———. *Quaestiones in librum quartum sententiarum*. Ed. R. Wood and G. Gál. St Bonaventure: St Bonaventure University, 1984.

———. *Quodlibetal Questions*. Trans. A J. Freddoso and F. E. Kelley. 2 vols. New Haven: Yale University Press, 1991.

———. *Scriptum in librum primum sententiarum ordinatio*. Ed. Girard J. Itzkorn. St Bonaventure: St Bonaventure University, 1979.

Williams, G. H., ed. *Spiritual and Anabaptist Writers: Documents Illustrative of the Radical Reformation*. London: SCM, 1957.

Wollebius, Johannes. *Compendium theologiae christianae*. In *Reformed Dogmatics*. Ed. and trans. John W. Beardslee. Oxford: Oxford University Press, 1965. 29–262.

Secondary Sources

Adams, Marilyn McCord. "Ockham on Will, Nature, and Morality." In *The Cambridge Companion to Ockham*. Ed. Paul Vincent Spade. Cambridge: Cambridge University Press, 1999. 245–72.

Almond, Philip C. *Heaven and Hell in Enlightenment England*. Cambridge: Cambridge University Press, 1994.

——, ed. *Demonic Possession and Exorcism in Early Modern England: Contemporary Texts and Their Cultural Contexts*. Cambridge: Cambridge University Press, 2004.

Angelo, Peter Gregory. *Fall to Glory: Theological Reflections on Milton's Epics*. New York: Peter Lang, 1987.

Armstrong, Brian G. *Calvinism and the Amyraut Heresy: Protestant Scholasticism and Humanism in Seventeenth-Century France*. Madison: University of Wisconsin Press, 1969.

Asselt, Willem J. van and Eef Dekker, eds. *Reformation and Scholasticism: An Ecumenical Enterprise*. Grand Rapids: Baker, 2001.

Barber, A. D. "The Religious Life and Opinions of John Milton: Part I," *Bibliotheca Sacra* 63 (1859), 557–603.

——. "The Religious Life and Opinions of John Milton: Part II," *Bibliotheca Sacra* 64 (1860), 1–42

Barker, Arthur E. *Milton and the Puritan Dilemma*. Toronto: University of Toronto Press, 1942.

——. "*Paradise Lost*: The Relevance of Regeneration." In *Paradise Lost: A Tercentenary Tribute*. Ed. Balachandra Rajan. Toronto: University of Toronto Press, 1969. 48–78.

Barth, Karl. *Church Dogmatics*. Ed. Geoffrey W. Bromiley and T. F. Torrance. 14 vols. Edinburgh: T&T Clark, 1956–77.

——. *Dogmatics in Outline*. Trans. G. T. Thomson. London: SCM, 1949.

——. *The Humanity of God*. Trans. John Newton Thomas and Thomas Wieser. Richmond: John Knox Press, 1960.

Bates, Catherine. "No Sin But Irony: Kierkegaard and Milton's Satan," *Literature and Theology* 11:1 (1997), 1–26.

Bauman, Michael. *A Scripture Index to John Milton's De Doctrina Christiana*. Binghamton: Medieval and Renaissance Texts and Studies, 1989.

———. *Milton's Arianism*. Frankfurt am Main: Peter Lang, 1987.

Beardslee, John W., ed and trans. *Reformed Dogmatics*. Oxford: Oxford University Press, 1965.

Beck, Andreas J. "Gisbertus Voetius (1589–1676): Basic Features of His Doctrine of God." In *Reformation and Scholasticism: An Ecumenical Enterprise*. Ed. Willem J. van Asselt and Eef Dekker. Grand Rapids: Baker, 2001. 205–26.

Bedford, R. D. "Time, Freedom, and Foreknowledge in *Paradise Lost*," *Milton Studies* 16 (1982), 61–76.

Benedict, Philip. *Christ's Churches Purely Reformed: A Social History of Calvinism*. New Haven: Yale University Press, 2002.

Bennett, Joan S. "Asserting Eternal Providence: John Milton through the Window of Liberation Theology." In *Milton and Heresy*. Ed. Stephen B. Dobranski and John P. Rumrich. Cambridge: Cambridge University Press, 1998. 219–43.

———. "'Go': Milton's Antinomianism and the Separation Scene in *Paradise Lost*, Book 9," *PMLA* 98 (1983), 388–404.

Berkouwer, G. C. *Divine Election*. Trans. Hugo Bekker. Grand Rapids: Eerdmans, 1960.

———. *Faith and Perseverance*. Trans. Robert D. Knudsen. Grand Rapids: Eerdmans, 1958.

———. *The Providence of God*. Trans. Lewis B. Smedes. Grand Rapids: Eerdmans, 1952.

Berry, Boyd M. *Process of Speech: Puritan Religious Writing and Paradise Lost*. Baltimore: Johns Hopkins University Press, 1976.

Bettoni, Efrem. *Duns Scotus: The Basic Principles of His Philosophy*. Trans. Bernardino M. Bonansea. Westport: Greenwood Press, 1978.

Bosley, Richard N. and Martin Tweedale, eds. *Basic Issues in Medieval Philosophy: Selected Readings Presenting the Interactive Discourses among the Major Figures*. Peterborough: Broadview Press, 1997.

Broadbent, John B. *Some Graver Subject: An Essay on Paradise Lost*. London: Chatto & Windus, 1960.

Brunner, Emil. *Dogmatics*. Trans. Olive Wyon et al. 3 vols. London: Lutterworth, 1949–62.

———. *Man in Revolt: A Christian Anthropology*. Trans. Olive Wyon. London: Lutterworth, 1939.

Bryson, Michael. *The Tyranny of Heaven: Milton's Rejection of God as King*. Newark: University of Delaware Press, 2004.

Bultmann, Rudolf. *Theology of the New Testament*. Trans. Kendrick Grobel. 2 vols. London: SCM, 1951–55.

Burden, Dennis H. *The Logical Epic: A Study of the Argument of Paradise Lost*. London: Routledge & Kegan Paul, 1967.

Bush, Douglas. *English Literature in the Earlier Seventeenth Century, 1600–1660*. Oxford: Clarendon, 1962.

———. *Paradise Lost in Our Time: Some Comments*. Gloucester: Peter Smith, 1957.

Campbell, Gordon, Thomas N. Corns, John K. Hale, David I. Holmes and Fiona J. Tweedie. "The Provenance of *De Doctrina Christiana*," *Milton Quarterly* 31:3 (1997), 67–117.

Carey, John. "Milton's Satan." In *The Cambridge Companion to Milton*. Ed. Dennis R. Danielson. Cambridge: Cambridge University Press, 1999. 160–74.

Christopher, Georgia B. *Milton and the Science of the Saints*. Princeton: Princeton University Press, 1982.

Citron, Bernhard. *New Birth: A Study of the Evangelical Doctrine of Conversion in the Protestant Fathers*. Edinburgh: Edinburgh University Press, 1951.

Clark, Mili N. "The Mechanics of Creation: Non-Contradiction and Natural Necessity in *Paradise Lost*," *English Literary Renaissance* 7:2 (1977), 207–42.

Conklin, George Newton. *Biblical Criticism and Heresy in Milton*. New York: King's Crown Press, 1949.

Copleston, Frederick C. *A History of Philosophy*. 9 vols. Westminster: Newman Press, 1946–74.

Cornforth, Maurice, ed. *Rebels and Their Causes: Essays in Honour of A. L. Morton*. London: Lawrence & Wishart, 1978.

Corns, Thomas N. *John Milton: The Prose Works*. New York: Twayne, 1998.

———. *Regaining Paradise Lost*. London: Longman, 1994.

———, ed. *A Companion to Milton*. Oxford: Blackwell, 2001.

Craig, William Lane. *The Problem of Divine Foreknowledge and Future Contingents: Aristotle to Suárez*. Leiden: E. J. Brill, 1988.

Crosman, Robert. *Reading Paradise Lost*. Bloomington: Indiana University Press, 1980.

Cross, F. L., ed. *The Oxford Dictionary of the Christian Church*. London: Oxford University Press, 1958.

Cummins, Juliet L. "The Metaphysics of Authorship in Milton's *Paradise Lost*." Ph.D. diss., University of Sydney, 2000.

Cunningham, William. *The Reformers and the Theology of the Reformation*. Edinburgh, 1862.

Danielson, Dennis R. *Milton's Good God: A Study in Literary Theodicy*. Cambridge: Cambridge University Press, 1982.

———. "The Fall and Milton's Theodicy." In *The Cambridge Companion to Milton*. Ed. Dennis R. Danielson. Cambridge: Cambridge University Press, 1999. 144–59.

———, ed. *The Cambridge Companion to Milton*. Cambridge: Cambridge University Press, 1999.

Davies, Brian. *The Thought of Thomas Aquinas*. Oxford: Clarendon, 1992.

Dekker, Eef. "An Ecumenical Debate Between Reformation and Counter-Reformation? Bellarmine and Ames on *liberum arbitrium*." In *Reformation and Scholasticism: An Ecumenical Enterprise*. Ed. Willem J. van Asselt and Eef Dekker. Grand Rapids: Baker, 2001. 141–54.

———. "Was Arminius a Molinist?" *Sixteenth Century Journal* 27:2 (1996), 337–52.

Diekhoff, John S. *Milton's Paradise Lost: A Commentary on the Argument*. New York: Columbia University Press, 1946.

Dixon, Philip. *"Nice and Hot Disputes": The Doctrine of the Trinity in the Seventeenth Century*. London: T&T Clark, 2003.

Dobranski, Stephen B. and John P. Rumrich, "Introduction: Heretical Milton." In *Milton and Heresy*. Ed. Stephen B. Dobranski and John P. Rumrich. Cambridge: Cambridge University Press, 1998. 1–17.

Dobranski, Stephen B. and John P. Rumrich, eds. *Milton and Heresy*. Cambridge: Cambridge University Press, 1998.

Donnelly, Colleen. "The Syntactic Counterplot of the Devil's Debates and God's Council," *Language and Style* 19:1 (1986), 58–73.

Driscoll, John A. "On Human Acts." In Thomas Aquinas, *Summa Theologica*. Trans. Fathers of the English Dominican Province. 3 vols. New York: Benziger Brothers, 1947–48. 3:3201–19.

Ebeling, Gerhard. *Luther: An Introduction to His Thought*. Trans. R. A. Wilson. Philadelphia: Fortress, 1970.

Eichrodt, Walther. *Theology of the Old Testament*. Trans. J. A. Baker. 2 vols. London: SCM, 1961–67.

Empson, William. *Milton's God*. London: Chatto & Windus, 1961.

Evans, G. R. *Anselm and a New Generation*. Oxford: Clarendon, 1980.

———. *Anselm and Talking About God*. Oxford: Clarendon, 1978.

Evans, J. Martin. *Paradise Lost and the Genesis Tradition*. Oxford: Clarendon, 1968.

Falconer, Rachel. *Orpheus Dis(re)membered: Milton and the Myth of the Poet–Hero*. Sheffield: Sheffield Academic Press, 1996.

Fallon, Stephen M. "'Elect above the Rest': Theology as Self-Representation in Milton." In *Milton and Heresy*. Ed. Stephen B. Dobranski and John P. Rumrich. Cambridge: Cambridge University Press, 1998. 93–116.

———. *Milton among the Philosophers: Poetry and Materialism in Seventeenth-Century England*. Ithaca: Cornell University Press, 1991.

———. "Milton's Arminianism and the Authorship of *De Doctrina Christiana*," *Texas Studies in Literature and Language* 41:2 (1999), 103–27.

———. "*Paradise Lost* in Intellectual History." In *A Companion to Milton*. Ed. Thomas N. Corns. Oxford: Blackwell, 2001. 329–47.

———. "'To Act or Not': Milton's Conception of Divine Freedom," *Journal of the History of Ideas*, 49:3 (1988), 425–53.

Farwell, Marilyn R. "Eve, the Separation Scene, and the Renaissance Idea of Androgyny," *Milton Studies* 16 (1982), 3–20.

Ferry, Anne Davidson. *Milton's Epic Voice: The Narrator in Paradise Lost.* Cambridge, Mass.: Harvard University Press, 1963.

Feuerbach, Ludwig. *The Essence of Christianity.* Trans. George Eliot. New York: Harper & Row, 1957.

Fiore, Peter A. *Milton and Augustine: Patterns of Augustinian Thought in Paradise Lost.* University Park: Pennsylvania State University Press, 1981.

———, ed. *Th' Upright Heart and Pure: Essays on John Milton Commemorating the Tercentenary of the Publication of Paradise Lost.* Pittsburgh: Duquesne University Press, 1967.

Fish, Stanley E. "Discovery as Form in *Paradise Lost.*" In *New Essays on Paradise Lost.* Ed. Thomas Kranidas. Berkeley: University of California Press, 1969. 1–14.

———. *How Milton Works.* Cambridge, Mass.: Harvard University Press, 2001.

———. *Surprised by Sin: The Reader in Paradise Lost.* London: Macmillan, 1967.

Flannagan, Roy. *John Milton: A Short Introduction.* Oxford: Blackwell, 2002.

Flint, Thomas P. *Divine Providence: The Molinist Account.* Ithaca: Cornell University Press, 1998.

Forsyth, Neil. *The Old Enemy: Satan and the Combat Myth.* Princeton: Princeton University Press, 1987.

———. *The Satanic Epic.* Princeton: Princeton University Press, 2003.

Frye, Roland M. *God, Man, and Satan: Patterns of Christian Thought and Life in Paradise Lost, Pilgrim's Progress, and the Great Theologians.* Princeton: Princeton University Press, 1960.

Gay, David. *The Endless Kingdom: Milton's Scriptural Society.* Newark: University of Delaware Press, 2002.

George, A. G. *Milton and the Nature of Man: A Descriptive Study of Paradise Lost in Terms of the Concept of Man as the Image of God.* London: Asia Publishing House, 1974.

Gilson, Étienne. *The Philosophy of St. Thomas Aquinas*. Trans. G. A. Elrington. New York: Arno Press, 1979.

———. *The Spirit of Mediaeval Philosophy*. Trans. A. H. C. Downes. London: Sheed & Ward, 1950.

Grace, William J. *Ideas in Milton*. Notre Dame: University of Notre Dame Press, 1968.

Graham, W. Fred, ed. *Later Calvinism: International Perspectives*. Kirksville: Sixteenth Century Journal Publishers, 1994.

Graves, Robert. *Wife to Mr. Milton: The Story of Marie Powell*. New York: Octagon, 1943.

Gregg, Robert C. and Dennis E. Groh. *Early Arianism: A View of Salvation*. London: SCM, 1981.

Greenlaw, Edwin. "A Better Teacher Than Aquinas," *Studies in Philology* 14 (1917), 196–217.

Grierson, Herbert J. C. *Cross Currents in English Literature of the Seventeenth Century*. London: Chatto & Windus, 1958.

———. "Milton." In *Encyclopaedia of Religion and Ethics*. Ed. James Hastings. 13 vols. Edinburgh: T&T Clark, 1908–26. 8:641–48.

Grossman, Marshall. *"Authors to Themselves": Milton and the Revelation of History*. Cambridge: Cambridge University Press, 1987.

Gunton, Colin E. *Becoming and Being: The Doctrine of God in Charles Hartshorne and Karl Barth*. Oxford: Oxford University Press, 1978.

Halewood, William H. *The Poetry of Grace: Reformation Themes and Structures in English Seventeenth-Century Poetry*. New Haven: Yale University Press, 1970.

Hamilton, G. D. "Milton's Defensive God: A Reappraisal," *Studies in Philology* 69:1 (1972), 87–100.

Hamlet, Desmond M. *One Greater Man: Justice and Damnation in Paradise Lost*. London: Associated University Presses, 1976.

Hanford, James Holly. *A Milton Handbook*. New York: Appleton, 1961.

———. "The Date of Milton's *De Doctrina Christiana*," *Studies in Philology* 17 (1920), 309–19.

Harrison, Peter. *"Religion" and the Religions in the English Enlightenment*. Cambridge: Cambridge University Press, 1990.

Hastings, James, ed. *Encyclopaedia of Religion and Ethics*. 13 vols. Edinburgh: T&T Clark, 1908–26.

Henry, Nathaniel H. *The True Wayfaring Christian: Studies in Milton's Puritanism*. New York: Peter Lang, 1987.

Heppe, Heinrich. *Reformed Dogmatics Set Out and Illustrated from the Sources*. Ed. and rev. Ernst Bizer. Trans. G. T. Thomson. London: Allen & Unwin, 1950.

Hill, Christopher. "From Lollards to Levellers." In *Rebels and Their Causes: Essays in Honour of A. L. Morton*. Ed. Maurice Cornforth. London: Lawrence & Wishart, 1978. 49–67.

———. *Milton and the English Revolution*. London: Faber, 1977.

———. "Professor William B. Hunter, Bishop Burgess, and John Milton," *Studies in English Literature, 1500–1900* 34 (1994), 165–88.

Hillerbrand, Hans J. *Encyclopedia of Protestantism*. 4 vols. New York: Routledge, 2004.

Hodge, Charles. *Systematic Theology*. 3 vols. Grand Rapids: Eerdmans, 1946.

Hoopes, Robert. *Right Reason in the English Renaissance*. Cambridge, Mass.: Harvard University Press, 1962.

Hunter, G. K. *Paradise Lost*. London: George Allen & Unwin, 1980.

Hunter, William B. "The Heresies of Satan." In *Th' Upright Heart and Pure: Essays on John Milton Commemorating the Tercentenary of the Publication of Paradise Lost*. Ed. Peter A. Fiore. Pittsburgh: Duquesne University Press, 1967.

———. "The Theological Context of Milton's *Christian Doctrine*." In *Achievements of the Left Hand: Essays on the Prose of John Milton*. Ed. Michael Lieb and John T. Shawcross. Amherst: University of Massachusetts Press, 1974. 269–87.

———. *Visitation Unimplor'd: Milton and the Authorship of De Doctrina Christiana*. Pittsburgh: Duquesne University Press, 1998.

——— et al., eds. *A Milton Encyclopedia*. 9 vols. Lewisburg: Bucknell University Press, 1978–83.

———, C. A. Patrides and J. H. Adamson, *Bright Essence: Studies in Milton's Theology*. Salt Lake City: University of Utah Press, 1971.

Isitt, Larry R. *All the Names in Heaven: A Reference Guide to Milton's Supernatural Names and Epic Similes*. Lanham: Scarecrow Press, 2002.

Jenks, Gregory C. *The Origins and Early Development of the Antichrist Myth*. Berlin: Walter de Gruyter, 1991.

Joseph, Miriam. "Orthodoxy in *Paradise Lost*," *Laval théologique et philosophique* 8 (1952), 243–84.

Kelley, Mark R., Michael Lieb and John T. Shawcross, eds. *Milton and the Grounds of Contention*. Pittsburgh: Duquesne University Press, 2003.

Kelley, Maurice. "Milton and the Trinity," *Huntington Library Quarterly* 33 (1970), 315–20.

———. "Milton's Debt to Wolleb's *Compendium Theologiæ Christianæ*," *PMLA* 50 (1935), 156–65.

———. "The Theological Dogma of *Paradise Lost*, III, 173–202," *PMLA* 52 (1937), 75–79.

———. *This Great Argument: A Study of Milton's De Doctrina Christiana as a Gloss Upon Paradise Lost*. Princeton: Princeton University Press, 1941.

Kelly, J. N. D. *Early Christian Doctrines*. New York: HarperCollins, 1978.

Kendall, R. T. *Calvin and English Calvinism to 1649*. Oxford: Oxford University Press, 1979.

Kendrick, Christopher. *Milton: A Study in Ideology and Form*. New York: Methuen, 1986.

Kerr, Fergus. *After Aquinas: Versions of Thomism*. Oxford: Blackwell, 2002.

Kierkegaard, Søren. *The Concept of Dread*. Trans. Walter Lowrie. London: Oxford University Press, 1944.

Klauber, Martin I. "Continuity and Discontinuity in Post-Reformation Reformed Theology: An Evaluation of the Muller Thesis," *Journal of the Evangelical Theological Society* 33:4 (1990), 467–75.

Knowles, David. *The Evolution of Medieval Thought*. London: Longman, 1962.

Kranidas, Thomas. *The Fierce Equation: A Study of Milton's Decorum*. The Hague: Mouton, 1965.

————, ed. *New Essays on Paradise Lost*. Berkeley: University of California Press, 1969.

Krause, Gerhard and Gerhard Müller, eds. *Theologische Realenzyklopädie*. 36 vols. Berlin: Walter de Gruyter, 1977–2004.

Leff, Gordon. *Bradwardine and the Pelagians: A Study of His De Causa Dei and Its Opponents*. Cambridge: Cambridge University Press, 1957.

Lewalski, Barbara K. "Innocence and Experience in Milton's Eden." In *New Essays on Paradise Lost*. Ed. Thomas Kranidas. Berkeley: University of California Press, 1969. 86–117.

————. "Milton and *De Doctrina Christiana*: Evidences of Authorship," *Milton Studies* 36 (1998) 203–28.

————. "Milton on Women—Yet Once More," *Milton Studies* 6 (1974), 3–20.

————. *The Life of John Milton: A Critical Biography*. Oxford: Blackwell, 2000.

Lewis, C. S. *A Preface to Paradise Lost*. London: Oxford University Press, 1942.

Lieb, Michael. "*De Doctrina Christiana* and the Question of Authorship," *Milton Studies* 41 (2002), 171–230.

————. *The Dialectics of Creation: Patterns of Birth and Regeneration in Paradise Lost*. Boston: University of Massachusetts Press, 1970.

————. *Theological Milton: Deity, Discourse and Heresy in the Miltonic Canon*. Pittsburgh: Duquesne University Press, 2006.

———— and John T. Shawcross, eds. *Achievements of the Left Hand: Essays on the Prose of John Milton*. Amherst: University of Massachusetts Press, 1974.

Loewenstein, David. *Milton: Paradise Lost*. Cambridge: Cambridge University Press, 1993.

MacKenzie, Iain M. *God's Order and Natural Law: The Works of the Laudian Divines*. Aldershot: Ashgate, 2002.

McColley, Diane Kelsey. "'All in All': The Individuality of Creatures in *Paradise Lost*." In *"All in All": Unity, Diversity, and the Miltonic Perspective*. Ed. Charles W. Durham and Kristin A. Pruitt. Selinsgrove: Susquehanna University Press, 1999. 21–38.

————. *Milton's Eve*. Urbana: University of Illinois Press, 1983.

McColley, Grant. *"Paradise Lost,"* *Harvard Theological Review* 32:4 (1939), 181–235.

———. *"Paradise Lost": An Account of Its Growth and Major Origins, with a Discussion of Milton's Use of Sources and Literary Patterns.* Chicago: Packard, 1940.

Martensen, H. L. *Christian Dogmatics: A Compendium of the Doctrines of Christianity.* Trans. William Urwick. Edinburgh, 1898.

Mascall, E. L. *He Who Is: A Study in Traditional Theism.* London: Longmans, 1943.

Maurer, Armand A. *Medieval Philosophy.* New York: Random House, 1962.

Miller, David M. *John Milton: Poetry.* Boston: Twayne, 1978.

Miller, J. Hillis. "How Deconstruction Works," *The New York Times Magazine* 9 (February 1986), 25.

Milner, Andrew. *John Milton and the English Revolution: A Study in the Sociology of Literature.* London: Macmillan, 1981.

Mintz, Susannah B. *Threshold Poetics: Milton and Intersubjectivity.* Newark: University of Delaware Press, 2003.

Moltmann, Jürgen. *God and Creation: A New Theology of Creation and the Spirit of God.* Trans. Margaret Kohl. London: SCM, 1985.

———. "Prädestination und Heilsgeschichte bei Moyse Amyraut," *Zeitschrift für Kirchengeschichte* 65 (1953–54), 270–303.

Mueller, Janel. "Milton on Heresy." In *Milton and Heresy.* Ed. Stephen B. Dobranski and John P. Rumrich. Cambridge: Cambridge University Press, 1998. 21–38.

Muller, Richard A. *After Calvin: Studies in the Development of a Theological Tradition.* Oxford: Oxford University Press, 2003.

———. "Arminius and the Scholastic Tradition," *Calvin Theological Journal* 24:2 (1989), 263–77.

———. *Christ and the Decree: Christology and Predestination in Reformed Theology from Calvin to Perkins.* Grand Rapids: Baker, 1986.

———. *God, Creation and Providence in the Thought of Jacob Arminius: Sources and Directions of Scholastic Protestantism in the Era of Early Orthodoxy.* Grand Rapids: Baker, 1991.

———. "God, Predestination, and the Integrity of the Created Order: A Note on Patterns in Arminius' Theology." In *Later Calvinism: International Perspectives*. Ed. W. Fred Graham. Kirksville: Sixteenth Century Journal Publishers, 1994. 431–46.

———. "Grace, Election, and Contingent Choice: Arminius's Gambit and the Reformed Response." In *The Grace of God, the Bondage of the Will*. Ed. Thomas R. Schreiner and Bruce A. Ware. 2 vols. Grand Rapids: Baker, 1995. 2:251–78.

———. *Post-Reformation Reformed Dogmatics: The Rise and Development of Reformed Orthodoxy, ca. 1520 to ca. 1725*. 4 vols. Grand Rapids: Baker, 2003.

———. "The Priority of the Intellect in the Soteriology of Jacob Arminius," *Westminster Theological Journal* 55 (1993), 55–72.

———. "The Problem of Protestant Scholasticism: A Review and Definition." In *Reformation and Scholasticism: An Ecumenical Enterprise*. Ed. Willem J. van Asselt and Eef Dekker. Grand Rapids: Baker, 2001. 45–64.

———. *The Unaccommodated Calvin: Studies in the Foundation of a Theological Tradition*. Oxford: Oxford University Press, 2000.

Musacchio, George. *Milton's Adam and Eve: Fallible Perfection*. New York: Peter Lang, 1991.

Musgrove, S. "Is the Devil an Ass?" *Review of English Studies* 21 (1945), 302–15.

Neander, Augustus. *Lectures on the History of Christian Dogmas*. Trans. J. E. Ryland. 2 vols. London, 1858.

Nicolson, Marjorie Hope. *John Milton: A Reader's Guide to His Poetry*. New York: Thames & Hudson, 1964.

Niebuhr, Reinhold. *The Nature and Destiny of Man: A Christian Interpretation*. 2 vols. London: Nisbet, 1941–43.

Normore, Calvin G. "Duns Scotus's Modal Theory." In *The Cambridge Companion to Duns Scotus*. Ed. Thomas Williams. Cambridge: Cambridge University Press, 2003. 141–45.

Oberman, Heiko A. *Forerunners of the Reformation: The Shape of Late Medieval Thought*. Philadelphia: Fortress, 1981.

———. *The Harvest of Medieval Theology: Gabriel Biel and Late Medieval Nominalism*. Cambridge, Mass.: Harvard University Press, 1963.

O'Keeffe, Timothy J. *Milton and the Pauline Tradition: A Study of Theme and Symbolism*. Washington: University Press of America, 1982.

Oldridge, Darren. "Protestant Conceptions of the Devil in Early Stuart England," *History* 85 (2000), 232–46.

Orr, James. *The Progress of Dogma*. London, 1901.

Pannenberg, Wolfhart. *Systematic Theology*. Trans. Geoffrey W. Bromiley. 3 vols. Grand Rapids: Eerdmans, 1991–98.

Parker, William Riley. *Milton: A Biography*. 2 vols. Oxford: Clarendon, 1968.

Patrides, C. A. *Milton and the Christian Tradition*. Oxford: Clarendon, 1966.

———. "The Salvation of Satan," *Journal of the History of Ideas* 28 (1967), 467–78.

Pettit, Norman. *The Heart Prepared: Grace and Conversion in Puritan Spiritual Life*. New Haven: Yale University Press, 1966.

Pieper, Josef. *Scholasticism: Personalities and Problems of Medieval Philosophy*. Trans. R. Winston and C. Winston. London: Faber, 1960.

Poole, William. *Milton and the Idea of the Fall*. Cambridge: Cambridge University Press, 2005.

Prestige, G. L. *God in Patristic Thought*. London: SPCK, 1959.

Pruitt, Kristin A. and Charles W. Durham, eds. *"All in All": Unity, Diversity, and the Miltonic Perspective*. Selinsgrove: Susquehanna University Press, 1999.

———, eds. *Living Texts: Interpreting Milton*. Selinsgrove: Susquehanna University Press, 2000.

Rajan, Balachandra. *The Lofty Rhyme: A Study of Milton's Major Poetry*. Coral Gables: University of Miami Press, 1970.

———, ed. *Paradise Lost: A Tercentenary Tribute*. Toronto: University of Toronto Press, 1969.

Raleigh, Walter. *Milton*. London, 1900.

Rehnman, Sebastian. *Divine Discourse: The Theological Methodology of John Owen*. Grand Rapids: Baker, 2002.

Revard, Stella P. "The Dramatic Function of the Son in *Paradise Lost*: A Commentary on Milton's 'Trinitarianism,'" *Journal of English and Germanic Philology* 66 (1967), 45–58.

Richard, Guy M. "Samuel Rutherford's Supralapsarianism Revealed: A Key to the Lapsarian Position of the Westminster Confession of Faith?" *Scottish Journal of Theology* 59:1 (2006), 27–44.

Robins, Harry F. *If This Be Heresy: A Study of Milton and Origen*. Illinois: University of Illinois Press, 1963.

Rosenblatt, Jason P. *Torah and Law in Paradise Lost*. Princeton: Princeton University Press, 1994.

Ross, James F. and Todd Bates, "Duns Scotus on Natural Theology." In *The Cambridge Companion to Duns Scotus*. Ed. Thomas Williams. Cambridge: Cambridge University Press, 2003. 193–237.

Rumrich, John P. *Milton Unbound: Controversy and Reinterpretation*. Cambridge: Cambridge University Press, 1996.

———. "Milton's Arianism: Why It Matters." In *Milton and Heresy*. Ed. Stephen B. Dobranski and John P. Rumrich. Cambridge: Cambridge University Press, 1998. 75–92.

———. "Stylometry and the Provenance of *De Doctrina Christiana*." In *Milton and the Terms of Liberty*. Ed. Graham Parry and Joad Raymond. Cambridge: D. S. Brewer, 2002. 125–36.

Rupp, E. Gordon. *The Righteousness of God: Luther Studies*. London: Hodder & Stoughton, 1953.

Russell, Conrad, ed. *The Origins of the English Civil War*. London: Macmillan, 1973.

Russell, Jeffrey Burton. *The Prince of Darkness: Radical Evil and the Power of Good in History*. London: Thames & Hudson, 1988.

Sandbach, F. H. *The Stoics*. New York: Norton, 1975.

Saurat, Denis. *Milton, Man and Thinker*. London: J. M. Dent, 1944.

Savage, J. B. "Freedom and Necessity in *Paradise Lost*," *ELH* 44 (1977), 286–311.

Schleiermacher, Friedrich Daniel Ernst. *The Christian Faith*. Ed. H. R. Mackintosh and J. S. Stewart. Edinburgh: T&T Clark, 1928.

Schreiner, Susan E. *The Theatre of His Glory: Nature and Natural Order in the Thought of John Calvin*. Grand Rapids: Baker, 1991.

Schreiner, Thomas R. and Bruce A. Ware, eds. *The Grace of God, the Bondage of the Will*. 2 vols. Grand Rapids: Baker, 1995.

Schwartz, Regina M. "Milton on the Bible." In *A Companion to Milton*. Ed. Thomas N. Corns. Oxford: Blackwell, 2001. 37–54.

Sellin, Paul R. "If Not Milton, Who Did Write the *De Doctrina Christiana*? The Amyraldian Connection." In *Living Texts: Interpreting Milton*. Ed. Kristen A. Pruitt and Charles W. Durham. Selinsgrove: Susquehanna University Press, 2000. 237–63.

———. "John Milton's *Paradise Lost* and *De Doctrina Christiana* on Predestination," *Milton Studies* 34 (1996), 45–60.

Sewell, Arthur. *A Study in Milton's Christian Doctrine*. London: Oxford University Press, 1939.

Shawcross, John T. *John Milton: The Self and the World*. Lexington: University Press of Kentucky, 1993.

———. *The Arms of The Family: The Significance of John Milton's Relatives and Associates*. Lexington: University Press of Kentucky, 2004.

———. *With Mortal Voice: The Creation of Paradise Lost*. Lexington: University Press of Kentucky, 1982.

Sherry, Beverley. "Speech in *Paradise Lost*," *Milton Studies* 8 (1975), 247–66.

Shoulson, Jeffrey S. *Milton and the Rabbis: Hebraism, Hellenism, and Christianity*. New York: Columbia University Press, 2001.

Silver, Victoria. *Imperfect Sense: The Predicament of Milton's Irony*. Princeton: Princeton University Press, 2001.

Sims, James H. "*Paradise Lost*: 'Arian Document' or Christian Poem?" *Études Anglaises* 20 (1967), 337–47.

Southern, R. W. *Saint Anselm and His Biographer: A Study in Monastic Life and Thought, 1059–c.1130*. Cambridge: Cambridge University Press, 1963.

Spade, Paul Vincent, ed. *The Cambridge Companion to Ockham*. Cambridge: Cambridge University Press, 1999.

Stavely, Keith W. F. "Satan and Arminianism in *Paradise Lost*," *Milton Studies* 25 (1989), 125–39.

Steadman, John M. "Milton and Wolleb Again," *Harvard Theological Review* 53 (1960), 155–56.

Steggle, Matthew. "*Paradise Lost* and the Acoustics of Hell," *Early Modern Literary Studies* 7:1 (2001), 9.1–17 <http://purl.oclc.org/emls/07-1/stegmil2.htm>.

Steinmetz, David C. *Calvin in Context.* Oxford: Oxford University Press, 1995.

Strong, Augustus H. *Systematic Theology: A Compendium.* Philadelphia, 1907.

———. *The Great Poets and Their Theology.* Philadelphia, 1897.

Stump, Eleonore and Norman Kretzmann, eds. *The Cambridge Companion to Augustine.* Cambridge: Cambridge University Press, 2001.

Summers, Joseph H. *The Muse's Method: An Introduction to Paradise Lost.* London: Chatto & Windus, 1962.

Tanner, John S. *Anxiety in Eden: A Kierkegaardian Reading of Paradise Lost.* New York: Oxford University Press, 1992.

Thomas, G. Michael. *The Extent of the Atonement: A Dilemma for Reformed Theology from Calvin to the Consensus, 1536–1675.* Carlisle: Paternoster, 1997.

Tillich, Paul. *Systematic Theology.* 3 vols. Chicago: University of Chicago Press, 1951–63.

Tillyard, E. M. W. *Milton.* London: Chatto & Windus, 1930.

———. *Studies in Milton.* London: Chatto & Windus, 1951.

Torrance, T. F. *Divine and Contingent Order.* Oxford: Oxford University Press, 1981.

Tout, T. F. and James Tait, eds. *Historical Essays by Members of the Owens College, Manchester.* London, 1902.

Trueman Carl R. "Puritan Theology as Historical Event: A Linguistic Approach to the Ecumenical Context." In *Reformation and Scholasticism: An Ecumenical Enterprise.* Ed. Willem J. van Asselt and Eef Dekker. Grand Rapids: Baker, 2001. 253–75.

Tyacke, Nicholas. *Anti-Calvinists: The Rise of English Arminianism, c.1590–1640.* Oxford: Clarendon, 1987.

———. "Puritanism, Arminianism and Counter-Revolution." In *The Origins of the English Civil War.* Ed. Conrad Russell. London: Macmillan, 1973. 119–43.

Ulreich, John C. "'Substantially Express'd': Milton's Doctrine of the Incarnation," *Milton Studies* 39 (2000), 101–28.

Venema, Cornelis P. *Heinrich Bullinger and the Doctrine of Predestination: Author of "the Other Reformed Tradition"?* Grand Rapids: Baker, 2002.

Wagenknecht, Edward. *The Personality of Milton.* Normon: University of Oklahoma Press, 1970.

Waldock, A. J. A. *"Paradise Lost" and Its Critics.* Cambridge: Cambridge University Press, 1947.

Walker, William. "Human Nature in Republican Tradition and *Paradise Lost*," *Early Modern Literary Studies* 10:1 (2004), 6.1–44 <http://purl.oclc.org/emls/10-1/walkmilt.htm>.

Warfield, B. B. *Calvin and Calvinism.* New York: Oxford University Press, 1931.

Webber, Joan Malory. "The Politics of Poetry: Feminism and *Paradise Lost*," *Milton Studies* 14 (1980), 3–24.

Werblowsky, R. J. Zwi. *Lucifer and Prometheus: A Study of Milton's Satan.* London: Routledge & Kegan Paul, 1952.

———. "Milton and the *Conjectura Cabbalistica*," *Journal of the Warburg and Courtauld Institutes* 18 (1955), 90–113.

Werman, Golda. *Milton and Midrash.* Washington: Catholic University Press of America, 1995.

Wetzel, James. "Predestination, Pelagianism, and Foreknowledge." In *The Cambridge Companion to Augustine.* Ed. Eleonore Stump and Norman Kretzmann. Cambridge: Cambridge University Press, 2001. 49–58.

Widdicombe, Peter. *The Fatherhood of God from Origen to Athanasius.* Oxford: Clarendon, 1994.

Wilding, Michael. *Dragons Teeth: Literature in the English Revolution.* Oxford: Clarendon, 1987.

———. *Milton's Paradise Lost.* Sydney: Sydney University Press, 1969.

Wiley, H. O. *Christian Theology.* 3 vols. Kansas City: Beacon Hill, 1940–43.

Wilkes, G. A. *The Thesis of Paradise Lost.* Melbourne: Melbourne University Press, 1961.

Willey, Basil. *The Seventeenth Century Background: Studies in the Thought of the Age in Relation to Poetry and Religion*. London: Chatto & Windus, 1957.

Williams, Thomas, ed. *The Cambridge Companion to Duns Scotus*. Cambridge: Cambridge University Press, 2003.

Winship, Michael P. *Making Heretics: Militant Protestantism and Free Grace in Massachusetts, 1636–1641*. Princeton: Princeton University Press, 2002.

Wood, G. A. "The Miltonic Ideal." In *Historical Essays by Members of the Owens College, Manchester*. London, 1902. 357–76.

Woodhouse, A. S. P. "Milton, Puritanism, and Liberty," *University of Toronto Quarterly* 4 (1935), 483–513.

———. "Notes on Milton's Views on the Creation: The Initial Phases," *Philological Quarterly* 28 (1949), 211–36.

Woods, Susanne. "Choice and Election in *Samson Agonistes*." In *Milton and the Grounds of Contention*. Ed. Mark R. Kelley, Michael Lieb and John T. Shawcross. Pittsburgh: Duquesne University Press, 2003. 174–87.

Yu, Anthony C. "Life in the Garden: Freedom and the Image of God in *Paradise Lost*," *Journal of Religion* 60 (1980), 247–71.

Indexes

Paradise Lost Index

Name Index

Wood, G. A., 1
Woodhouse, A. S. P., 2, 9, 97
Woods, Susanne, 1

Yu, Anthony C., 10

Zall, Paul M., 56

Subject Index

Abdiel, 56, 138
absolute power, 28, 47, 57, 61–62
Adam and Eve, 16–17, 20, 30, 36–37, 54, 74, 88–91, 98–99, 103–5, 108, 109, 111–12, 113, 115–42, 143–45, 154, 156–62, 164, 165
alternativity of choice, 25, 30, 36–37, 93, 94, 96–97, 112, 114, 121, 122, 123, 125, 128, 132, 141–42, 152, 164–65
Amyraldism, 8, 44–47, 49, 77, 91–92, 108, 119, 150, 164
angels, 53, 56, 62, 67, 99–102, 109, 116, 122, 124–25, 150
    see also Abdiel; Michael; Raphael
anti-Calvinism, 13–14, 57–71, 78, 88, 141, 163
arbitrariness, 47, 57, 61–63, 67, 70, 81
Arianism, 2, 7, 94, 102–9, 112, 166
Arminianism, 9–10, 40–44, 46, 47, 49–50, 51, 59, 61, 64, 66, 68, 69–70, 71, 76, 77–80, 83, 86, 87–88, 90, 91–92, 94–97, 110, 112, 114–15, 117, 118–19, 123, 124, 133, 136, 139–40, 141, 146–47, 150, 153–55, 160–61, 163–65
Augustinianism, 7, 15, 20, 21, 134
autonomy, 14, 21, 23, 44, 73, 89–90, 92, 109–11, 116, 132, 163, 165

Beelzebub, 58, 61–63, 65
Belial, 59, 63–65
blasphemy, 56, 70

Calvinism, 8–9, 35, 40, 43, 50, 57–71, 88, 136, 163
    see also anti-Calvinism; Reformed orthodoxy
causation, 23–24, 25–26, 28, 34, 38, 39, 43, 48–49, 90, 99, 102, 114, 116–17, 127, 128, 131–33
certainty, 19, 26, 38, 85–86, 89–91, 126, 129, 131
compulsion, 18, 32, 33, 65–66, 97, 115, 128, 130
concurrence, 116–17
    see also providence
condemnation, 17, 43, 47, 62, 78, 84, 86, 92, 109
conscience, 71, 162
conservation, 152–53
    see also providence
contingence, 14, 23–26, 28–29, 37, 44, 50, 93–96, 98, 102, 103, 105–8, 110, 112, 113–25, 126, 128, 130–33, 138, 142, 162, 164–66
conversion, 33–34, 37, 43, 46–47, 80, 143–62, 165
    see also grace; regeneration
corruption, 17, 30, 32, 34, 36–37, 41, 46, 83, 133–42, 144, 147, 149–50
    see also total depravity
counter-Reformation theology, 35, 51, 80, 146
creation, 23, 24–25, 28, 37, 39, 45, 54, 56, 60, 71, 74–75, 89, 91, 93–102,